TABLETOP
ANALOG GAME DESIGN

Design & composition by Ethan Gladding and Maya Irvine

CONTENTS

TABLETOP

ANALOG GAME DESIGN

INTRODUCTION

Much has been written about the videogame revolution, which is often portrayed as springing spontaneously from the forehead of Nolan Bushnell, like Athena from the brow of Zeus. In a scant thirty some-odd years, we've grown from nothing to one of the world's largest entertainment forms, grossing tens of billions annually, with games being the mainstay of entertainment and acculturation for most of the planet's youth.

Works that discuss the evolution of the game industry from an historical perspective generally talk about the connection between the pre-digital arcade and the earliest digital games; I've even heard some claim that "without the arcade, videogames would not exist."

This is, of course, bosh. Early creators such as Crawford, Garriott, Bunten, and the Brothers Gollop were not inspired by coin-drop amusements, but by tabletop games, either of the board or roleplaying variety. Without the arcade, we might have fewer twitch games and more that require cerebration, but that is another story.

Indeed, you can draw a direct line of descent from, say, *Tactics II* to *Call of Duty*, or from *Dungeons & Dragons* to *World of Warcraft* – or, for that matter, from games like *Rail Baron* to *Farmville*. If, as I do, you accept that digital and non-digital games are not different in essential nature, you must conclude that our history extends far longer than thirty years; as Stewart Cullin documented in a series of landmark works for the Smithsonian at the turn of the century, every Neolithic culture that survived into the modern era has its own games, and one can presume that this was true millennia ago as well. Even if you prefer to draw a line between what David Parlett (in the *Oxford History of Board Games*) calls "folk games," and games intentionally designed by identifiable creators, our history can be said to begin with Don Casimir Freschott's *Map Game*, published in 1680 in Venice; or perhaps with *Cribbage*, designed by the poet Sir John Suckling in the early 17th century; or with *A Journey Through*

Europe, the first English-language boardgame ascribable to a creator, designed by John Jefferys and published in Britain in 1759. The last is perhaps the most important of the three, since it is followed in subsequent decades by dozens of other original games, the first time what we can reasonably call a "game industry" appeared, an evolution that led directly to the 19th century efflorescence of boardgame publishing.

And far from being crippled by the advent of digital games, tabletop games have flourished in the same era – with ups and downs, to be sure, as waves of innovation have washed over them: the rise and decline of wargames, roleplaying games, and trading-card games followed, today, by increasing interest in Eurostyle boardgames.

As many game studies programs have discovered, tabletop games are particularly useful in the study of game design, because their systems are exposed to the player, not hidden in code. It is easy to misunderstand the essential nature of a digital game, if you focus on graphics or narrative without appreciating the way in which system shapes the experience, a fundamental failing of the narratological school. Tabletop games may have an intimate connection to narrative (as with roleplaying games), and certainly the nature of their graphics and components has an impact on the feeling of play; yet the system of rules they use to shape the experience are explicit and immediately graspable. Digital games can be far more complicated, in terms of the algorithms they use and the number of elements in play than tabletop games, but they are controlled, in the final analysis, by algorithms that, like those of tabletop games, create gameplay loops, provide positive or negative reinforcement, and pose challenges to players they must work to overcome.

In other words, whether your interest is in tabletop games themselves, in game design as a discipline, or in the historical evolution of the form, tabletop games are worthy of study.

In this volume, we have asked people of diverse backgrounds – tabletop game designers, digital game designers, and game studies academics – to write about tabletop games. Some have chosen to write about their design process, others about games they admire, others about the culture of tabletop games and their fans. The results are various and individual, but all cast some light on what is a multivarious and fascinating set of game styles.

This volume is not a definitive study of the field, nor of the design of tabletop games, nor of their history; it is not intended to be. Rather, we trust that readers will find in these pages, interesting and different views on the pleasures to be gained from tabletop games; and perhaps, in reading, will discover a renewed interest in playing and designing them.

Greg Costikyan

DESIGNING TABLETOP GAMES

THE THREE-PLAYER PROBLEM
Lewis Pulsipher

In quantum or classical mechanics, there's a well-known class of problems that has traditionally proven very difficult to solve, complex problems that model the motion of three particles or objects such as the sun, earth, and moon: the "three-body problem."

In games, the equivalent of this is the "three player problem." There are actually two problems. In a three-player conflict game without a definite end, the two players who are behind will usually beat on the one who is ahead, resulting in a perpetual stalemate. This can be avoided by placing a time limit on the game. However, as soon as you add a definite end to the game, such as a number of turns or a number of points, the situation changes drastically. Perpetual stalemate is no longer possible. But it is frequently possible for one player (call him "A"), if he believes he will lose and cannot catch up in the remaining duration of the game, to determine which other player wins. That is, late in the game the losing player exerts all his efforts against another player "B," which tends to let the third player "C" win. R. Wayne Schmittberger (long-time editor of *Games magazine*) called this the "petty diplomacy problem" in his book *New Rules for Classic Games*. "Petty" here is derived from "pettiness," I believe, implying that the player who thinks he'll lose often chooses for petty reasons which of the others to take with him to defeat.

This is not usually a problem in games where players can do little to affect other players, such as most race games. If a player can hardly affect the other players (as though each were playing alone), then the "petty diplomacy problem" goes away. Many "Euro"-style board and card games (which are often for three or four players) have been called "multiplayer solitaire," a popular style partly because it avoids the "petty diplomacy" problem.

But it can be a big problem in wargames and other conflict games. And this is why we rarely see such games that are "naturally" good for three players. Generally most conflict games are best for two, or four to five. When there are four or more players, a single player has less influence on the outcome, mitigating the effects of "I'm going to lose so I'll make sure *you* don't win."

I've discovered a number of ways to retain a strong competitive aspect in a game yet make it work well for three players. The example games I'll describe are non-electronic but these solutions apply just as well to videogames. I'm going to follow the examples with a discussion of problems that occur in any game with more than two separate interests, all of which can be applied to the three player problem.

The general description of the two solutions is:

1. The victory condition must be one that can be attained in a single move/turn, and that can change over time, yet players can usually (but not always) anticipate that it might occur. This enables two players to "gang up" on the third to stop him. If they succeed, the game returns to an equilibrium until one player once again threatens to win. Even without a time limit, the game will eventually end.

2. Have a situation where changes in the state of affairs are quite small, so that no single move can make a very large difference in the state of things, in who is ahead and who behind and what the margin is. Only late in the game will a player be able to recognize that he's not going to win. By that time, he usually cannot make enough difference in the short run that remains, to throw the game to another.

Actual examples will make this clearer.

Law & Chaos

In my prototype titled *Law & Chaos* (in the publishing queue with Mayfair Games, and likely to have the name changed), I serendipitously discovered how the first method can work.

The game is played on a simple hexagonal board (61 hexagons) with one kind of piece. The game is an example of one that arises from components, as I wanted to devise a way to use in a game the colored glass beads or "stones" so common in flower-arrangements nowadays. (In the end, I had to abandon those pieces because they weigh too much, as publishers usually pay for shipping to distributors!)

Unadorned hexes and one kind of piece don't offer much room for variety, and I settled on using cards to provide that variety. There are three types of cards:

*   Victory conditions. These specify patterns a player can form to win the game, such as a row of six stones

*   Capture methods. These specify patterns that let a player capture opposing stones

*   Action cards. These enable the player to take/cause a specified action (such as preventing the replacement of a victory condition card)

Each player has cards in hand, and there are cards on the table that apply to players selectively. Each turn a player either places a piece on the board (which could also result in one or more captures) or plays a card. The key for our discussion is that anyone can win at any time by having the right victory card in combination with the corresponding pattern on the board. The card needs to be face up on the table already, or it must be played from the player's hand; in the latter case the other players have one round to try to break up the pattern. (There are more details than this, especially about player interaction, that will await the game's publication.)

Players soon learn the possible victory patterns (which are also illustrated on a separate sheet), and can either see that another player has the right victory card on the table for a pattern he can soon form, or can anticipate that it is in the player's hand, as that player builds patterns.

When the other players see this, they tend to gang up on the "leader" to thwart his plan. If they succeed, then they play once again in a kind of equilibrium. If one player is far behind (it's possible to have no pieces on the board), the others will usually concentrate on one another, which gives the third a chance to catch up. But sometimes the other players will fail to see that the "leader" is threatening, or will be unable to stop him or her.

In the end, it is that rarity, a game that is not only good but outstanding for three players, and best played with three, though it can be played by two or four.

The "sudden victory that can often be forecasted and prevented" characteristic is the key. Unlike many wargames, some information must be uncertain or hidden, or players will always know who is threatening to win. It is also important that the victory conditions themselves can change over time.

Any kind of foreseeable/definite time limit helps "petty diplomacy" rear its ugly head. Using a criterion of victory by reaching a set point total, very common in boardgames these days, is unsuitable because the end is fairly predictable. On the other hand, a margin victory criterion– for example "have 20 points more than the next highest player"--means no one knows for sure when the game will end, because the players behind can catch up and the margin can get smaller as well as larger. When the player who is furthest behind can still hope to catch up, he's not likely to give up and "suicide" against another player. If a set total of points determines when the game ends, then at some point the player furthest behind will realize he doesn't have time to catch up, allowing "petty diplomacy" to kick in.

So this kind of game needs an open end, probably with some mechanism that prevents the game from going on forever but does not arbitrarily end it. In *Law & Chaos* I added that mechanism when playtest games among expert players stretched to more than two hours, much longer than the average. The mechanism comes into play at a certain point, by increasing the number of ways players can win.

The game doesn't work as well with two or four players. With two, when a player "gets it going," there's a steamroll effect that's hard to stop. With four, it's too easy for three to gang up to stop one, and that led to a variation of the game, recommended for four players, that limits what a player can do to stop someone else because they do not have a hand of cards.

A military version of this kind of game

How might this apply to a military game rather than an abstract one? Occasionally we see three-way, rather than two-way, historical struggles for supremacy. The one that first comes to mind for me is Athens, Sparta, and Persia in the fifth century BC. Athens and Sparta joined together to defeat the great Persian invasion of 480 BC. Then Athens' sea empire became dominant for a while, and Sparta abandoned the alliance against Persia. By the end of the Peloponnesian War, Persia controlled Greek Ionia, and gave subsidies to Sparta, enabling the Spartans to build fleets to defeat Athens. In the fourth century it was Sparta's turn to be pulled back, this time by Thebes in conjunction with Athens. Finally, the Macedonians conquered Greece, and soon after conquered Persia with the help of the traditional Greeks.

In other words, one power or another threatened to become completely dominant, but was defeated by the other two, until yet another more-or-less Greek power defeated them all.

How can this be represented in a game? The key will be a card for each round of play that will indicate a victory condition for one of the nations (or perhaps all three). If the condition is attained, the game will end right there. The order of play will change from round to round to help give nations a chance to thwart the one closest to a win, and some mechanism that abandons the move-all-units-in-your-turn tradition might be desirable as well. There's also a possibility for a point game here, with the card specifying the points that can be earned by achieving certain objectives, and if any nation reaches a given point margin over the next highest, it wins. In essence, in many if not all rounds we want at least one nation to have a chance to win while the others must thwart that nation, possibly ignoring their long-term interests in favor of defeating the temporary leader.

Because there have been at least two Peloponnesian War games published in the past few years, I have not tried to develop this game.

Other Historical Wargames

Now what about the second version of a natural three player conflict game? I call this the "equilibrium" method. I have a prototype *Britannia*-like game called *"Frankia: the birth of France and Germany,"* that includes three scenarios, 406-814 AD, 843-1215, and 1215-1492. As in my game *Britannia*, each player controls several nations in the course of the game, and victory is determined by points. The first two scenarios are for four players, as with almost all *Britannia*-like games, but the last one is for three. I decided to try this because the situation in this scenario is so different from the typical *Britannia*-like game. The typical situation sees major raids and invasions from external sources, and a considerable turnover of nations and locations–which is the situation in the first two scenarios. In 1215-1492 in this part of the world, the nascent nation-states of modern Europe could already by discerned, there were no external invasions or raids at all, and in part thanks to geography, borders did not shift a great deal over time.

I was fortunate insofar as I had changed two of the fundamental systems of *Britannia* for *Frankia*, the combat system and the economic system. The three player scenario would not work as well with the combat system used in *Britannia*, in which casualties can be quite high. (Roll a die for each army in a battle; a 5 or 6 kills an opposing army.) *Frankia* uses a card-based, diceless combat system that does not eliminate more than one army in a fight, and often none at all. Sometimes, in fact, the battle ends with both participants jointly occupying the area they've contested.

The economic system depends on the number of armies a nation already possesses, so that Powers tend to reach an equilibrium until they can conquer more territory. Your economy must pay to maintain existing units before you can get new units. In contrast, in *Britannia*, the number of new units you receive depends only on the economic value of the areas you hold, regardless of how many units you already have. Armies are also a representation of population, so you can build up armies until you reach your population maximum. In *Frankia*, the cavalry and infantry armies are more specialized, not representing the population as a whole.

Finally, the number of units is relatively low, in part because the stacking limit, the number that can be in a given area, is lower than in *Britannia*. In particular, there is no unlimited-size stack. When you cannot concentrate large forces, it is harder to make a sweeping invasion.

The result is that this scenario is even less a "conquest game" than normal *Britannia*. Much of the time in *Britannia*, you protect what you have rather than attack, until your next big invasion comes into play. In *Frankia*, you don't have the forces to launch a big invasion, nor can you kill the enemy fast enough to overwhelm them. It is a case of nibbling a little here, a little there, trying to be on top of an equilibrium. And that is what we need to help us avoid the "petty diplomacy problem."

Another situation that lends itself to this kind of game is eighteenth century Europe. This was an era of "the laws of war," a reaction against the excesses of the Thirty Years War. Professional, not mercenary, armies relied on long supply lines guarded by highly efficient earthwork fortifications. The "civilized rules of warfare" prohibited living off the land (the commonplace in the Thirty Years). The aims of warfare were usually limited to wearing out the opponent while gaining bits of land (and fortresses) here and there. It is another case of "nibbling", though in the game ahistorical events can occur, just as in other games with this long chronological scope.

My prototype (tentative title, *Struggle for Hegemony in Europe, 1689-1789*) also sees each player controlling several of twenty-two nations–there are no uncontrolled neutrals. The game is for three to five players. The dice-based combat system once again rarely results in casualties, with much of warfare revolving around sieges and the occasional assault on forts. The lines of forts tend to prevent sweeping invasions. A submission rule allows small nations to become subordinate to an attacker (at a cost) rather than be wiped out. The economic system once again considers the number of armies and fleets you already have, and there are maximum numbers of units as well reflecting the general difficulty of maintaining large armies and fleets.

As "sweep of history" games, both of these have a definite number of turns, but that is tolerable for an "equilibrium" game. More changes occur in nation positions in this game than in the real world–the purpose is to have a good game–but it is largely a situation in equilibrium, which we need to avoid "petty diplomacy". The scoring system also contributes to this. Prussia, for example, doesn't score any points for areas in France, or deep in Austria, or in Russia or the Ottoman Empire. The Prussians may (rarely) invade France in order to reduce the French score, but gain no points from it themselves. If they're pursuing their self-interest as indicated by their scoring areas, they are unlikely to stray far from home. The English might, in some games, conquer Spain with Portuguese help, but they won't gain points for every area in Spain, any more than the French would.

The right situation, then, combined with appropriate combat, economic, and scoring systems, allows these two wargames to be played by three players while avoiding the petty diplomacy problem. It is still possible for two players to decide to try to wipe out the third, but when they choose to do that early in the game, the victim has the opportunity to throw his forces against one of his two tormentors with sufficient effect to throw the game to the third. The threat of doing so actually tends to help restore the situation to something close to equilibrium. Late in the game, with all that has passed before, the simple two-against-one is much less likely to occur, and will be less effective.

Of course, another possible way to avoid the three player problem is a wargame in which almost all information, including information about who is winning, is hidden from the players. If you don't know you're losing, or who's winning, the petty diplomacy problem goes away. Then we have a kind of race, or something that wouldn't be much of a game, in most cases.

Another Abstract

I'm going to go back to abstract games for a moment to describe another solution. What makes this game work for three players is that it isn't really a conflict game, it's a positional game. That is, while player interaction is high, you cannot throw or exert force against another player, though you may be able to temporarily eliminate one of his pieces. You can block a player from scoring, but this may help the third player more than it helps you.

The game is played on a four by four square grid with stackable pieces (tentative title, which is likely to be changed when a theme is attached, is *Four by Four*). To score you must get four in a row or four in a square–a little like *Tic-Tac-Toe/Noughts and Crosses*--and the scoring pieces are then removed. There are stack size limits depending on the number of players.

Some of the pieces have special powers, such as the "Top" piece that another player cannot place a piece on top of, and the "Order" piece which freezes the order of pieces in a stack. The pieces alone might not be very interesting, but each player also has a hand of cards. The sequence of play is that all play one card simultaneously, then play two rounds of placing pieces on the board. The cards have "initiative numbers" that determine order of execution both for the current card round and for the following placement rounds, so there is no question of consistent advantage for playing first the way there is with *Chess* and many other games. The cards allow various manipulations of the pieces, such as moving the bottom piece in a stack to the top or allowing you to move a piece (not necessarily one of yours).

Each time a player achieves the scoring condition he gets a point, and play goes to three points, or fewer if players agree. Sometimes when one set of scoring pieces is removed, another score is revealed, and it is also removed. It is not unusual for one player to be behind, but come back to win the game. As the game progresses, a player must often choose whether to prevent a score by another, or to work toward a score for himself. Late in the game you know who's threatening to win, because you can see the score. The time of ending of the game is uncertain, but there is a mechanism to end it rather than go on indefinitely (when a player has no more pieces to play). The game can also be played by two or four, with rather different tactics in each case.

In some ways the three-player problem can be seen as a subset of problems that occur in many games involving more than two sides. I'll discuss some of those next.

Problems with Multi-sided Games

Boardgamers call any game with more than two players "multiplayer", but this term is used in the videogame world for "more than one player;" and in videogames, a "multiplayer" game often has just two teams, as in *Team Fortress*. So I use the term "multi-sided,"meaning more than two separate interests regardless of the number of human players.

Certain kinds of problems crop up in three player games just as they do in multi-sided games for more than three. These potential problems exist to a lesser or greater degree in most multi-sided games, but in the extreme become obstacles to enjoyment. These are:

- Turtling
- Leader bashing
- Sandbagging
- Kingmaking

Turtling

A player sits on the sidelines, avoiding conflict, while other players fight a debilitating war; then the turtle steps in and wins the game because the others are too weak to stop him. In videogames this is often called "camping", although "campers" often choose the tactic because they can occupy a very good defensive position and kill many opponents without dying often. In boardgames, the player may avoid combat altogether.

How is turtling avoided? The clearest method is with a zero-sum game, such as *Diplomacy*. You can only gain units by taking supply centers from another player: the general definition would be, a player can only gain something that another player loses.

Most games are not zero-sum. However, if a player stands to gain more by attacking than by turtling, the turtle tends to fall behind. This requires that there be a positive rather than negative economy, that is, that a player can acquire additional force/capability over time through the game economy. This is what makes turtling somewhat dangerous in *Risk*, because the players controlling more areas gain more new units. Nonetheless, the entire system of gaining new armies through cards exists, in part, to encourage players to attack rather than turtle (if you don't successfully attack in a turn, you don't get another card).

In many tactical battle games, there is no economy (or, to put it another way, there's a negative economy, as both sides gradually lose units). If there are only two sides, this is not a problem. If there are more than two, it becomes a big problem. Three player *Chess*, for example, is likely to be an exercise in turtling. Even if a player is awarded control of all remaining opposing pieces when he checkmates a king, this may not be enough incentive to attack rather than turtle.

Turtling can happen in a two-sided game. For example, in *Chess* a player may try to create a very strong defensive position and wait for his aggressive (or computer) opponent to make a mistake, then attack.

It is very common for beginning designers of multi-sided conflict games to allow, even encourage, turtling, because there is not a positive economy.

Another way to discourage turtling may be extreme uncertainty about the overall situation. The turtle needs to know when other sides have been debilitated to the point that he can attack and probably win. If he doesn't have enough information to know when that occurs, he may decide he needs to go forward rather than turtle. But this is not a desirable solution, especially in a boardgame. It is more practical (and more often used) in card games, where the cards provide a simple, natural means of hiding information.

Finally, victory conditions can discourage turtling. In a game where points are scored periodically throughout the game, a player who turtles may not be able to score well. This will certainly be true if those point awards involve holding certain locations, or destroying numbers of opposing units. Even if the victory conditions only apply at the end of the game, as in *Axis & Allies* (where the objective is to hold enemy capitals, with no predetermined time/turn limit), the turtle is less likely to hold these areas at game end. Yes, if everyone else wears themselves out without achieving the victory criterion, the turtle may be able to sweep the board and then achieve the victory. In *A&A*, because there's a positive economy as well, and because there are only two sides, turtling doesn't happen.

Leader Bashing

Leader Bashing is simply the tendency to attack whoever is ahead. This is a necessary component of multi-sided conflict games, though generally absent from race games. It becomes a problem when the typical thing to do is to attack whoever is in the lead, regardless of one's own position.

In my game *Britannia* and other *Britannia*-like games, there are two elements to discourage leader-bashing. First, players score at different junctures of the game, so it's difficult to actually know who is ahead at a given time. For example, the Romans score a lot early on, because they conquer much of Britain. The (yellow) Romans can have more than a hundred points in turn five, more than any other color, but yellow would be well behind *overall* because the average Roman score is about 125. (The average score for each of the four colors at game end is around 217.) Experienced players understand whether the yellow color is doing better or worse than average, but even then, this must be seen in relation to the scores of the other three colors. As the game goes on through sixteen turns and seventeen nations, discerning who is ahead becomes more complicated. In other words, there can be honest differences of opinion as to who is actually ahead, and you'll often hear players over a *Britannia* board each explaining (sometimes disingenuously) why they are behind and someone else is ahead.

Further, the latest version of *Britannia* includes scoring markers. If players agree not to track the scores on a scoresheet, the scoring markers provide further uncertainty about who is ahead. In a game like the Hasbro version of *History of the World* this kind of uncertainty is absolutely necessary to avoid rampant leader-bashing.

Second, in a four player game, if you expend your efforts trying to "stop the leader" at the cost of your own score, then the other two players benefit. In *Britannia* each nation has historical scoring objectives that sometimes conflict with other nations, but not necessarily the one that you want to "bash" right now. This doesn't work as well in a three player game, because only one other player benefits, not two, but it certainly helps in *Frankia* and *Struggle* (described above) which use a simpler version of the *Britannia* scoring system.

Sandbagging

Sandbagging is the reverse side of leader-bashing. Sandbagging is pretending to be worse off than you are, to somehow disguise how well you're doing. In some games in which leader-bashing is easy, that is, each player is able to exert some influence and exert it against any other player regardless of positioning on the board, then it makes sense to try to be slightly behind the leader near the end of the game. In a game such as *Vinci* this is a common strategy. Either you need to be fairly far ahead when the end of game approaches, or you need to be in second or third place in order to win when others bash the leader(s). (How this works depends on the players, of course: some refuse to attack the leader, concentrating only on how best to maximize their own score.)

The easier it is for other players to see the reality of the game situation, the harder it is to sandbag.

Kingmaking

Kingmaking is the more general term for "petty diplomacy problem". If it is too easy for one player to affect another sufficiently to cause him to lose, regardless of the number of players, the game suffers for it. Obviously, as there are more separate interests, each player can have less effect on the game as a whole, and kingmaking becomes less problematic.

Of course, in games allowing negotiation, a player with a weaker position can try to persuade a stronger player to leave him alone because "if you attack me I'll throw my entire force against you and you won't win." If players can significantly hinder one another, this kind of negotiation strategy cannot be avoided.

Further, in some games a player can influence any other, while in other games there are circumstances of geography or even of turn order that reduce the effect some players can have on certain others. For example, in *Diplomacy* (World War I), the English player can try to influence others to attack Turkey, but he cannot affect Turkey with his units until late in the game, because the nations are on opposite corners of the board.

As with the specific case of the petty diplomacy problem, if players don't know that they're losing, they're less likely to try kingmaking.

Insofar as uncertainty tends to mitigate the petty diplomacy/kingmaking problem, the problem is less likely to occur in card games than in board games. Cards naturally hide information, whereas boards naturally reveal information. In this respect, videogames are often more like card games, naturally hiding information from the players.

In summary, here are some ways to deal with the three-player problem:

- A race or "multi-sided solitaire"; players cannot do enough to hinder/harm another to make a significant difference in the end portion of the game

- Sudden victory that can frequently be forecasted and prevented, with changing victory conditions

- "Equilibrium", no side can drastically alter the situation in a single turn

- A game that is almost entirely positional

- Extreme uncertainty about who is winning and losing

Britannia references:

Wikipedia: http://en.wikipedia.org/wiki/*Britannia*_%28board_game%29

Boardgamegeek: http://boardgamegeek.com/boardgame/240/britannia

Publisher's Site: http://new.fantasyflightgames.com/edge_minisite.asp?eidm=42&enmi=Britannia

SIMULATION GAME DESIGN
James F Dunnigan

My specialty is historical simulations. I designed over a hundred (that got published), and ran Simulations Publications, Inc (SPI), a company that published over 400 of these games while I was there (1969-80). Most of these were wargames. Peace games don't sell as well, which says something about us all. We'd rather fight. Kill for peace and all that.

Wargames have been around for thousands of years, with *Chess* being the most obvious example. *Chess*, as we know it, is still a pretty accurate simulation of ancient battles. Over the centuries, there have been many variants on the *Chess* idea, and in the last two centuries, the idea of adapting the *Chess* concept to contemporary military operations, took hold. Over the last century, more and more of these "wargames" have been published as entertainments for those interested in such things. Military professionals took the same basic concepts and developed more complex "*Chess* variants" for planning and training. These were very successful, and are still used in a limited way.

I entered the business in the late 1960s, with the belief that the games could be a bit more accurate, and informative, without becoming a lot more complex. It turned out that there were many others out there with the same idea, but I got the ball rolling with some new ideas on how to go about quickly turning history, or current events, into a playable game. The main reason for this was curiosity. I, and many others, wanted to do more than read about history, we wanted to see a convincing model of how historical events worked, and have the ability to explore "what ifs" in a believable fashion. Most importantly, we were creating historical games that convincingly allowed the players to make the same historical decisions, and get the same results. But, most importantly, you could make other decisions, and see an accurate alternative result.

My basic premise was, and still is, that any situation can be turned into a useful model/game/simulation. Naturally, I developed a tool set to accomplish this. Here are the tools, along with some examples. The following discussion assumes that you are seeking to create some kind of conflict simulation (the term we coined to describe these kinds of games).

But remember, these guidelines can be used to create games on anything. And I mean anything. I first realized this in the 1960s. Late in that decade, Tom Shaw, the guy who was running game publisher Avalon Hill, had doubts about this. He challenged me. I told him to name any situation, and I would deliver a publishable (entertaining and easy to learn) game within a month or two. He responded with, "do a game about getting lost in the woods." I did, he did, and *Outdoor Survival* became a best seller. I've taken up that challenge many times since, often in casual conversations, and always came up with a solution. So be confident as you proceed. For more examples (visual and otherwise), surf over to: http://www.hyw.com/Books/WargamesHandbook/Contents.htm. But the basic tools are as follows:

The Tool Of Understanding

It's easy enough to do a game on a subject you are interested in, if you are the only one who is going to use it. But if others are involved, especially a client, the situation can become difficult. Know what the user/customer wants. It's difficult enough knowing what you want to do when you are doing a model for yourself. It's easy to start building a model with a vague idea of what you want, and then sharpen your focus as you proceed. It's impossible to complete an adequate model unless you have developed a precise idea of what you want it to do. If the user is someone else, you have to help them figure out what they want it to do. This is not easy, and is often avoided because of the difficulty. Don't avoid it, be difficult if you have to. In the long run, this is the easy way out. To define the needs of the project, apply this checklist. It will get you started in defining the model users need. If you can't define your project adequately, you'll waste a lot of time and effort. You probably won't complete your project, either. The last thing you want to hear from the user is, "that's what I asked for, but it's not what I want."

1. Determine the Process to be modeled. Many different aspects of your model must be defined before you can proceed. Scale (Strategic, Operational, Tactical), Environment (Land, Air, Naval, Combined), Intensity (Low, Medium, High), Basic Aspects (Movement, Combat, Order of Battle), Special Aspects (C^3I, Logistics, Doctrine & Tactics, Fog of War--Is the situation highly dependent on one, or both, sides being in the dark about what is going on? If so, you will have to model this aspect of the situation.)

2. What do you want it to do? There are several different tasks you can direct your modeling towards. These can include training, research, analysis, etc. For example: You may want to test a hypothesis. This can be historical, contemporary, or future. It can be about weapons, tactics, organization, or whatever. Be rigorous in defining your hypothesis. A model/wargame will eat you alive if you are sloppy. Perhaps you want to better define a process. You may want to break down an existing system into only its essential parts. A wargame building exercise is excellent for this.

3. How do you want the game to go about its work. Do you want to use a map (most common with wargames), or cards, or a computer interface? The customer, or user, might not even be sure which form of game would work best. You have to figure this out before you proceed.

The Rule of Plagiarism

Start with an existing model. For example, to create a wargame for contemporary ground combat operations, you can wander off to your local game or software store and see what the commercial designers are up to. There are also companies that deal in out-of-print games that may be of use. If there are any gamers in your area, buy them a beer and pump them shamelessly for leads. There's also a lot of previous work in the non-commercial sector waiting to be plundered. No sense reinventing the wheel, especially since that approach is sure to lead to exceeding your budget and missing deadlines. Don't endanger your career. Plagiarize. There's no copyright on ideas and most of the ones you need have already been thought of and thought out by more experienced designers. I know, I often steal from myself (as well as others, that's why I'm an expert).

The Rule of Self Knowledge

Be sure you know what you know. Pick a subject you have a keen interest in, or have gained a perceptive knowledge of. This will eliminate a lot of time-consuming research. You wouldn't be doing this if you weren't an expert in something.

The Rule of Digging

Compile information. Once you have agreed upon what you want to do, you must gather information. Here is a sample checklist.

- Area of Operations- Where, in time and geography, is the conflict to take place?

- Scale- What is to be represented on the map, a few square miles or a continent?

- Significant Terrain- For the Terrain Effects Chart, this is a winnowing process, in which you reduce all the terrain information you have gathered into a usable format.

- Order of Battle- Units involved, their movement capability, combat capability, and other characteristics.

- Victory Conditions- This is a critical element, and often slighted or overlooked. What were the goals of the combatants?

- Combat Results- Attrition rates in combat, with adjustments for other factors as needed and likely distribution of results for use with non-deterministic (unpredictability of combat) procedures.

- Sequence of Play- The sequence that appears to work best in most situations is: 1-Planning and preparation operations, 2-Movement, 3-Combat, 4-Post operations checks (victory, morale, command control, etc.).

The Rule of Taking a Chance.

This is all about the "Integration Phase." The Big Moment, when you create the prototype. This is where you assemble the first working version of the game. The Prototype is usually quick and dirty. Just get it working, quickly. Once that is done, you can make many minor changes to get it to work (produce a certain result using a certain sequence of moves). Whether the game is manual or computerized, you should have probability tables that can be easily changed to adjust the game's outcomes in a controllable fashion.

Finally, a note on "Pre-Dawn Madness & The Bleeding Edge of Technology." There is a bit of magic involved while creating the prototype. The model must be exercised, errors noted and modifications made, and the process repeated. Strange things will happen and you will often find yourself spending more hours working on this phase than you realize. This is the Pre-Dawn Madness most programmers are familiar with. Don't expect to understand everything that's going on in the prototype. If it works, leave it be and move on. Don't be any more inventive than you have to be. Beware the Bleeding Edge of Technology. Stay with the simple and don't get cute.

The Truth Rule

This is all about testing and user acceptance. First there is Alpha Testing, where first you and then some typical users must be able to reproduce the Historical Event, or the defined hypothetical event. If the game can't do this in the hands of others (the people who created the game sometimes unconsciously make the game work by, well, cheating), you have to tinker with it until it does. That's the truth, and you cannot ignore it. Once you have done this, you can proceed to Blind (or Beta) Testing, where the game is handed to typical users without you hovering over them ("blind" to you). These people may break the game, but mainly, this crew will point out the many errors you made in writing the instructions and laying out the components. All games, and especially commercial products, should have a degree of addiction to them. As commercial game developers like to say, while developing such a game, "is it crack (cocaine) yet?" Lastly, there is ongoing testing after installation/publication. No model is ever truly finished.

And now, there is the bad news. These types of simulations/games appeal to a small number of people. While *Chess* is played by about twelve percent of the U.S. population, that's ten to twenty times the number of people who are interested in these simulation type games. I know this because I ran surveys and other forms of market research for over a decade, in an attempt to discover how big the market actually was. Turns out that while there are forty million chess players in the United States, less than one percent of Americans are willing (deep interest in history/current affairs), or able (knowledge of math and operations research concepts, consciously or subconsciously) to handle these kinds of games. In the 1970s, we came to call wargaming, "the hobby of the over-educated." The manual games further restricted the number of users, because these games are more time consuming to learn and play. Computerized versions of these games appeal to a wider audience, but still a niche audience -- An audience of under a million people. While complexity frightens the many, it appeals to the few. Thus wargames are often lumped into all things geekish. Guilty as charged.

People who are into playing or designing wargames do not think like the rest of us. Actually, this applies to most people in the sciences, or anyone who uses the scientific method (testing hypotheses until you get a proof in the form of a reproducible result). Wargamers look at wars, and most other things, in a more analytical fashion, taking into account historical precedents and antecedents. When I started designing games on contemporary (wars not yet fought) situations in the 1970s, I discovered again the old adage, "the past is prolog to the future", still applies. But the basic rules of historical simulations still applied. Or, as we put it back then, "If you can't predict the past, you can't predict the future."

But take heart. This stuff really works. If you have the analytic and math skills, you don't have to be a military history buff to make this work. These techniques really can be applied to anything. Over the years, I have been approached with many requests for advice on how to apply these tools. Most had nothing to do with warfare. For example, I once had a fellow from the New York City Health Department come in asking for help in training inspectors, stationed at the ports and international airports, to screen people for rare diseases (like AIDS, this being the 1970s). I came up with a card based system, where the inspectors could be presented with a wide array of "people with suspicious diseases" and exhibiting an even wider array of symptoms. Sort of a play on flash cards, but with some branching and game play. The NY Police Department wanted help in building training simulations for commanders who had to cope with public disorder. Turned out the NYPD had a lot of details on past disturbances. So we discussed, "if you can predict the past, you can predict the future." That, plus the fact that the police department has a disproportionate number of wargamers in their ranks. Then there was the guy from the U.S. Forestry Service (walking into my office wearing cowboy boots and a ten gallon hat). That was more like war, and the forestry service, like the cops, had lots of good data to mine, from past wild fires. I think that's what they ended up calling the game, *Wildfire,* which eventually evolved into the current computerized, and very accurate, version. Then a group of academics at a Mexico City university wanted help in simulating rural agriculture, and the impact of some new ideas on productivity, and local politics. Some of these guys were already into wargames, and they immediately grasped the concept of modeling media and political factors. More recently, a NATO country wanted help in building a crisis simulation for senior political and military leaders. In this case, politics and media reaction played a major role in their most likely crises. The two guys who were my main contacts (they had gone to graduate school in the U.S.) were wargamers, and immediately understood what I needed when I asked for a media "Order of Battle" for their country. Within weeks, I received an elaborate spreadsheet, containing all the major national media (and that of some neighboring nations), along with the critical characteristics of each media outlet. It was smooth sailing from that point. The military angle, it turned out, was the easy part.

If you know some wargamers, or can spot those who could be (are analytic, practical and good at turning the news into numbers), but aren't, they are the ones who can make this happen. Unless you are the one, in which case you can get straight to work.

RANDOMNESS, PLAYER CHOICE, AND PLAYER EXPERIENCE
John Kaufeld

When people complain about boardgames, what do they complain about the most? Luck! Many games at many tables around the world (but particularly in the United States) end with a variation on the classic line, "If I just rolled a nine, I would have totally owned you in that game! You can't call that a 'win.' The dice just liked you better tonight."

All games contain a certain balance between randomness and player choice, but different levels of that balance appeal to different types of players. To be successful it in the market, a game requires the right combination of features to appeal to its target audience. As long as the game meets the needs of the intended audience, and does so in an entertaining and engaging way, the game has a shot at success.

We see this idea demonstrated in the market with everything from simple, mass-production children's games to high end European boardgames.

Bouncing into the Random World of *Candyland*

The classic children's game *Candyland*, for example, is entirely based on chance. Player skill has nothing to do with the outcome of the game.

After setting up the pieces and shuffling the deck of colored movement cards, players simply flip over the top card of the deck, move their pieces, and wait to see which of them will draw the right combination of colors to reach the finish line first.

Before the first player even drew a card, the game already selected the winner; it just hasn't told anyone the outcome yet. The act of "playing" the game reveals which player the game selected. There is no decision-making, no strategy, and no player choice. If you substituted a dog, monkey, or pile of building blocks for one of the human players, the replacement would still have exactly the same chance of winning as the human player did.

As a children's game, though, this mechanic delivers a benefit for its audience. First, it's simple. It requires no reading, so young children can play. Because the board and cards are color-coded, players can easily figure out where to move their pieces.

The mechanic also creates an interesting by-product: the ability to play the game alone. By taking player choice completely out of the game and substituting a simple card-flipping mechanic, the designer made *Candyland* into a completely functional activity for one young player. A creative child can completely engage in a game "against" a couple of stuffed animals or other toys. She can entertain herself the whole time with imaginative commentary as play goes on. Because the game gives entertainment value through this capability, the game continues selling well today. By meeting a need for its audience and delivering value, a game that completely ignores player choice and interaction becomes a viable, profit-making product.

Peeking at the Realm of Pure Strategy

At the other end of the scale, we find pure strategy games. These games boil randomness entirely out of gameplay, creating an experience that focuses on player choice, skill, and interaction.

In games like *Blokus*, *Quarto*, *Chess*, and *Go*, players see the entire strategic situation laid out in front of them. There is nothing hidden and nothing unknown, apart from the other player's strategic plans. Players use completely balanced groups of pieces against each other. A player's success or failure in the game relies entirely on his ability to plot out a solid strategy and react to what his opponents do. No random event will suddenly appear out of nowhere and turn the outcome of the game.

Cityscape adds a twist to the "pure strategy" concept by letting players set secret goals for each row of buildings in their city. The goals add an element of surprise to the game's outcome, although the playing style itself relies on pure strategy and player choice.

At the beginning of each round, players decide their goals for each section of the board, and then record their choices by placing a standard 6-sided die into a scoring block. Only they can see their goal dice during game play.

During a turn, players draw one block from a shared pool, and then place that block onto one of the board's sixteen spaces to build part of their city. Since the pool contains a limited number of each size block, players sometimes find their choices limited. At the end of the round, players lay their blocks down and show their choices to all players. Finally, all players count their score.

Are these game designs somehow better because of their high strategy? Are games that use a more random concept in their design automatically inferior? Again, you need to go back to the experience of the player, because the player is the final judge on these questions.

Losing in a pure strategy game clearly, plainly, and somewhat painfully demonstrates that a player made less successful choices than the winner. While that's fun for highly competitive, thoughtful, strategic and serious players, not everyone shares that vision.

Tempering Strategy with Randomness (and Vice-Versa)

Many people look to games as a form of light mental challenge, relaxation, and a handy excuse to get together with their friends. In those situations, most players look for an experience that mixes pure strategy with randomness, rewarding players who make good decisions, while giving people with lower skills a fighting chance for victory at the same time. The vast majority of games on the market today fall into this broad category, although with wildly different mixtures of their key ingredients.

Even Eurogames known for their high strategy include some random elements to keep the playing experience fresh and provide different challenges. In the highly-rated European strategy games *Power Grid* and *Puerto Rico*, randomness touches the gameplay experience like seasoning in a fine meal: you notice it and you know it's there, but it only nudges the game experience, not defines it.

Examining the Mix in *Puerto Rico* and *Power Grid*

The random element of *Puerto Rico* comes from the blind draws of plantation tiles during each Settler round. Players need plantation tiles, along with matching production facilities, to create goods that give them money and victory points in the game. Tiles representing plantation fields for the five production crops come into the game in random order. This limits player options and forces them to make the most of the available choices in any given round.

Although the random element impacts each player's strategy, it does not define that strategy. Players can still follow their own directions and make their own choices. For example, a player might really want a coffee field this round, but if no coffee is available on their turn to choose, they can shift their strategy a bit to make use of the many sugar fields that appeared during the last draw, for example.

In *Power Grid*, randomness controls the supply of plants available for the power plant auctions. Players need plants to power the distribution grids they build in the game. Each plant supplies power to a certain number of cities while using a specific type and amount of fuel (powering up to three cities by burning two units of oil, for example). In addition, each power plant card has an identification number which represents the opening bid to own the plant, and figures into how players determine turn order. Those variables make each plant unique in the game. This creates a lot of tension in the power plant auctions, because a plant's value depends on each player's growth strategy, the quantity and type of fuels available, the type of power plants owned by the other players, and how close players are to ending the game.

During setup, players pull nine "starter" power plants out of the deck, then shuffle the remaining plants to create a randomized draw deck. Every game begins with the same eight starter power plants in the auction supply. The ninth starter power plant card sits at the top of the draw deck, waiting to enter play as the first new card drawn.

As players purchase power plants from the auction, they restock the auction supply with replacement power plants drawn from the deck. Starting with the second draw, randomness takes control of the power plant auction supply. After six to eight auctions, players clearly see the effects of randomness in the game as the original plants disappear, replaced by progressively more efficient plants which randomly join the game.

But the designer did not completely leave random chance in charge of the auction supply. The game's auction system includes two mechanics that maintain the balance of power by managing the availability of plants in the auction.

The first mechanic governs which plants players can purchase at auction. Of the eight cards in the auction supply, only the four lowest-numbered plants are available for purchase. Players can see the other four higher-numbered cards, but can't bid on them yet. When a new plant comes into the game from the draw deck, it goes into auction supply according to its identification number. Depending on its number, the new plant might immediately be available for purchase or it might force a lower-numbered plant into the available for purchase section.

The second mechanic works much more simply. At the end of each turn, the highest-numbered power plant in supply goes back to the bottom of the deck. Players immediately draw another plant to replace it, using the regular restocking rules to position that plant in the auction supply.

If a designer increases the random element in a game, she will often put the randomness inside some constraints to limit its impact. The constraints blunt the impact of random chance, giving the players' choices and strategy more power over the game's outcome.

Can't Stop Dealing with Dice in Settlers of Catan and Formula D

The much-vaunted *Settlers of Catan* uses two dice to drive resource production each turn. Although dice are a common source of randomness in any game, *Settlers* constrains the randomness with a predetermined grid of production numbers placed on the board's resource tiles. The production numbers enforce a standard bell curve distribution on resource production.

Since the players can clearly see which tiles are more likely to produce goods, they can make informed, strategic decisions about the placement of their settlements and roads in the game. Their strategy drives those choices. The production numbers on the board serve as extra information to help players guide their choices and achieve their strategy, but they also constrain the impact of randomness on the game's outcome.

The racing game *Formula D* (formerly known as *Formula De*) accomplishes the same thing by using custom-numbered polyhedral dice. Each die in the game represents a different gear in the car's transmission. Although the dice are of standard polyhedral sizes ranging from four-sided to thirty-sided, the numbers on each die use different ranges than normal.

For example, the first gear die is four-sided, but only displays the numbers one and two on its faces. Likewise, the twenty-sided die that represents a car's fifth gear only rolls numbers ranging from eleven to twenty. The distribution of numbers in that range is exactly even, so you stand the same chance of rolling an eleven as you do of getting a blazing twenty. The custom dice protect you from complete chance because of their restricted range of numbers.

The classic Sid Sackson game *Can't Stop* is entirely focused on rolling four standard six-sided dice, but it still gives players a lot of control over their success. This game constrains randomness and improves player choice through its board layout and how players use the die rolls on each turn.

The board is shaped like a classic stop sign, and displays a column of movement spaces for each number in the range from two to twelve. The columns for two and twelve sit in the shortest sections of the board, along the outside edges on each side. As you move toward the middle, you find columns for each number. The columns are in order by the probability of rolling that number on two six-sided dice. The center of the board belongs to the column for the number seven, the most-rolled combination.

In the game, players roll four six-sided dice each turn. That takes care of the randomness component, but what about player choice? Players set their strategy by splitting the four dice into two pairs. The players put markers onto the board according to the pairs of numbers they generated.   Players can choose to lock in their score with the markers as they already are, or they can take a chance and continue rolling. If they roll again, they must be able to make one of the numbers from which they previously scored on two of their newly-rolled dice, or they lose all of the points they scored this round.

Because the players have complete control over how they pair the dice, they effectively get to choose the probability of success on future rolls. If they feel lucky, they might choose a low probability number like two or twelve, because the scoring tracks for those numbers are much shorter than the tracks for higher probability numbers such as six, seven, and eight. Regardless of the outcome, the players still get to make the decisions that drive their strategy and the outcome of the game.

Is There a Single Right Answer?

There's no "right" setting when it comes to the balance of randomness and player choice in a game. Instead, it all depends on what the players enjoy and how the randomness elements fit into the greater design of the game.

The balance of randomness versus player choice in a game's design dramatically affects the player experience. Knowing your target players helps you refine the game experience to meet their needs. The more a game entertains and challenges its players, the more players your game will get. And that, after all, is the name of the game!

DICE AS DRAMATURGE
Chris Klug

"Well, I don't know what to do, you tell me." We were playing *DragonQuest*, an older pencil-and-paper RPG which I was helping develop for SPI. A good friend of mine was playing an RPG for the first time ever that Sunday. He and I had forged our game-playing friendship over *Strat-O-Matic Baseball*, a dice-and-cards centric baseball simulation, and he wanted to try this 'fantasy' thing with me. He knew I designed games for a living, was willing to give anything I was working on a try, but fantasy wasn't normally his cup of tea.

This game session, however, was a particularly bad one to serve as his introduction to the world of fantasy role-playing. The party had encountered a troll, the negotiations had gone badly, one of the group had decided to take a swing at the 'big ugly,' and a couple of fumbles on their part later, the only party member left standing was the character run by my newbie friend, and all he was armed with was a dagger.

My friend (Todd by name) understood the dynamics of baseball sims; he understood odds, and even though he didn't quite know for sure what a 'troll' was, he had just seen it wipe the floor with the other party members, and he also knew the character he played was about as green a character as he was a player, it being the first game session for both player and character. He tried to come up with a baseball metaphor to describe the situation his character was facing, one that he and I would both understand.

"This is kinda like Koufax against Choo-Choo Coleman, right?" (Koufax is, of course, Sandy Koufax, the all-time great Los Angeles Dodger lefty pitcher who mowed down batter after batter during the *1960's*, while Choo-Choo Coleman was a starting catcher on the 1962 Mets, they who still hold the all-time single season record for least wins as a team in a season. Coleman epitomized that team).

I thought for a second. "Well, while it may look that way, I think you have a better chance to suceed than Coleman did."

"That's not saying much," he whined a bit. Todd never liked to lose.

"In *Strat*," I continued, "Koufax dominated lefties, and since Coleman batted lefty, he'd have absolutely no chance of hitting a homer against Sandy."

Todd looked glum. "Don't I know it."

"However, *DragonQuest* has a system that does allow you a chance, albeit a small one," I said.

"What's that?" Todd looked up.

"We have a Critical Hit System. If you roll really, really well, you can do a hit that avoids the troll's natural armor and you can do a lot of damage," I explained.

Todd brightened. "Well, that sounds like I should stay and fight this guy," and he started to shake the two D10s in his hand.

"Whoa," I cautioned. "Before you choose to stand your ground, let me explain your chances. First, you're rolling D100."

"You explained that already." Did I mention Todd was impatient?

"Hang on. You need a 02 or less to do a Crit."

"That doesn't seem like much of a chance."

"You are only a new character, remember?"

Todd just stared at me silently.

"Ok, so IF you roll an 02 or an 01, you do a Crit, which does max damage for that dagger."

Todd thought a sec. "That still wouldn't kill him, would it?"

"Nope."

Todd was getting frustrated. "Well, so even if I do hit him with a Crit, then he's gonna take a swipe at me and I'll end up like so much hamburger!"

I sighed. "More than likely."

Another player, Steve, chimed in. "Wait, wouldn't Todd then get a roll on the Critical Hit Table?" That table was one of my favorite toys in *DQ*. In addition to just doing max damage that avoided armor, when you generated a Crit, you rolled D100 and looked up a viscerally descriptive additional result on this table. Most of the time, the table added flavor to the result, such as "Your blade has caught in the target's right elbow joint and been ripped from your hand. You are now without your weapon but the target's right arm is totally useless for the remainder of the fight." or "Your attack found a particularly vulnerable chink in your opponent's armor, the damage done from the blow is doubled." Nasty stuff.

However, in addition to these descriptive results, some results were based on the type of weapon used (crushing weapons might break a bone, stabbing weapons might injure an internal organ) and these results were particularly effective but very rare.

"Let me see that," Todd asked. He skimmed the table, skimming some of the more lurid descriptions, and handed it back to Steve. "That seems pretty cool, let's just have at it."

"You sure?" I asked.

"Yup," Todd replied. "And, after all, I can always just create another character, right?"

"Right," I said. "Roll."

Todd shook the two D10s in his hand. They were read sequentially, with the first die (numbered one to zero) read as the 'tens' digit and the second die (also numbered one to zero) read as the 'units' digit. So, rolling a '4' and then a '6' was read as a '46.' If the first die read a '0', that meant the second die was just read as the single digit, with a '0' and a '7' being read as '7.' If, however, two zeros were rolled, that result '00,' was treated as '100.' So, Todd needed to roll a zero ('0') on the first die and a '1' or a '2' on the second die to generate a Crit in the first place.

As he always did, he rolled to two dice one after the other rather than at the same time (a habit that most players found annoying but this time added to the suspense). The first die read '0.' "Whoa, cool," he said. Then rolled the second die and his face lit up. "Two!" Indeed the second die read '2' which meant he had rolled '02,' or a Crit. "Whoa, whoa, whoa!" he yelled. "How much damage does that do?"

"Well, the max damage of the dagger is 8 points, so all of that counts against the trolls' total hit points."

"Which is?"

"17."

Silence.

"And after this, he goes, right?" Todd was hoping I'd reply in the negative.

"Uh, yeah." I tried to say that in as hopeful a way as I could.

"And that means he's gonna kill me right?"

"Probably."

"Oh, well." Todd began to crumple the character record. Steve chimed in again. "Man, don't forget your roll on the Crit Table."

"Whatever," and Todd grabbed the two D10s and just tossed them carelessly across the Battlemat. They stopped rolling.

We just stared. The two D10s came up "0" and "1". Steve was quiet "I think that's a good thing." I looked at the table. It read:

"01: If weapon is a stabbing type, the attacker has managed to lodge the blade in the eye of the target, driven very deep with great force into the target's brain, killing the target instantly. Target is dead."

Todd screamed. Steve screamed. I beamed quietly, knowing that this singular event had created a gaming memory for everyone at the table, and cemented Todd's participation in the campaign for ever more. To this day, when we see each other and we talk about gaming, Todd doesn't talk about *Strat-O-Matic* (well, not TOO much, anyway) but never fails to bring up that Sunday afternoon at my gaming table in Elizabeth, NJ. The drama, the impossible odds realized, the improbability of the event, all combined to cement the memory in all those present. Forever.

One of tools for evoking player emotion that modern computer RPGs have taken away from game designers is the ability of the player to directly manipulate, understand and experience game systems themselves. The physical interaction of player and the game systems, if those systems are designed well, induce emotion in the players just from the way they work and how the players use them. In this essay, I'd like to discuss and analyze examples of this effect: the effect dramatized in the actual events depicted above. Yes, while embellished slightly (the event happened in the summer of 1982, almost thirty years ago, so the dialogue is dramatized), the details of the event are as they actually happened. This event underlines my premise, and allows me to discuss this player/game system interaction in detail, because the easiest game system with which to show this effect is to use the way dice systems work in roleplaying games (RPGs).

RPG dice systems have a particular bonus in the way they invoke player emotion, as those dice systems determine success or failure of the player's actual alter ego, his character. In the best of those designs, dice not only provide randomized conflict resolution, they also provide a foundation for the emotional experience; tangibly manifesting the world to the players as they manipulate the world's totems - the dice.

Like most things, game design is cyclical. The passions and likes of the gamer audience wax and wane with time, often coming back to enjoy popular motifs heretofore out-of-fashion time and time again. My roots as a game designer are in the fertile turf of board/pencil-and-paper game design, and I migrated into computer/video design more to make a living as a designer, rather than from a particular passion for that style of gaming. Don't misinterpret me; however, I enjoy playing *World of Warcraft, Call of Duty, Railroad Tycoon* and *SimCity* just as much as the next geek, but there is something 'visceral' to me about boardgames and their younger, geekier sibling, roleplaying games, that always have a soft spot in my heart.

Part of this fascination, to my way of thinking, resides in the physicality of the game props and systems, including lovely printed four-color game boards, cards, pieces, and, the focus of this essay, the dice. While one could debate with some validity the impact of images appearing on the screen of a video game as opposed to the impact of printed game parts, the dice to me have a particular fascination as they do not have a direct equivalent in the video game world. Part random number generator, part talisman, these objects viscerally connect the player with the game systems, precisely because the player manipulates the outcomes of these systems by rolling the dice. Talk all you want about digital media being 'interactive,' I posit that there is no greater degree of interactivity than the kind a player gets when they have the dice in their hand and are trying to manifest a particular result to appear, face-up, on any particular throw of the dice.

One reason for the power of this activity, I believe, is a kind of 'head fake' where the player, because she is holding the random number generator in her hand, believes that they can affect the roll in some fashion. While the left-brains amongst us would claim they don't really believe this is possible, almost every game player I've ever met feels as if they can, indeed, affect the roll. I happen to believe that you can affect the result, but that belief does not affect my game designs and is a topic for another discussion.

Owing to this feeling of connection, the act of rolling dice carries with it an emotional charge which, if the designer is aware of it, can be leveraged to deepen the game experience. Additionally, if the designer is a master of this game prop, the actual use of the random properties inherent in a random result generated for the audience to see can also aid in telling the game story.

In order to illuminate my point, this article will describe the mechanics of a simple thirty-year-old RPG system, the D100 system used by Chaosium's games, called Basic Role Playing (BRP). It was used specifically in *Call of Cthulu* and *RuneQuest*, and the rules have shown a remarkable resiliency even in this day of the 'D20' system made ubiquitous by Wizards of the Coast. The rules are still in print and available here: (http://www.chaosium.com/article. php?story_id=246). While possibly not the most elegant RPG dice system ever invented (Greg Gorden's exponential dice system he created for Mayfair's *DC Heroes* might win that award if I were voting), I used the D100 system for a very long time in my RPG campaign, I adapted it (er, was 'inspired by it') for the dice system I created for the *James Bond 007* game I designed for Victory Games, and was always cognizant of the impact dice systems had on players. BRP was very flexible (Chaosium used it for more than a dozen titles over its long life) but when WOTC made the D20 system openly available in the 1990s, it was all-but abandoned as a viable RPG system.

The D100 BRP system was born in an era when *D&D* was the newly crowned king of the gaming world. *D&D*'s original dice system, in case you were unaware, introduced many new exotic kinds of dice to the world: D4s, D8s, D10s, D12s and D20s. These new (to most gamers) dice were part of what gave *D&D* its appeal, and some of the 'magic' of that game was the 'ooh, cool dice!' factor for players. One of the things you could do with the D10's, however, was roll two of them and read the pair sequentially, thus generating an equally weighted number from 1 to 100. If the first die read '0' and the second die read '1', this was read as '01,' or simply '1'. If the first die read '0' and the second die read '0,' that was read as '100.' First die '4' and the second die '5,' and you had '45.' *D&D* used this D100 system mainly with random lists of up to 100 items. Each entry on such a list would have a 1/100th chance to being generated, which facilitated long detailed lists of esoteric objects. Lots o' fun.

While I'm not exactly sure whether the events occurred in this sequence, my memory is that after *D&D* was released, the people working on *RuneQuest* took the ability to generate a number from 1-100 and built their conflict resolution system around that pillar. While *Rune-Quest* (hereafter *RQ*) included D4s, D6s and D8s (you almost had to include those kinds of dice in role playing games published around 1978 in order to be taken seriously as an RPG), none of those dice were used for combat resolution in BRP. Instead, they were all used to calculate the amount of damage done if you did hit. To see whether you *did* hit or not, you rolled a D100. Your chance to hit something was expressed as a 1-100 number as well -- for example, '67.' Thus, if you roll a 67 or less with your D100, you hit. Rolling a 68 or greater meant you missed. This kind of system emulated the state of the art at that time in *D&D*, where they used a D20 to resolve the 'hitting' thing, generating either success or failure.

Degree of Success

To this basic system, however, the *RQ* designers added what I later called 'degree of success' (I'm not sure whether they gave it a name quite like that). The dice system not only determined success or failure, but *how well or how badly* the player succeeded or failed. Two layers of success were added: 'Critical Success' (hereafter referred to as a 'Crit') and a 'Special Success,' hereafter called simply a 'Special.' Failure had only one additional layer, that of a failure so bad it was termed a 'Fumble.'

The D100 roll needed to achieve these results were calculated as a percentage of the players' original success chance: a Crit was determined by multiplying the Success Chance by 5%, and a Special was determined by multiplying the Success Chance by 20%. Crits were better for the player than a Special, and a Special was better for the player than a Normal success. Success in combat was measured first by hitting the opponent, and then additionally by the amount of damage done.

For example, if the player's Success Chance was 60 (rolling a 60 or less on D100), 5% of that was a Crit (rolls 01, 02, and 03), while 20% of that was termed a Special (rolls 01-12, with 01-03 being a Crit and 04 or above being a Special). If the player rolled a Special, more dice were rolled for damage, and the blow was harder to Dodge (in fact, it needed a Special Dodge on the defender's part). If a Crit was rolled, the maximum possible damage was done and the defender only avoided being hit by rolling a Crit Dodge. In that game system, a Crit was a devastating blow indeed, because the character did maximum possible damage AND all the defender's armor was ignored.

Fumbles were calculated as were Crits, but the dice range was placed at the other end of spectrum and was calculated from the Failure chance. So, if the player's Success chance was, say, 20 or less, his failure chance was 80, and his Fumble chance was 5% of 80 (or 4 chances out of 100), thus the failure roll was 97-100. This may sound complicated, but there were look-up tables to handle the calculations.

It is important to understand that the very fact that 'success' was placed at the low end of the dice result possibilities and 'failure' at the extreme high end also expresses my theory. Players would desire to 'roll low' to get a good result and they would try to avoid 'rolling high' so as not to get near a fumble.

That note actually brings us to the reason why this system was troublesome for some players: the math. The feeling the game system delivered to players worked just fine, thank you, but the simple mathemetical manipulations needed to get there were problematic. Intellectually, the system seemed fine; a 1-100 system gave the GM the opportunity for fine gradations in success chances ("hmm, I'll give you a +8 to your success chance for coming up from behind him, but he gets a -6 for his Sixth Sense, so that's an overall +2 for you, your adjusted chance to hit goes from 57 to 59.") That seemed like an advantage, but in practical terms there was a lot of adding and subtracting.

As a little generational observation, the system worked a *lot* better 'back in the day,' as players of my generation handled the addition and subtraction in their heads with a lot greater ease than do the 'youngun's' of today do (perhaps not as used to having to do that kind of math on the fly). I GM'ed a campaign using this system in the 2007-2008 timeframe and players in their mid-20's really enjoyed the visceral nature of the system (the 'emotional manipulation' the system delivered as described in this essay) but they relied on us 'oldtimers' at the table to handle all the math. That campaign had a little bit of 'oldtimer' cool to it; I GM'ed while Zeb Cook (of *AD&D* fame) played.

Anyhow, I digress. The point of the system is this: players really enjoyed rolling for the goals they knew to be present and visible. "What do I need for a Crit and what do I need for a Special?" were often uttered just as the players were shaking the two D10's in their hand prior to their roll. And, if the roll was just short of a goal, there was a very palpable feeling of being 'almost a crit.' If the player needed a 15 for a Special and rolled a 16, cries of agony rose from the table, even though the system resolved the 16 identically as a roll of, say, 47 (assuming both were a success).

Let me just amplify this a bit: having the dice system deliver a described result (Critical, Special, Normal and Fumble) not only enabled and encouraged the players to visualize what those results might be in their noggins, it allowed the players to translate dice results that *almost* reached one of those thresholds and enjoy the drama of the 'not quite' nature. Knowing what they had to roll, and knowing how close (or far) they came, increased their visualization of the gameplay.

Now, if the player rolled a Fumble, well, the pain and anguish were tangible. It was more than simply the fact of failure; when the description of the fumble was read to the player (example: "adventurer slips on the blood-covered floor and his weapon is thrust into the leg of the nearest companion, impaling them") this act of ineptitude begat a legend of its own (assuming the players' characters survived the evening, of course). These incidents created much more than the math and damage done would simply generate numerically. They created drama.

While the D100 system functioned well enough as a game system, the drama that came as a result of understanding (and pre-visualizing) the potential outcomes and how to maximize success, combined with the always-present potential for outright disaster with a fumble (regardless of how high the player's chance of success might be) as well as the glorious success of a crit, gave every single roll a sense of the dramatic that the players enjoyed. All of this drama came from the simple fact of life in these games: the game system was visible to the players, they generated the random numbers needed to make the system work themselves, and thus 'created' the game as they played. They did not just watch as a computer resolved every swing and applied the damage. Designers of those systems didn't need to search for ways to make the players feel more involved; those players were involved from the word go.

Using Dice Systems to Tell a Story

In addition to the simple resolution of combat, the Chaosium systems have also used dice to help players visualize the action in a visceral way as well as to deliver the world story to them. I'll describe both of those facets now.

RuneQuest Hit Location System

RuneQuest's Crit system, combined with a Hit location system, delivered a distinct flavor to the gameplay. The Crit system basically communicated that at almost any time, with a series of very good dice rolls, anyone could kill anyone else. Thus every combat had drama built in. Their Hit Location system, which was based on research done by one of their designers into the way sword fighting was done in Society for Creative Anachronism battles, also added a degree of the visceral. But, it also altered strategy. In typical *D&D* battles, where an opponent was viable until dead, every fight lasted until one side or the other reached zero hit points (dead). With the *RQ* system, a viable strategy was to just 'take out the legs' of an opponent, because once they went down, they couldn't follow you any longer, and you could move on to another opponent. Certain types of wounds were as good as a kill. The result in play was that the battlefield was littered with wounded characters and monsters instead of piles of dead. It just 'felt' different, and thus the kinds of adventures you created as gamemaster differed as well.

Demon Armor

In another variant of the BRP system, *Elric!*, certain types of armor a character could wear were imbued with the power of a chaotic demon. This power gave the armor more protection points than a set of comparable normal armor. The system stated that when damage was applied to a target from a successful hit, the armor protection rating was subtracted from the damage first before it was applied to the target. So, if your character did 8 points of damage but the monster was wearing 3-point leather, you did only five effective points of damage (8 - 3) = 5.

However, if a demon inhabited the armor, the exact amount of protection the armor afforded was determined at the moment of impact by a die roll. For example, a suit of leather demon armor might protect for 2+D4 points. When an attack hit the armor, you rolled a D4; the armor (for that hit only) might protect for 3 (2 + a roll of 1 = 3) or it might protect for 6 (2 + a roll of 4 = 6). You couldn't tell. More powerful demons used larger dice to determine their possible protection, but also *more chaotic demons had a bigger swing* of protection values.

So, one demon might have an armor value of 5+D12, a range from 6 through 17. Another demon might have an armor value of 5+2D6, also a range from 6 through 17. The first demon's range had an equal chance of a 6, an 11, or a 17. However, the second demon's distribution, because the 2D6 roll was a bell curve, had a much greater chance of a 12 (right in the middle of the distribution) than it did of generating a 6 or a 17. Thus, the second demon would be viewed as more 'predictable' while the first demon would be viewed as more 'chaotic.'

The D20 System: Simpler, but less drama?

Once RPGs proliferated, the challenges of the genre for the gamer became the expanding variety of systems. Just because you know how to play, say, West End Games's *Star Wars*, didn't mean you know how to play SPI's *Universe*, or GDW's *Traveller* (even though all these games were science-fiction RPGs). Players would play one system, begin to know it intimately, then perhaps a new system would arrive and the gaming group would discuss the option of giving that system a try. But someone would bow out because they just didn't want to invest the time to learn something new. Game companies were aware of this, especially Chaosium, who proposed all their games use a similar system so players might move from one game system to another as painlessly as possible. All the Chaosium game systems (*Elric, RuneQuest, Call of Cthulu*) had similar conflict resolution systems (married to slightly different skill lists).

As long as you were a fan of Chaosium's product line, and stayed there, the system switches were relatively painless.

But many companies tried to distinguish themselves with innovative game systems. The hobby market has faced this problem over and over. In response, Wizards of the Coast created the D20 system. Well, they didn't create it so much as make the system 'open source.' The D20 system was at the heart of *D&D*, and what Wizards did was say "hey, anyone can use the D20 system if they want to, all they need to do is acknowledge that the system is ours, and that they are using our system, and they're home free." And many companies, seeing the economic advantages of using the system, adopted it. The advantages were numerous: RPG players wouldn't need to learn multiple systems, just one; adventures published for one system would, with a little tweaking, work for other systems; and those companies wouldn't have to invent their own systems any longer, they could just co-opt the D20 system. But the sense of the dice design embodying the essence of the IP of the game world evaporated with these advantages. That facet of RPG game design lost its steam, and, in my opinion, also lost much of the possibility of dice systems evoking emotion in gameplay.

Computer Games

Today's computer games hide all the calculations from the player. This can be an advantage, in that the designer can utilize calculations of much greater complexity than ever before. This allows a greater range of game possibilities. But designers struggle to find ways to weave back into gameplay some sense of the dramatic. Luck isn't the only thing that drives a dramatic conflict resolution system. Doing exactly the right thing at exactly the right moment is crucial for great storytelling. But knowing what that moment is, and how slim your chances really are, can be challenging for videogame designers.

I recently spoke to a colleague working on an MMO, where small, almost undeterminable 'adds' are the way most of those games are designed. This is almost required, as players desire to accumulate pieces of armor and such as they play, and you can't max out the system too easily by this kind of accumulation. The downside of this is that no 'magical' aid is very dramatic, and at the end of the day everything just tends to fade into the background, and nothing seems to matter. At least to this observer, nothing seems to matter.

My colleague complained about this very issue, as he is also a dramatist and a writer, and yearns for those moments as well. His staff systems designer, an MMO veteran and someone who revels in those minute differences, can't see what the big deal is about my colleague's concerns. He worries about 'balance' and 'max/min' play styles, and in his job, I suppose he should. But something is lost, and my colleague and I both sense it.

Visible, rolled-by-humans dice and the ability they bring to add the unexpected, definitely add drama to games. As someone who came of age playing games where I could tell how tough or easy something was, I desperately miss that kind of drama when I play computer or video games. I always try to figure out a way to add that back into play. Games sometimes can be shallow experiences without that kind of drama.

DESIGNING FOR PUBLISHING
JT Smith

Designing tabletop games is a far more challenging undertaking than anyone first expects. There are many factors to take into account that can quickly turn a seemingly simple project into something much more complicated.

Just like writing a book, when designing a game you have to identify your audience: Who are they? What do they know? What are their biases? How will their knowledge and biases affect gameplay? How does it affect what mechanics you'll use? How does it affect how you write the rules? Just like a good book, knowing what to leave out is often more important than knowing what to put in.

In addition to establishing your audience, you should anticipate the special needs of your target players. Are they color blind? About 8% of males and 0.5% of females have some form of color blindness. Is your target player a child? If so, you'll have to get your game CPSIA certified. If they are in the infant to toddler range then you'll likely need all paper components laminated with plastic for the drool factor. Are your target players older than 40? If so, make sure there is no fine print or they may have trouble seeing it. And the list goes on.

Games must also be packaged to sell. A sign of a newbie game designer is failure to take into account the retail experience when designing the game. There are many reasons why all game designers should keep this under consideration. Will the game be sold primarily in brick and mortar stores? If so, there are specific form factors that those retailers prefer. If the game will be sold at multi-lingual venues you should include multi-lingual text on the outside of the box, and multi-lingual instructions. Did you take into account that 60 to 70% of the retail price of your game will be divided between distributors and retailers? You should also research the prices of other similarly sized games of the same or related genre to make sure you are asking a reasonable price for yours.

All of these things are important, but there's another factor that's becoming more and more important: designing your game for the publishing process, including manufacturing, marketing, and distributing.

Traditional Game Publishing

It used to be that every game went through the same publishing and sales process. A game would be picked up by a publisher, they would print 3,000 to 5,000 copies on an offset press, and then they'd push the game out the door through their various distribution channels. If the game was successful, they'd print more copies and repeat. Virtually every game you see in your local game store from *Settlers of Catan* to *Ticket to Ride* has gone through this path.

The only variant in this formula is that some people choose to do a vanity run (self-publish). Most of these fail due to lack of distribution. There are many reasons a distributor decides against picking up a game from an indie publisher. Often, the games just aren't very good because indie developers didn't invest time in playtesting. Most of the time, a small publisher won't have the means or knowledge to do the market research to see if their game is actually a niche product. And don't forget that buyers are creatures of habit who pretty much always prefer buying a product from a name they recognize.

Regardless of whether or not you use a publisher or do a vanity run, the process for manufacturing and distributing the game remains the same. You design high-resolution artwork, print several thousand copies, and get custom game parts made and included in the box. Then, you make deals with distributors and retailers to sell your game. Your out-of-pocket expense for manufacturing and distribution can be around 90% of the retail price of your game, and you end up the proud owner of $5,000 to $50,000 worth of game inventory. If you want to make sure this doesn't happen to you, make sure you keep your manufacturing costs in line with the retail price of the game. A good rule of thumb is that the manufacturing cost should be no more than 17% of the retail price.

The biggest benefit of this route has always been, and will always be, that you can do pretty much anything you want. You can print game components to be as large as the offset press will allow, which is usually pretty large. You can get custom plastic or wooden game parts made and included in the box. You can design custom packaging to fit any specification. The sky is really the limit.

The only strategic considerations you have to take are whether to use plastic parts or wood, and how few components you can use to keep the game playable, yet profitable. You might also think about whether to use a four color printing process, or just a one/two color process. These are the basic variables you can play with, and almost everything else is just the cost of doing business.

The Rise of Print and Play

In the mid-1990's, with the mainstream adoption of the Internet, a new publishing process, known as print and play (PNP), was widely adopted by indie game designers. Print-and-play games are games that are published as PDFs to the web, sometimes for charge, but usually for free. It is the player's responsibility to print the game components on a home printer, and use parts (pawns, dice, etc) from other games they already own.

Board Game Geek's Canonical List of PNP Games

http://www.boardgamegeek.com/geeklist/7603/the-canonical-list-of-free-print-and-play-games-0

With this new medium came new design challenges. You want to make your game look good, but you also have to keep the artwork low resolution so that your target players can easily and quickly download it. You have no means of distributing parts with your game, so you have to make do with what you think your players will have on-hand. You also have to take into account that the player's printer may only be black and white, and likely can't print on anything larger than 8.5" x 11".

Print and play also brings new business challenges. PNP offers virtually no opportunity to regain the cost of large production artwork, so as a game designer you have to decide whether to do it yourself, pay for professional artwork, or make friends with an artist. You also have to decide what you will charge for the game, if anything. Ask yourself if you are you doing this because you want people to play your game, or are you doing it for money? Many designers such as Scott Slomiany choose to go free and gain massive popularity, like he did with his game *Pocket Civ*, which has since been turned into various computer and cell phone games. Others put their print and play games up for charge and are able to make a small profit, like those on www.wargamedownloads.com. Yet others fail altogether, just like in the traditional publishing process.

Print and play has a nice advantage in that the web is a built-in distribution mechanism. There's no need to find a distributor, because it's relatively easy and cheap to set up a web site, although a bit more difficult and expensive to set up an e-commerce web site if you intend to sell your game. However, this also means that 100% of the profit from any sales you make go directly to you.

In this new era of print and play, savvy game publishers soon realized that they had a new means of vetting potential games. If a print-and-play game was getting a lot of attention, game publishers could strike a deal with the designer to make a production version of the game. Print and play helped level the playing field a bit by removing part of the gamble from the publishing process. The publisher gained because the game could prove its popularity first, and the game designer could gain attention with little upfront cost.

Print on Demand Emerges

Around the turn of the century a new technology emerged known as Print on Demand (POD). With this technology things like books and game mats could be printed one at a time, when the customer ordered them. At the very least it allowed you to do very short runs (10 at a time). It was no longer necessary to print thousands of copies of a game and hope that they would sell. This blew the market wide open for indie game developers, especially those developing RPGs. Companies like RPGNow.com specialize in POD books for gamers. Unfortunately, it wasn't until the mid 2000's that board and card game designers could start making use of this technology via companies like Guild of Blades (www.guildofblades.com). It turns out it's a lot harder to make a deck of cards one at a time than a book.

Like Print and Play, this new publishing mechanism once again opened the way for designers. You could now get nearly the same quality of components that you'd get out of a traditional print run, but you didn't have to buy 5,000 copies of a game that would only ever sell 500 copies. POD would open the market for niche games.

As a designer, designing for POD is virtually the same as designing for traditional offset printing, although your color options are now black and white or full color. You can't do a single non-black color, and it is the same cost to print two colors as it is four. The ultimate quality you get isn't quite as good as a large run printing, but it's certainly good enough. The main challenge you face as a POD publisher is that your cost per game is increased by about double what a traditional run will cost per game.

Just like with an offset printing company, you must design your game to fit a printing and die template, whether that be for game boards, books, or cards. So you design your artwork, put it into a specific layout to exacting specifications, then ship it out to the POD printer.

POD printers typically print on smaller paper stock than an offset press, which opens up a new variable for printing card games. This new technology means that you're printing 12 to 20 cards per sheet rather than 40 or more. With each piece of paper your cost goes up, so designing a deck around the printing process can save you money. If it's a 16 card process, then make sure your deck size is a multiple of 16.

Unfortunately, POD suffers from one of the weaknesses of print and play. You aren't going to get any game parts, unless you source them separately and add them to the box yourself. Therefore, as you design your game, you have to take into account what parts the player may have on-hand.

POD also has no built-in distribution channel. You get a few copies printed in advance, and then you have to sell them yourself to retailers, or individuals, or whomever.

Many of the bigger publishing companies have started using print on demand to make prototypes of their games, or to get small runs of their new games manufactured to test sales at trade shows. This advantage can also work for indie designers as they can get production quality copies made for playtesting, or to ship to large publishers to be added to their line-up.

Web to Print Arrives

Recently, print on demand has evolved into something new called web to print (W2P), which has completely changed the game for designers. For independent designers, W2P is pretty much the best possible scenario. There is one company which set the standard for how web to print game publishing works, The Game Crafter (www.thegamecrafter.com).

Full Disclosure: The author of this essay is one of the principal owners of The Game Crafter, LLC.

The Game Crafter's web-to-print process provides the same print quality you get with print on demand, but your costs are a bit lower, and the process is much easier. Black and white and color printing cost the same, which enables you to design whatever works best for your game. You can choose to make one game at a time, or you can order in bulk. You also get a wide selection of parts to flesh out your game, so your target player doesn't need to have anything on-hand. The Game Crafter also provides the flexibility of allowing you to design cards, game boards, player mats, tiles, tokens, and instructions to meet the needs of your game. When your game is ready, you can put your game up for sale right on their online store and collect royalties.

The design process for web to print is a bit easier than POD. Instead of designing all your pieces of art and then formatting them into some sort of printing/cutting template, you simply upload your artwork one piece at a time (or in bulk via FTP) and the software automatically positions your artwork in the best possible position to maximize quality and minimize production costs. You also have digital proofing tools at your disposal, so you have a good idea of what each component is going to look like before you print anything. The Game Crafter also provides a wide array of parts to choose from so you don't need to make sacrifices when designing the mechanics of your game around the parts the players may have.

W2P also provides a built-in distribution mechanism in the form of an online store, which is not available in POD or traditional vanity publishing. It's still your responsibility to market your game, to take it to trade shows and play it at game shops, but you don't have to worry about warehousing and shipping, and you get paid at the end of each month for the copies you sell. Perhaps the best part is that you can still order copies at cost for yourself to take to trade shows or to play with your friends.

W2P doesn't have the weaknesses of print and play either. W2P allows you to easily make physical prototypes during play testing. If your game becomes popular, it's more likely to get picked up by a large publisher, because the game was never released as a free PDF, and you don't have to try to set up your own e-commerce web site to sell it.

W2P's only weaknesses come to light when compared to a traditional publishing print run. The cost per unit is higher so you likely won't be able to sell your game through traditional distribution channels. Also, you have to design your components to meet the sizes and shapes that the W2P allows, which is less flexible than a traditional run. However, you have no up-front costs or warehousing, and you don't need to find a publisher willing to pick up your game.

Making the Choice

Now that there are more ways to publish, you need to choose the publishing type that's right for you. In doing so you'll need to take into account the pleasures and perils that each has to offer. There's no right or wrong answer, and you don't even need to settle on one. Just as many video game companies publish CDs to sell in brick and mortar stores and digital copies to download from various online distributors, you too can implement more than one publishing strategy. The important thing is that you know your options up front, and design your game to fit within the constraints of your strategy.

SIMPLY KNIZIA – THE ART IN KEEPING GAME DESIGN SIMPLE
Kevin Jacklin

Reiner Knizia designs simple boardgames, easily learned and most playable in less than one hour. However that does not necessarily mean that they are simplistic; the converse is often true. Knizia designs are often richly themed, the themes deeply embedded into the game mechanics. This article explores how Reiner Knizia game designs reflect a philosophy of sufficiency ("enough and no more") that leaves space to promote social interactivity and enjoyment. Additionally, these deep designs reward players who are prepared to follow Knizia's lead into that play space and explore for themselves.

Playing games is instinctive for young minds. A reading of the Knizia ludography[1] reveals that a large proportion of the games are children's titles. By necessity these are simple and straightforward games, usually with a single game mechanic – *Kangaroo* and *Schildkrötenrennen* being typical examples. To be successful, a game for children must relate to the common experiences of young players: shopping baskets or animals or fruits or tractors or dragons. That is to say, it must be highly thematic. A recognisable theme is part of the 'way in' to the game.[2] Once that theme is acknowledged and understood, then the game rules will describe a simple underlying relation between the components (a shopping basket can hold six bananas but only two pineapples). Game success comes with realising (learning) that simple relation. The same goes for adult titles, but the underlying ideas are more nuanced.

Take the game *Modern Art*. Auctions are real-life activities that lend themselves to a natural game mechanic, and selling art at auction needs little explanation. Other games explore the same theme. *Modern Art*, however, manages to reveal two more underlying truths: a market in particular artists is created, thereby making the works of some more lucrative than others; the auction process inherently lends itself to natural role-playing as each auctioneer attempts to promote the artist they are selling. There isn't even a rule for this – many players do it naturally and unconsciously. Thus the players, by bringing something of themselves to the game, make it a more social activity.

What *Modern Art* does so well is build an underlying structure that players are free to expand, fill in, and explore among themselves. Arguably *Modern Art* is Knizia's most successful role-playing game. The inclusion of excellent artwork on the cards adds positively to the atmosphere, and helps promote the communal 'willing suspension of disbelief' that good games engender. [3]

Finding themes that are generally accessible to a broad audience is a balancing act. If the theme is too obscure, sales will suffer. The very largest games manufacturers will usually only countenance a new game that can either be explained in the course of a thirty-second television commercial, or one which exploits an already popular licence. Knizia's best-selling game is *Lord of the Rings*, originally published by Parker/Hasbro.[4] The game recreates the struggle of Frodo and his companions to dispose of the One Ring without being overcome by the corrupting influence of Sauron. It is successful in recreating the sense of overwhelming dread as great and dark forces wheel around the heads of the players, and as they are challenged by a seemingly never-ending series of perilous events. The game above all – like Tolkien's novel – demonstrates that struggle and sacrifice for the good of the mission may have to come before personal safety. The lavish game components and outstanding artwork help put the players in a 'Middle Earth' frame of mind.

Lord of the Rings is probably at the complexity limit of a mass-market boardgame, since learning to play it is perceived as somewhat daunting. Not only are there a large number of components, but players are required to cooperate with each other. The strong theme, however, incentivises new players to persevere with the rules and – once the basics are understood[5] – *Lord of the Rings* plays straightforwardly. Discussions (or indeed disputes) among the players ("You can't be so selfish! If we don't summon Gandalf, then Sauron will eat us for breakfast!") become the interesting issue, not the rules of game itself.[6] It is only now, some ten years after the first appearance of *Lord of the Rings*, that cooperative games are finding some greater acceptance among the gaming public. It may be a little while longer before a mass market breakthrough is achieved, although this may appear in the online console market, as people learn to interact socially via the Wii and Playstation, rather than over a boardgame.

Still popular among games players is Knizia's second title, *Lord of the Rings: the Confrontation*, which is a 'simple' two-player game using few components and a small game board. It recreates the 'fog of war' felt between the forces marshalled by good and evil in the War of the Ring. Players have just nine tiles to represent their forces, and a very simplified map of Middle Earth. Not an overwhelming set of materials, but it is sufficient to achieve its goal. Most games last just twenty minutes, but by the finish players have had the experience of an epic struggle - although the first reaction is often to want to have another attempt at vanquishing one's foe.

What both *Lord of the Rings* titles demonstrate that that an epic theme does not require an epic game length, nor hundreds of components. Knizia shows that a theme can be distilled to an essential core, and that showing the essence is all that is needed. Knizia trusts players with the imagination to 'fill in the gaps' for the remainder of their enjoyment, in the same way that the pictures are better on radio. Those same gaps also leave room for the social interaction that allows a game to breathe, and for players to bring something of themselves to the table.[7]

Where the theme is rich enough, with a variety of viewpoints that merit examination, then it is possible to produce a series of games that explore different aspects of that theme. Knizia has achieved this with merchant rivalry in Renaissance Italy in the *Medici – Strozzi – Bardi* series. All of these use as their foundation the trading rivalry among the great houses of Renaissance Italy, but each has its own distinct play mechanics and feel. We may not be particularly surprised that writers and film-makers explore a subject from a variety of angles (detective, historical and fantasy series abound), but it is a rare feat with popular boardgame designers.[8] There is a danger in taking an idea too far and stretching it ever-thin; movie sequels abound, and some mass-market game titles are constantly being repackaged. But with care, a game publisher can make it easier to gain public acceptance by producing a series of thematically linked game titles.

Knizia has recently taken a step further in producing a series of games linked not by theme but by game mechanics – and these are purely abstract games. With almost no theme to pull in the casual games player, abstract games are notoriously difficult for publishers to market. The best-known example from Knizia must be *Keltis* [9]– but even this game was delivered to the publisher as a themed boardgame.[10] Kosmos [11] however believed that the recognition factor for a Knizia title would be a sufficient draw in itself and – combined with attractive artwork and some streamlining of the rules– would work better in the German market.[12] The consequent success of *Keltis* meant that it became widely-known in Germany very quickly, thus Kosmos were confident in commissioning further titles from Knizia that played variations on the original game mechanic. Knizia has ensured that all subsequent titles have the *Keltis* feel, even though they play differently.[13]

If asked about his abstract games, Knizia is most enthusiastic about the *Einfach Genial/ Ingenious* series[14], as these were purposely designed as abstract games (as opposed to the happy accident of *Keltis*). Using a series of stock components (conjoined hex pieces with symbols printed on both sides) Kniza delights in the varying ways he can link these pieces (and score them). Abstract games are not for everyone (but then, neither are roleplaying games or sushi or Shakespeare); however for those willing to trust the designer and follow his lead, working out the best way to set up a line of tiles while simultaneously blocking one's opponents' opportunities, can be *very* rewarding. These 'sociable' aspects still play a key part even in the driest of abstract settings. For abstract designs, without the easy 'way in' offered by a theme, the 'extraneous' factors of component quality, board, and box design become even more important in the enjoyment of the game. There are currently four major *Einfach Genial*[15] titles published, but Knizia has (allegedly) even more waiting in the wings, such is his enthusiasm for the opportunities that the *Einfach Genial* series affords.

Thus we have moved from enjoying the new perspective that a game can – via its mechanics – cast on a game world (which may be real or fictional), through to playing directly with those mechanics. It's the interconnections themselves that become interesting. Since Knizia's doctorate is in mathematical integration theory, we can understand why he enjoys this aspect of games design. In *Lord of the Rings* Knizia is imparting to us the struggle of the hobbits against an implacable foe; in *Einfach Genial* he is able to get players to start thinking in terms of conceptual lines of power. Enjoyment can come in sharing the emotional predicament of the hobbits, and equally from the balancing of competing scoring imperatives.

It's a cliché that abstract games can be simple to learn, but the best of them are notoriously difficult to master. The sparest of designs allow for the deepest game play. The best of the Knizia titles demonstrate this. Where a theme is 'deeply embedded' (a very spare design) there is some ambiguity over whether it is there intentionally. There is an ongoing debate over whether *Tigris and Euphrates* is actually a war game, for example ("Where are the armies?").

Equally some Knizia game designs appear over a period of time (and geographies) with a variety of themes 'overlaid' onto them – some more radically differing than others.[16] Does the fact that this can happen actually invalidate the theme? As has been noted above, *some* theme is useful in attracting the casual player into the game initially and so is valuable in that context at least. One argument often overlooked, however, is that the same underlying structure can inform more than one theme. In literature it has been said that there are only seven basic plots, but the book trade shows no signs of stopping after just seven novels! Some of the more intriguing insights come when comparing two themes by using the same structure, or in some cases exactly the same words.[17] *Gem Dealer* has recently reinterpreted the original mechanism of *Attacke*, but both games work well on their own terms.

In the design process, Knizia will frequently devise an interesting game mechanic, and then search for themes with which to relate it. Often a mechanic hints at more than one potential theme, and some thought needs to be applied as to which will be most suitable. In the best instances, a good theme goes on to inform further refinements of the game mechanic. In some cases a theme is temporarily attached to a design (usually to establish the 'way in' to the game, as described above) before another theme subsequently emerges. Early versions of a mountain expedition design eventually were replaced by a 'golden-age' movie-making theme and resulted ultimately in *Traumfabrik*. It takes a strong imagination now to envisage anything other than a Hollywood background to that design.[18] Thus a design informs the theme and vice versa.

That's not to say that Knizia will always start a game design with a mechanic in mind. In many cases the theme will be the first inspiration. Knizia's design vault contains many unused/discarded/undeveloped mechanics waiting for the day when a theme needs one. The majority of commissions undertaken by Knizia are theme-led; it is rare indeed for a publisher to request a purely abstract design.[19] Knizia has, however, had some recent success in persuading publishers to take on a non-commissioned abstract design.[20]

Whether theme- or design-led, Knizia's aim is always to provide a framework that players can enjoy. Success is achieved when players have consciously forgotten the game rules, and start playing within that framework space. This is analogous to learning to ride a bicycle or operating a videogame controller, or becoming totally absorbed in a book or a movie; the delivery mechanism becomes secondary to the experience. Enjoyment is subjective of course; those who thrive on the cut and thrust of the auctioneering world in *Modern Art* may not be the same as those who enjoy mastering the lines of power within *Einfach Genial*. However, it is through simple, natural, and elegant game rules that Knizia ensures that barriers to enjoyment are kept to a minimum, so that everyone has the opportunity to share Knizia's vision.

With the best Knizia designs, the nuances of the game only begin to reveal themselves after several plays, despite the game's apparent simplicity. For those players who are prepared to follow Knizia's lead, diligently and patiently aiming towards achieving mastery of a game, going with the flow to see where it takes them, the results can be extremely fulfilling.

[1] http://www.convivium.org.uk/kgludography.htm

[2] Conveying the theme successfully to the players relies on a combination of factors; including the quality of the components and playing pieces, attractive artwork, and box design. These, together with commonality of experience/purpose, provide the 'gateway' for gameplay and merit a separate discussion.

[3] *Modern Art* has been published in a variety of editions, many with different works of art. The most recent is *Masters Gallery* (Gryphon Games, 2009) which utilises 30 'classic' paintings from Van Gogh, Renoir and others.

[4] The original *Lord of the Rings* commission came from Sophisticated Games of Cambridge, England.

[5] The basics of *Lord of the Rings* are most easily and rapidly learned under demonstration conditions (i.e. someone in the group has played it before).

[6] There is a point in every game where its mechanics are learned sufficiently well to allow social interactions to take place, and the theme to emerge more strongly. The height of such a bar, the game designer's intent (or otherwise) in setting it, and its appropriateness in relation to the theme, game setting and marketplace are the basis of a separate discussion.

[7] The debate between the US-centric 'card/pawn for everything' vs. the Euro-game 'less is more' philosophy is a lively one, and won't be resolved any time soon.

[8] Knizia does not always succeed: the 'missing' quarter of the board in *Beowulf – the Legend* hints that he has more to say on the subject than was allowed for in the original publication.

[9] *Keltis* – awarded the 2008 Spiel des Jahres in Germany.

[10] *Lost Cities – the Boardgame* was published in the US in its original incarnation. The US publisher Rio Grande felt a theme (as well as being an already well-known and popular game) would be more suited for the domestic US market.

[11] Kosmos Verlag, of Stuttgart Germany, is a large boardgame publisher. Kosmos released the original two-player *Lost Cities* in 1999, subsequently licensing it to other publishers around the world.

[12] German spielwaren (games stores) are known to promote some games with their designer's name prominently displayed on the shelves, in the same way that bookstores do for their authors. Knizia game titles from the very beginning have almost always had their designer's name on the box, thus promoting recognition.

[13] Ironically the very large success of *Keltis* in Germany meant a change of plan for other markets. Originally *Keltis* was destined for Germany only, with the rest of the world going with *Lost Cities – the Boardgame*, which after all had some existing recognition, and would likely benefit from the association. Such was the positive publicity generated by the Spiel des Jahres, however, that it became clear it would be a better commercial decision to also publish *Keltis* in markets outside of Germany.

[14] Knizia is a doctor of mathematics; its disciplines underlie all his designs. With *Einfach Genial* he enjoys 'playing' with pieces unconstrained by thematic requirements.

[15] The original game, then *Einfach Genial-Knobelspass* (puzzle game), *Einfach Genial-Kartenspiel* (card game) and *Genial Spezial*. *Ingenious Challenges*, published in the US by Fantasy Flight Games, incorporates the card game along with a dice game and tile challenge. There is also a two-player Travel Edition, *Einfach Genial-Mitbringspiel* (minigame), *Einfach Genial Junior* a CD-ROM and hand-held computer versions.

[16] *Honeybears* and *Bucket Brigade* share an identical game mechanism, but have very different thematic interpretations.

[17] Shakespeare is extraordinarily adaptable. Insights are found when setting *Henry V* in modern day Iraq; or by transforming *The Tempest* into the movie *Forbidden Planet*.

[18] Subsequent versions of *Traumfabrik* from other publishers have all used a movie-making theme, albeit with more contemporary Hollywood setting.

[19] Even *Einfach Genial/Ingenious* came about as a request to design a game suitable for the British Mensa society, and was originally published under the title *Mensa Connections*.

[20] *FITS* and *Callisto* were both published in 2009.

FILTERING FEEDBACK
Ira Fay

One thing I love about being a game designer is getting feedback. Of course, I hate that sometimes too, but most of the time, receiving feedback is an ultimately helpful experience. The sting of critique passes quickly if it leads to a better game, especially when given honestly and with good intentions. While it is impossible to make a game that appeals to everyone, playtesting is a vital tool in a designer's toolbox, and should be used generously at all stages of development.

Currently, my favorite boardgame is *Agricola* by Uwe Rosenberg (number two on board-gamegeek.com as of this writing). *Agricola* is a one- to five-player game in which players take on the role of 17th century farmers, striving to feed their families and build a large farm. It is a fairly complex Eurogame and takes approximately two hours to play. In this article, I will spend only a little time explaining the rules of *Agricola*. If you are not already familiar with the game, you can read the rules online.[21] Furthermore, any aspiring boardgame designer should be familiar with the Top Ten games on boardgamegeek.com!

Agricola was originally published with four different decks, and several more decks have now been published. I recently had the pleasure of being a designer for a crowd-sourced expansion, the G deck (Gamers deck). In this article, I will analyze what makes *Agricola* great and then discuss how I strove to make it even better with the G deck expansion. I will also cover the role of player feedback in our development, and how you can use it to improve your games.

As Lewis Pulsipher notes in his article on the Three Player Problem,[22] most Eurogames, including *Agricola*, resolve the king-making problem by limiting direct player conflict. Fortunately, players still interact and are faced with interesting decisions. Within the genre of Eurogames, *Agricola* is great for many reasons, which I have grouped into five categories:

- Lots of content
- Excellent theme
- Supports one to five players
- Multiple paths to victory
- High replayability

Content

The first thing that most new players notice when they open the box, is that there are many bits and pieces. *Agricola* contains 360 cards and approximately 400 other markers, counters, and tiles. While there is some risk that the player might feel overwhelmed, most players who are trying out *Agricola* for the first time are open to complex Eurogames. The player is most likely excited to explore all the possibilities. When I play *Agricola* with my friends, we still discover cards or combinations that we have never seen before, even after dozens of games. The sheer volume of content included in the game creates excitement for the players. Obviously all the different cards contribute to high replayability as well.

There are many excellent boardgames that have minimalistic content, such as *Go* or any game played with a standard deck of cards. Therefore, you should not feel compelled to create games that have lots of content. On the other hand, if you do choose to include unique cards, ensure that you include enough to keep games fresh and interesting.

Agricola also has excellent attention to detail in all the cards. For example, there are house tiles that everyone uses; if you look closely, some of those tiles show people playing *Agricola* in their house! Another example is that the art for the Scholar card matches with the Bookcase. Throughout the game, observant players will be pleasantly surprised.

Theme

Agricola is well-themed. All elements of game play are related to farming, which is fun for players because it makes it easier to learn the game and to deduce basic strategy. The cohesiveness of the game rules is elegant and pleasing. Furthermore, the game includes good iconography, consistent language and keywords. For any game, it's important to employ systems, images, and words that help players learn and retain the rules.

For example, players score points in many ways, including having vegetables at the end of the game. Vegetables are a relatively small part of the game, but all of the following cards are related to vegetables: Bean Field, Turnip Field, Lettuce Patch, Giant Pumpkin, Pumpkin Seed Oil, Greenhouse, Schnaps Distiller, Schnaps Distillery, and many more. It makes sense that those cards relate to vegetables, simply based on their card names. Such strong theming facilitates learning for new players, and helps them retain what they learn.

One to Five Players

By allowing one to five players per game, *Agricola* can be played in many different situations. Furthermore, due to some small but significant changes in the setup, the game plays very differently depending on the number of players, which also promotes replayability. When designing your games, it's valuable to consider the number of players required to play. The greater the range, the more valuable the game is to your players, since they will be able to play it in more situations.

Of course, the catch is that the game must still be fun regardless of how many players are playing, within the advertised range. This is one area where playtesting can be valuable. When you are designing your games, try experimenting with the number of players required to play. Stretch your boundaries and see what happens. Through playtesting, you can refine the gameplay for a varied number of players.

Multiple Paths to Victory

Agricola also excels at providing players many different strategic options, all of which are viable under the right circumstances. While some strategies tend to win over others, the player generally enjoys a sense of freedom in choosing his or her strategy. Experienced players tend to use a draft variation of the setup, which gives even more opportunities to customize strategy.

Multiple paths to victory are only possible if each path is well-balanced against the other options. In my experience, such precise balance is only possible through playtesting and iteration. The original game had 138 playtesters credited,[23] with approximately 200 playtest games.[24] That amount of feedback allowed Uwe to fine tune each card and strategy to be balanced against each other. I mentioned the benefits of massive content above; while it's certainly great for the players, balancing all those cards and ensuring they are fun will add design time, which is important to consider for your development timeline.

High Replayability

Strategic depth and variation, lots of content, diversity of number of players needed to play, and some randomness all combine to yield a high level of replayability in *Agricola*. Every game has exactly fourteen rounds, and in each round a new action becomes available to the players. The new actions appear in a slightly different order each game. That small variation creates a large impact on gameplay, which is elegant, fun, and results in greater replayability.

The G Deck

Now that I have extolled the virtues of the basic version of *Agricola*, I'd like to discuss the G deck expansion, and how a group of dedicated fans set out to make a great game even better. One particularly dedicated fan created an online implementation of the game (with permission), and a community began to form (play-agricola.com). As the site caught on, the players started creating new cards for fun. Soon, Uwe noticed the momentum and requested a full expansion. Each designer had his or her own reasons for participating, but I got involved for the sheer fun of it. My goals for the expansion included:

- Have fun during the design process

- Increase strategic depth by providing interesting, new choices

- Improve game balance to increase possible winning strategies

Have Fun Designing

It can be a challenge to design a game under any circumstances; it's especially difficult to design with sixty-six other people! The amount of feedback that everyone generated during development was nearly overwhelming. In nine and a half months of design, we had sixty-seven people discussing the cards, 311 playtesters, over 1300 games played, and more than 5400 forum posts.[25]

Any idea that is tested by so many games and players will tend to lose its rough edges and end up more polished. Certainly our final product was far from perfect. Nonetheless, the process of convincing other people about the value of a particular design tends to yield good results, as long as the people involved in the discussion are committed to quality, are well-informed, and have good judgment. In the case of our expansion, I believe that to generally be the case.

To share ideas, each proposed card had its own discussion thread in the forums. Anyone could comment on the card, and each person got one vote per card: yes or no. It was a pure democracy, with the most popular ideas making the final deck. Once we picked the top 125 cards, we had several months of fine-tuning with those cards to ensure they worked well together and with the previously published decks.

There were many times during development that someone would propose an idea for a new card, and the feedback on the forum was disparate. It quickly became obvious who had playtested with the card and who had not. From the beginning, designers could watch live games in progress, and we built additional tools that let us replay games asynchronously and link to them on the forums. Once everyone playtested the card, we reached consensus much more quickly. It was easy to filter out feedback from anyone who had not actually seen the card played in a game.

When designing your games, it's important to gather lots of feedback from many different players. As you use the feedback to make design changes, ensure that you give the most weight to feedback from people who actually played the game, and people who fit your target audience.

Increase Strategic Depth

To increase strategic depth, we created a few new mechanics, while still remaining true to the original game. Since the basic version was so well liked, we did not want to stray too far. For example, there is no auction mechanic in the original game; I designed a card that introduced a small auction that awards resources to players, yet does so in a way that is consistent with other cards from the original game.

For example, here is the original card text that I proposed:

Auctioneer, Occupation (4+ players)
Place 4 Wood, 4 Clay, and 3 Stone on rounds 7, 9 and 11, respectively. At the start of these rounds, all other Players (starting with the starting player) bid once in Food for the resources (no ties allowed.) The highest bidder gets the resources and you get the Food.

When we playtested this card, we found that a player would rarely play this occupation for fear of giving other players too large a benefit. Therefore, I changed it to:

Auctioneer, Occupation (4+ players)
Place 4 Wood, 4 Clay, and 3 Stone on rounds 7, 9 and 11, respectively. At the start of these rounds, all players simultaneously bid Food for the resources (place Food in your hand, then reveal simultaneously.) The highest bidder gets the resources and you get the Food. If you win, pay your Food to the supply. Ties are broken in player order. (The starting player wins all ties.)

This second revision increased speed of play since the auction is simultaneous, and also allows the Auctioneer to bid on the resources. The drawback of the change was longer card text, but it was within reasonable limits. When we tested the second version, we found that it got played more; it was still too weak because large piles of resources didn't command large enough prices. We solved that by having 4 smaller auctions. Here is the final version:

Auctioneer, Occupation (4+ players)

Place 2 Reed, 3 Wood, 3 Clay, and 2 Stone on rounds 7, 9, 11 and 13, respectively. At the start of these rounds, all players simultaneously bid Food for the resources (players secretly place Food in their hands, then reveal.) The highest bidder gets the resources and you get the Food. If you win, pay your Food to the supply. Ties are broken in player order. (Starting player wins all ties.)

Improve Game Balance

As you might anticipate, the players who sought out this project were some of the most hardcore players of *Agricola* on the planet. There was general consensus among us that certain strategies were slightly weaker than others, and therefore we used the G deck to make the weaker strategies more viable. For example, we felt that baking and early fences were slightly too weak, and therefore we created several cards that benefit those strategies (Baker's Daughter, Carrot Cake Baker, Fence Helper, Hoe Maker, Hammer, and more). I hope that we succeeded in improving the game balance, and I feel confident with our final tuning considering all the playtesting data we examined. Of course, no game is ever perfect, and I look forward to even more *Agricola* expansions in the future.

Keep it Simple

When advanced players create new designs or give feedback on existing designs, they may develop overly complex rules. This pitfall can also catch game designers, who are likely the most experienced players of their own games. During development of the G deck, we were careful to keep new ideas as simple as possible. When addressing feedback on game balance, strive to avoid exceptions and special cases when a simplification would work just as well. For example, here is the original text of the Headmaster occupation:

Headmaster, Occupation (3+ players)

Whenever another player plays an Occupation using an occupation space, place the Food paid on this card. Whenever you play an Occupation, you must pay using Food from this card if possible, otherwise you pay normally. At the end of the game, you receive Bonus points equal to the number of Food remaining on this card divided by the number of opponents, rounded up.

As you can see, that text has complex restrictions about how the food must be paid, and how it's scored at the end. The core idea is great: an occupation that benefits directly from other people playing occupations. While there were some occupation-related cards in the original game, this idea is new and interesting. Through playtesting and iteration, the final text was streamlined as follows:

Headmaster, Occupation (4+ players)

Whenever another player plays an Occupation, place 1 Food from the supply on this card. Whenever you play an Occupation, you may pay any costs using Food from this card. At the end of a 4/5 player game, you receive 1 Bonus point for every 3/4 Food on this card.

As a final example of the value of simplicity and the challenges of collaborative design, here is the text of a G deck card:

Shared Wall, Minor Improvement

Your home now creates a natural border for pasture(s). You may not extend your home into pastures created in this way. You may still build all 15 fences.

This card was the fourth most-debated card in the set, and here was the alternate text we considered:

Shared Wall, Minor Improvement

Any fences you build that are adjacent to your home cost no wood.

When we playtested this card, a few players were confused by the first text, but it is slightly more powerful. I argued for the latter text because it is shorter and simpler, even though it is slightly weaker. In the end, I was out-voted because most designers felt like the first text was sufficiently easy to understand. Which would you have picked?

When designing your next game, I hope that you will find some these concepts helpful. Playtesting and gathering feedback from your players will be your most reliable tool to balance and polish your game.

21 Agricola Rules, http://www.zmangames.com/boardgames/files/agricola/Agricola_Rules.pdf

22 Page 17.

23 Agricola Rules, http://www.zmangames.com/boardgames/files/agricola/Agricola_Rules.pdf

24 Agricola by Uwe Rosenberg - Retrospective, http://jogoeu.wordpress.com/2009/09/01/1373/

25 G Deck Statistics, http://play-agricola.com/forums/index.php?topic=1569

15 GAMES IN 15 YEARS
Stone Librande

Making Games

For as long as I can remember I have been making my own card and board games. One of my earliest game design memories is converting a box of my father's old business cards into a random boardgame generator. On the blank side of each card I scribbled simple instructions such as "Move ahead 4 spaces" and "Lose 2 turns". My friends and I would shuffle the huge deck and then lay out the cards in a long winding trail that swerved along the concrete floor of the basement.

As I grew older I continued making my own games as a hobby. In junior high I made sci-fi games based on *Star Wars* and *Battlestar Galactica*. In high school I designed entire fantasy worlds and adventures for our *Dungeons and Dragons* group. (I was not interested in role-playing a character; I always wanted to be the dungeon master.)

After college my passion for games led me to a career in the videogame industry, where I am currently employed as a designer. Every day I work with a talented team of programmers and artists, using the latest technologies in an attempt to produce the next hit game that will be played by hundreds of thousands of people. A typical videogame production involves years of work, millions of dollars, and the coordinated effort of more than a hundred creative and brilliant people. But I find more personal satisfaction working alone late nights on my own small games, using only cardstock, an X-Acto knife and a bottle of white glue. Many of these games are designed for an audience of two: my sons.

The first of these games was for my two-year old son. It was a simple color matching game that we made together to celebrate Christmas. I did not know it at the time, but that was the beginning of an annual tradition—what we now call the "Christmas Game." For each of the next fourteen Christmases I would continue to design and build a new game, wrap it up, and place it under the tree. On Christmas morning I would watch anxiously as my sons opened the present and examined the pieces. Then we would spend several hours on Christmas afternoon playing the game and modifying the rules in response to the kids' feedback.

What follows is a brief description of the fifteen Christmas Games that were constructed over the last fifteen years. I am not including the actual rules to the games (that would take up far too many pages). Instead I will focus on the design philosophies, production techniques, and core mechanics of each game. It is important to note that these games were not meant to be sold or published. My goal was not profit. The only motivation was to create age-appropriate games that could be enjoyed by the entire family.

Hidden Reindeers

My two-year old son, Jordan, was interested in all the Christmas decorations that my wife had placed around the house. To his dismay, he was constantly hearing, "Don't touch that!" as he explored the fragile ornaments, the blinking lights, and the ceramic Nativity figures. To keep his little hands busy I got out some construction paper, paint, a few bottles of colored glitter glue, and a small wooden reindeer figure. We spent the next hour playing in the sparkling mess.

When we had finished I took three of Jordan's masterpieces and rolled each of them into a cone. Then I placed the reindeer, now painted red, under one of them and asked, "Where's the reindeer?" He pointed at the correct cone. "You win!" I exclaimed, as I lifted up the cone. I put the cone back down. This time I mixed them up before I asked him to find the reindeer. I was proud to see him point it out on his first try.

This game was too easy. I decided to add in a few new rules to see if he could handle some extra complexity. We got a second wooden reindeer and painted it green. Then I cut out a small cardboard disk and Jordan squirted red glitter glue on one side and green on the other. After our new pieces had dried, I put the two reindeer under two different cones, shuffled them around and had him toss the coin into the air. "Red!" I exclaimed as the coin landed on the table. "Where's the red reindeer?" It took him a short while before he understood the relationship between the coin, the cones and the colored reindeer, but with each coin flip his success rate steadily improved.

We played *Hidden Reindeers* for short bursts throughout the holiday season. Then it was packed up in early January along with the rest of the decorations, stored in the attic, and forgotten for the next eleven months. But every December it comes back out of the box and I am reminded of the simple fun that we had with the first Christmas Game.

Fishin'

The next year I was looking forward to making a new game, but I wanted to do something less spontaneous and more elaborate. I decided to construct a fishing game that Jordan could play from his bed, as if he were fishing from a rowboat out at sea. The game featured a colorful fishing pole (a hand-painted lime green dowel) from which dangled a thin rope anchored with a magnetic disk. There was also an assortment of wooden pieces such as a starfish, a shark, an angelfish, a boot, and a tire. Hammered into each piece was a large-headed nail which acted as an attractor when the magnetic hook was near.

The idea seemed simple enough. I had seen similar fishing playsets in the toy store, but they were cheaply made out of one-colored molded plastic. I wanted to make something more solid and unique. Something durable enough to last for a generation. Unfortunately, I quickly discovered that my intentions were far beyond my capabilities. I had neither enough money nor space for a jigsaw. Luckily, my father has a large, well-supplied workshop in his basement and my mother is a whiz with a jigsaw, so I was able to enlist their help. I sent off a copy of my illustrations for her to use as a template and, a week later, the perfectly cut wooden pieces arrived in the mail. That was the easy part.

Fig. 1: The template illustration that was used to create the wooden pieces.

I also had to build the pole, which turned out to be frustratingly difficult. A fishing pole seems like such a basic object until you try to build one from scraps in your garage. I started with the obvious piece – a long length of wooden dowel – but problems arose right away. What is the reel made of? How is the reel attached to the rod? How does it turn without falling off? Is it easy enough for a three-year old to operate? Is it strong enough to survive a play session with a three-year old? There were so many problems that I was still trying to piece it all together after midnight on Christmas Eve.

Despite the mechanical troubles, and the late night crunch session, the game components came out fine. There were no formal rules to accompany them, but that did not matter. That night Jordan and I fished off his bed and we created our own challenges as we played. Who can hook the blue fish first? How many fish can you catch before you catch a shark? Try to catch something while your eyes are closed.

We never did make any official rules for *Fishin'*, and I am convinced there should never be any. It is a game about experimentation and camaraderie, not score keeping or adhering to rules.

Alpha Zoo-tauri

Jordan was just beginning to read and I wanted to make him a game that would help him learn the alphabet. More importantly, I wanted to avoid a big production (and the associated problems) that had tripped me up the previous year. It was time to go back to basics. Armed with a large black piece of poster board and some trusty bottles of glitter glue, I enlisted Jordan as the lead artist for another boardgame art project.

I marked out twenty-six areas on the poster board and helped Jordan "draw" multicolored swirls that represented planets, asteroids and nebulae. Next to each one I wrote a letter from A to Z. Then we connected the neighboring stellar objects together with a crisscross web of "hyperlines" that were used for traveling through the galaxy. I purchased a deck of alphabet animal flash cards to represent the beasts we were trying to capture for our personal intergalactic zoos. Two matchbox-sized spaceships, taken from a drawer of loose toys, were used to mark our positions on the map.

The rules, as with all of the games described in this chapter, evolved as we played. Jordan's feedback and opinions were the ones that mattered most. (His younger brother, Dylan, who was now only one, would soon begin expressing his opinion, too.) If the play mechanics were too simplistic then they were made more complex. Features that caused laughter and engagement were strengthened, while confusing and tedious mechanics were rapidly eliminated. This interactive form of game design is the main reason that the Christmas Games are strong reflections of the children's developing cognitive personalities.

The goal of *Alpha Zoo-tauri* is to collect the majority of the twenty-six animals. The flash cards are shuffled and the top three are revealed and placed on the matching alphabet letter (Elephant on "E", Ostrich on "O", and Donkey on "D"). On your turn you move your ship along one hyperline, moving from one sector to the next. If you land on an animal you pick it up, add it to your zoo, and place a new random animal from the deck into the appropriate sector of space. Players are not allowed to be in the same sector at the same time, so it is possible to block the other player's path as you swoop down and grab his Zebu one step ahead of him.

This game not only helped teach Jordan alphabetic and phonetic relationships, it was also a way for him to play with the concepts of spatial and temporal relationships. Furthermore, the stricter rule system and competitive score-keeping showed a maturing of his ability to understand fundamental structures of game design.

RoboBall

By now it was clear that the Christmas Game had become an annual tradition so I started working on this year's game a month before the Christmas deadline. I wanted to make a game that was suitable for both Jordan, who was in kindergarten, and Dylan, who was now two years old. *Alpha Zoo-tauri* required a lot of counting and planning, and I wanted to make a less cerebral game with more action and chaos. Both kids had been playing with small plastic robot toys called Z-Bots and I thought they would be perfect as game pieces. I had also been thinking about classic kids' games, and decided that using marbles would be a good starting point. Robots plus marble shooting? The game practically designed itself!

Fortunately, that year my family spent the holiday season at my parents' home. Being far away from the workplace meant that I had plenty of free time and I was excited to have access to the table saw, belt sander, and paints in their expansive basement workshop. With the correct tools and resources at my disposal, I decided to ramp up the production.

For the next few nights I stayed up late building and painting the *RoboBall* arena. This was a heavy hexagonal piece of wood, about two feet across, with sloped walls nailed in around the perimeter. A hexagonal grid of small divots was drilled in the arena floor to act as traps that would stop slow rolling marbles.

Dylan did not have the dexterity to shoot a marble the traditional way, so to even the playing field between him and his brother I made two "shooters." These are eight-inch long strips of wood with a groove down the middle. The shooter acts much like a pool cue. The player places one end of the shooter on top of the arena wall and then angles and tilts the opposite end to form a ramp. Then the marble is placed on the high side where it rolls down the groove and drops into the arena.

The first set of rules was simple and intuitive. Each player starts with six robots that they place in the arena anywhere they want. Then the players take turns rolling marbles in an attempt to knock over their opponent's robots first.

There were two main problems with this game that we discovered on Christmas afternoon. First, since the plastic robots were all unique, some of them were clearly better than others. The best robots were the short squat ones with large feet and a low center of gravity; the worst were the thin upright androids that would sometimes fall over for no apparent reason. The second problem was that the game lacked replay value and each new play session felt similar to the last.

To fix these problems I made a "trading card" for each robot. Each card had an illustration of the robot on the top and special ability printed along the bottom. The robots that tended to tip over more often had strong abilities ("Can move anywhere on the board") while the stable robots had weak abilities ("Cannot move"). The game starts out with a drafting phase in which players take turns choosing a robot for their teams. Do you draft a tougher squad of sturdy robots or try to out-finesse your opponent with your powerful abilities? Not only did this fix the robot balance and replay problems, but it also added personality to the robots. Instead of colored pieces of plastic, the robots now had names and unique characteristics. This added an unexpected level of immersion and emotion to the game as the players could now "personify" the robots. In fact, it worked so well that I now try to use this design trick in all my games.

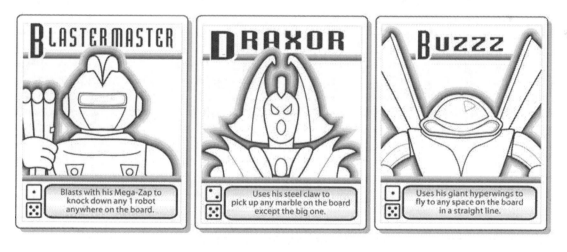

Fig. 2: Three of the *Roboball* trading cards that described the robots' special powers.

Maze

A few years before the kids were born I had worked on a boardgame called *Maze*. (This was loosely based on the commercial children's game, *Labyrinth*.) When we moved from Massachusetts to Northern California *Maze* had been packed up and stashed in the garage along with other boxes of seldom used items. Five years later, I decided to dust it off and give it to the kids as a gift.

The game features a seven by seven board made out of ceramic tiles that can slide in horizontal and vertical rows. Each tile has a piece of a dungeon corridor painted on it. Some tiles have T-shaped corridors and others are L-shaped. As the tiles move some of the corridors form connections while others become blocked. In the center of the dungeon lurks a dragon that will eat any hero who gets too close. The goal of the game is to slide the maze in such a way as to form connections to the other players and blast them with your spells. The last surviving wizard wins.

Maze had four fantasy miniature figures (the kind used in *Dungeons and Dragons*) that the players would use to mark their positions. Even though they looked different they were functionally identical. But based on my success with the *RoboBall* robots, I decided to give each of the figures in *Maze* a unique power. The Wizard drew spells for free; the Barbarian moved faster than any other character; the Druid controlled the dragon as a pet; and the Wraith had the power to move through walls. This addition substantially improved the game and helped immerse the players in the experience. When people play *Maze* it is not uncommon to see them role-playing as if they move their chosen hero through the dungeon.

The spell deck contained many aggressive spells—such as fireballs and lightning bolts—that a player used when attacking his opponents. When my wife, Toby, saw these cards she asked, "If this game is for the kids then why does it have to be about battles and fighting? Don't the kids see enough of that on television and in videogames?"

I tried to explain to her that the game would be boring without combat, but my arguments were not convincing to her. She issued a challenge to me, "If you're a good designer then you could design this game so that it didn't need combat."

That ended the discussion. I did not know how I was going to do it, but I knew I had to try. The first step was to remove the hit points, damage spells and the "kill or be killed" goal. But what would be left? Over the next several weeks I play tested many different versions of *Maze*, and eventually came up with a new goal that emphasized cooperation over destruction.

Instead of every man for himself (one vs. three), the game now had two teams of two players each (two vs. two). And instead of fighting, the teams were racing to collect the majority of nine small treasure chests placed near the dragon. The spells emphasized movement (teleport, haste, switch and freeze) instead of attack (the aforementioned fireballs and lightning bolts). Even the dragon lost the ability to eat the characters. Instead, if he entered a hero's square the hero would just be forced to teleport back to his or her home corner. The end result is a game that feels fresh and plays differently from most games that feature heroes, dungeons, spells, and dragons.

Of all the games I have created, *Maze* is the one that is played most often. It is enjoyed as much by my friends as it is by my kids and their friends. Even after more than a decade it continues to evolve and improve. Old spells are removed and replaced with upgraded versions. New heroes are added (there are twelve now). Some special powers are made more powerful, while others are weakened based on player feedback. *Maze* has taught me that there is no reason to ever declare a game "final." As long as people continue to play it then there will be new ideas to try.

Junkyard Bots

Maze is one of my personal favorite games, but it is not particularly well suited to young children. The turns require deep thinking and it can take several minutes of thought per player. For my sixth Christmas game I wanted to make something with high energy, a lot of noise, and turns that would last less than a minute. As an added bonus, I wanted to the components to be so playful that when it was not your turn you could still have fun fiddling with the pieces. The game that met these criteria is called *Junkyard Bots*.

In this game, each player is a robot trapped on a planet-wide battlefield of discarded robot parts. The goal is to collect different pieces—arms, wheels, eyes, mouths and bombs—and assemble a custom robot that will either blow up the other robots or teleport itself onto an orbiting space cruiser and escape the planet forever. (The second goal was added later, to make it possible to play the game in a non-violent fashion.)

The robot parts were printed on sticker paper and applied to one face of a wooden cube. The remaining five sides have a varying number of pips, in a fashion similar to a standard die. There are three different sizes of cubes: small, medium and large. Small cubes have either no or one pip per side, medium cubes have one to three pips, and large cubes have two to six pips. As is typical for a Christmas Game, I was overwhelmed by the amount of production work required to assemble the game and I ended up working late on Christmas Eve sticking tiny stickers onto more than 120 cubes.

One of the design challenges was creating illustrations that could be connected together in many different configurations. A robot might have only one eye and a small pair of legs; or it might have five eyes of different sizes, tank treads, and an extended arm with a clawed hand. Above all, I wanted the robots to reflect the personality of their creators. The mouth could be turned one direction and would look like a smile, or it could be rotated 180 and it would look like a frown. Eyes could be placed in a way that made the robot look as if it were sad or angry. As far as the rules were concerned, the position of the parts did not matter. But that fact the robots could be customized in hundreds of different ways adds a lot to the playfulness of the game.

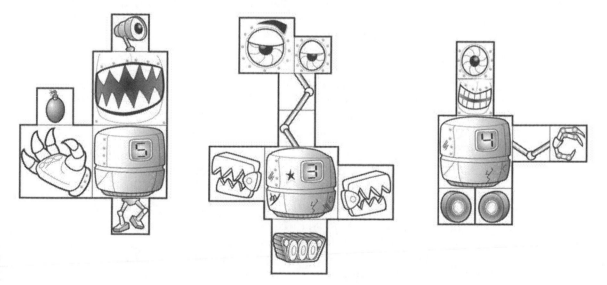

Fig. 3: A variety of robots created with *Junkyard Bots* dice.

Players start the game with a basic robot made up of mechanical eyes, a body, and small legs. The rest of the cubes are placed face-down in a central "junkyard". Each turn the player picks a task for their robot (look, grab, eat, throw, or teleport) and rolls the appropriate parts to determine if the task succeeds or fails. For example, the player can roll all of the robot's eyes to peek at the face-down cubes. Or, a player could roll all the mouths to eat energy. In general, the bigger the part the more powerful it is, but also the higher you need to roll to collect from the junkyard.

Junkyard Bots was a family favorite for many years. The dual victory conditions and the large variety of custom robots gave it excellent replay value, and the rapid fire turns kept everyone engaged throughout the session. Because the core of the game is based on rolling dice, the victor is predominantly determined by luck. This worked well when the kids were young, since anyone could win regardless of age or experience. But as the kids grew older the randomness turned into a negative and the game has not been played for years.

Kongzilla

When September rolled around I was already thinking of new ideas for the next Christmas Game. I had a few thoughts, but nothing seemed special enough. Then, while visiting a local comic book shop, I saw what I knew had to be the centerpiece of my next game. High on the shelf behind the cashier was a two-foot tall, hand-painted resin statue of Kongzilla! (According to the box, Kongzilla is a genetically designed monstrosity made from skin tissue found on the ground in the aftermath of a Godzilla vs. King Kong battle.) I immediately pulled out my wallet, eager to buy the statue without even a clue as to what to do with it. Then I saw the price tag: $100! I sheepishly put my wallet back in my pocket.

Kongzilla would make an incredible game token and my desire to go back to the store and purchase him grew stronger each day. I made a deal with myself. I could only buy Kongzilla *after* I designed the game that would feature him. No design, no Kongzilla. This was all the incentive that I needed.

I had a few high-level design goals in mind. First, I didn't want a fixed playing field. I wanted a game could be played on any floor, which would allow the players to arrange furniture and obstacles to create custom battlefields. Secondly, movement would be freeform; there would be no grid or measuring tapes. Third, there would be no hit points or damage calculations. In fact, I did not want any numbers in the game; combat needed to be physical, not computational. Finally, I wanted an asymmetric game. One player would control the mighty Kongzilla and the other would command an army of soldiers and tanks.

After weeks of thought and several dead ends I came up with the basic concept for the game. It took weeks of shopping to find all the necessary components: three plastic office buildings from a hobby shop's model railroad department; tanks, jeeps and soldiers from the toy store; two laser pointers from an electronics store; small square mirrors from a hair stylist. And, most importantly, Kongzilla himself!

The construction work was fairly straightforward. I removed the plastic turret guns from the jeeps and replaced them with mirrors. They were mounted in such a way that some mirrors could rotate around a vertical axis, while others could only tilt up and down. The laser pointers were mounted on tank turrets and could be aimed in any direction. Instead of solidly gluing the walls of the office buildings together, I attached them together using only small pieces of Velcro. When Kongzilla's fist or tail connects with a building it falls apart with a satisfying plastic crash (and can be quickly reassembled for the next game).

The goal of the Kongzilla player is to advance across the floor and knock over the three office buildings. (The players are free to place the buildings, and Kongzilla's entry point, anywhere they want.) The goal of the army player is to shoot Kongzilla with a laser, but the beam must bounce off at least one mirror first.

To move Kongzilla the player chooses one leg to act as a central axis. The other leg is free to rotate around the axis by any amount. By alternating between the left and right foot Kongzilla can be made to walk forward with a slow, shambling gait. As Kongzilla pivots, his arms and tail sweep arcs through the air. If he comes in contact with any army piece then it is instantly destroyed and removed from the game. If he crashes into an office building then it will crumble to the ground.

The army player can either move or shoot each turn. If he chooses to move then he drives his vehicles to any position on the battlefield. If he chooses to shoot he aims a laser pointer at any mirror and fires! If the bright red dot of the laser hits Kongzilla in the face then the game is over and the army wins.

Kongzilla feels like two games, depending on which side you choose to play. Controlling the army is like playing pool. You have to carefully align your mirrors to bounce a shot into Kongzilla. But since you cannot move and shoot in the same turn it is necessary to aim the mirrors on a spot where you think he will be next turn, not where he is now. On the other hand, as Kongzilla there is little reason to strategize or plan ahead. The best option is to race towards the buildings. You do need to be careful not to move too predictably or the army player will surely catch you in a trap.

All these rules work fine…when they are followed. In practice, once the game is set up then the kids quickly ignore the rules. Giving children access to laser pointers (with strict "not in the eye" warnings, of course), a giant monster, tanks and collapsible buildings tends to invoke freeform imaginative play experiences. A rigid rule set cannot contain the awesome power of Kongzilla!

Monster Hunter

I had been playing a lot of *Diablo II* and wanted my sons to join in the on fun, but Toby adamantly refused. (Something about corpse explosions, if I remember correctly….) Well, if I couldn't bring the kids to *Diablo* then I'd bring *Diablo* to the kids. Could I distill the essence of *Diablo* into a family friendly card game? From this idle thought sprung the most labor intensive of all the games I have created: *Monster Hunter*.

It seemed simple enough at first. I would just download all the weapon and monster statistics (damage, health, armor, etc.) from Blizzard's web site and print the information onto cards. I soon realized that this would never work. The problem was that the number of stats was overwhelming. When a computer is performing all the combat calculations then a rich set of data is fine, but I did not want to make a calculator a required component of my card game. I wanted the player to experience the feeling of starting out as a regular villager and becoming a god-like powerhouse at the end. I did not want the player to feel like an accountant.

I mocked up the basic elements using index cards and a pencil. The first task was assembling a collection of heroes, monsters, weapons, and potions. In about thirty minutes I had scribbled fifty simple cards and started the first playtests. Combat was fast with a minimal amount of math. (The hero rolls one die and adds his or her speed to the result. The monster does the same. Whoever rolls the highest value does damage to the loser.) Heroes gain gold when they defeat a monster, which is used to buy more powerful items in the store. Powerful items help the hero fight larger monsters, which drop larger amounts of gold, which allow the purchase of even better items. Like *Diablo*, this cyclical process is repeated until the hero is powerful enough to take down the final boss monster and win the game.

After a few iterations the game played surprisingly well. Now it would only be a matter of cleaning up my prototype art and making the final set of cards. Or so I thought. At first I tried creating my own original artwork, but it did not take me long to figure out that the game would never be finished in time for Christmas. I tried printing art directly from the *Diablo* web site but the pixilated sprites looked terrible on paper. At this point I decided to abandon the *Diablo* theme and instead I used art scanned from the *Dungeons and Dragons* manuals.

Production started out deceptively easy. I would scan in the art, copy it onto a template (nine playing cards arranged in a three by three grid per sheet of cardstock) print it, and then cut out the individual cards. Unfortunately, playing cards made from a single sheet of cardstock are too flimsy and are slightly see-through. This meant that I had to print the backs of the cards on another sheet of cardstock, cut them out, and then glue them to the faces to make the final card. As a final polish step I rounded the corners of each card. The end result was a sturdy, professional looking playing card.

Unfortunately, that level of quality came with a high price: it was taking me over an hour to make nine cards…and I needed over 400! Needless to say, I worked many late nights in a failed attempt to get the game ready by Christmas morning. When the kids opened the box they did not find a playable game, but were instead greeted with many sheets of uncut cards. It took me several days after Christmas to get the game to a point where it could be played. It was a lot of work, but well worth the effort.

Monster Hunter is one of the most popular of the Christmas Games and still gets played to this day. Its main drawback is that a single game can take around four or five hours and usually has to be played over multiple sessions. Unfortunately, as the kids have grown older it has become increasingly difficult to find enough free time to play.

It is worth noting that *Monster Hunter* helped me get my first job in the videogame industry. Up until this point in time I was working as a programmer at a computer graphics company. When the company went out of business I took several months off to do some soul-searching. What would be the best job for me? Of course, I wanted to make videogames! (In retrospect, it seems obvious. But before that time I had never considered getting paid to make games; it was something that I did on my own time for fun.) Shortly after I made that decision I managed to get an interview at Blizzard North (the creators of *Diablo*). I took *Monster Hunter* with me as a portfolio piece and spent an hour playing it with several of the team members. They liked the game so much that I ended up getting a job there and eventually became a designer on *Diablo III*.

Hyperline

Not surprisingly, Jordan, now age eleven, had become an avid gamer and loved to play strategy games. At the top of his Christmas list that year was the PC game, *Masters of Orion 3*. I was also looking forward to playing it since I had enjoyed the previous two games in the series. Unfortunately, the game had been delayed and was not going to release until several months after Christmas. As a consolation present—and based on my success at translating *Diablo* into a card game—I decided to try converting *Masters of Orion* into a board game.

Masters of Orion is a space conquest game that follows the "4X" formula. First you explore the planets and stars nearby your home system. Then you expand your empire by colonizing the best planets. You exploit your neighbors as you build up territory and technology. Then you exterminate everyone that gets in your way as you race toward galactic domination. It is also a game of numbers: technology levels, planetary output, fleet sizes, travel distances, etc. Some people refer to it as "playing a spreadsheet."

I knew that boardgames and mathematical calculations are not the best of companions, so I gave myself a design challenge: Can I make this game without any numbers? To achieve that goal I needed to concentrate on the feel of the "4X"s and not on the computational data prevalent in the videogame.

The final game, *Hyperline*, consists of a nine by nine board divided up into sectors. Each sector is blank when the game starts, but gets filled in with a random tile as the "explore" phase progresses. Some tiles contain planets, asteroids, or black holes, while others have "hyperline" connections, which are like train tracks through space and dictate how space-ships move from planet to planet.

Next, you "expand" your power by moving your ship along hyperlines to visit neighboring planets and acquiring their technologies. Each planet offers a different technology such as a weapon (lasers or torpedoes), engine (warp or combat), or shield (armor or energy). These new systems are also printed on tiles that are pieced together to augment your ship. One player may opt to build a ship with a lot of engines, while another one adds extra weapons. Ships can never lose parts so the power level continues to grow throughout the game. Simple scouts evolve into weapon-studded battlecruisers as the game progresses.

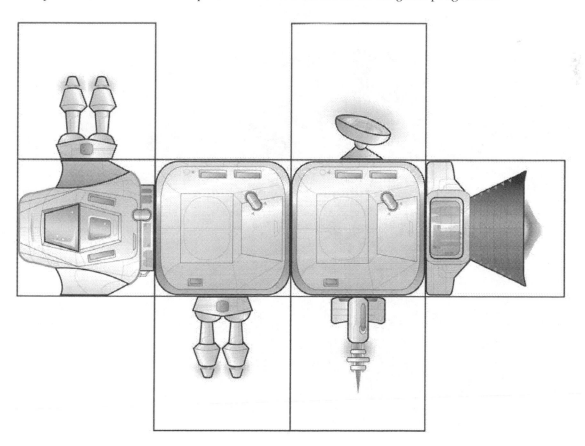

Fig. 4: A *Hyperline* ship made up of several components.

As the ships increase in power the "exploitation" phase begins. The stronger ships are able to hold territory while the weaker ones must dodge around them. Finally, as the game nears the end, the players race to "exterminate" each other to determine the ultimate winner.

Hyperline was a hit with the boys. They especially enjoyed building up powerful spaceships. (Sometimes they would purposefully delay the ending of the game just to have more time to add new pieces onto their ships.) But it was not a hit with Toby, who did not like the "fight and die" goal. To address this problem we altered the victory condition. Instead of battling for the win, the players now had to research Nexxus, a radioactive planet in the center of the board. A new part, the scanner, was added to the game to make research more effective. Now it was possible to win the game in a peaceful, scientific race, without ever firing a shot.

A few years after I had created *Hyperline*, I was cleaning out a closet and I came across the *Alpha Zoo-tauri* game, forgotten and unplayed for more than six years. At first glance I was struck by the huge gap in production quality between the two games. *Alpha Zoo-tauri*

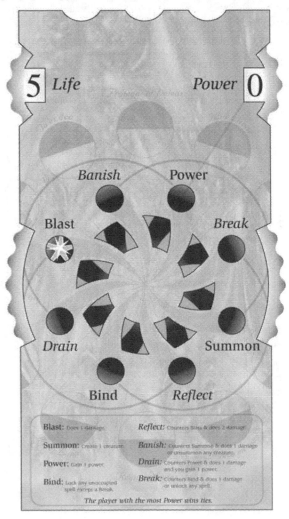

Fig. 5: *The Spellbind card. The central wheel can spin, allowing a player to select a secret spell each turn.*

was made in one afternoon with glitter glue and poster board, while *Hyperline* took months of work and featured crisp, full-color, laser-printed artwork on precise 1.5 x 1.5 inch tiles, all framed by a wooden board. But after a bit of nostalgic reflection, I realized that the games were, surprisingly, the same at the core level. In both games you traverse a web of connections in an attempt to acquire items (alphabet animals in one and interphasic shields in the other) before your opponent gets to them first. While I was working on *Hyperline* I had never consciously thought about *Alpha Zoo-tauri*, but somewhere in the back of my mind my old designs were still exerting their influences.

Spellbind

It was my responsibility to drive the kids to school each morning. Jordan was now in junior high and Dylan was in fourth grade. The trip only took about ten minutes but—as would be expected for boys that age—there was plenty of time for them to get into petty fights in the backseat of the car. For Christmas I thought it would be interesting to make them a game that could be played during our brief morning commute. The design parameters were fairly rigid:

- It had to take less than ten minutes to play so that it could be finished in one car trip.
- It could be suspended at any time, and resumed in the same state at a later time. I did not want the kids to stay in the car upon arrival if the game was not quite finished.
- It could not have loose pieces that would be lost in the cracks between the seats.
- All the rules had to be printed onto the game itself. An extra rules sheet would quickly be lost.
- It had to be small enough and thin enough to fit in the seat pockets in front of them.

I thought back to the old Car Bingo games I used to play with my siblings when we were on car trips. Each player had a cardboard grid of windows with pictures printed in them. If you saw an object outside the car that matched one of the pictures you would slide down a small red piece of plastic to mark it. ("I see an airplane!"– "I just found a fire hydrant!") When one player marked a complete line across the board then they shouted, "BINGO!" and won.

I made a quick trip to the toy store and was surprised to find that these Car Bingo cards were still being made. I purchased a few and took them home to dissect. The construction turned out to be simple in principle: three layers of cardboard, with the middle layer acting as a series of guides to keep the red plastic windows in place. Unfortunately, it turned out be extremely hard to duplicate on my own using only a straight-edged metal ruler and an X-Acto knife. But despite the construction difficulties, I knew this was the right direction.

Over the years I have learned the importance of playtesting thoroughly before jumping into final production. (I was still working at Blizzard at this point so it was easy to find people that were eager to help me with my designs.) So before I began to work on a complex paper-cutting project I mocked up a version of the game that used beads and a hand-drawn board. By necessity I knew the game had to be easy to play, so I started with a basic rock-paper-scissors mechanic. Each player would simultaneously choose an action, reveal it, and determine the outcome. To give the game more atmosphere and depth, I wrapped a spellcasting fiction around the game and made eight different spell choices (four attacks and four defends). The initial playtests revealed that the game was too random and lacked any strategy. But it took less than an hour of iteration before we homed in on an interesting game.

Each player begins with five life and zero power. The goal of the game is to reduce your opponent to zero life or for you to increase your power to five. The eight spells are arranged in a circle and alternate between attack and defend. Each turn you can only choose a spell if it is adjacent to your previous spell choice. You can also "center", which means you are selecting no spells this turn, but next turn can then select any spell of your choice. You can also spend one power point to select the same spell again. So unlike rock-scissors-paper, where each player always has exactly three options to choose from, *Spellbind* alternates between eight options, three options, and four options, depending on the circumstances. This breaks up the repetition, decreases randomness, and allows for longer term planning.

While it only took an afternoon to design the game, it took months to actually build it. I not only needed to figure out how to make the red plastic windows slide up and down, but I also needed three spinning dials (one for life, one for power, and one for selecting your spell), and three sliding tabs (to track the monsters each player summons). After studying a book on "paper engineering" I learned several tricks of the trade and—with much frustration—was able to glue together two cards, one for each player.

The game worked great and it occupied the kids' attention on numerous car trips. Surprisingly, after a month of playing with the game cards they had memorized the game to the point that they could play it in their heads. Instead of spinning the dials to keep track of life and power they would count, "One…Two…Three…Blast! One…Two…Three…Reflect! One…Two…Three…Bind!" and use their fingers to keep track of their power and life. The game cards that had taken me weeks of intricate cutting and meticulous gluing were no longer necessary.

Fridge

Each year it seemed that the Christmas Games were taking longer to design and produce. Sadly, as the kids grew older we were also playing them less. The family members' schedules were always full. Piano practice, soccer games, karate tournaments, and business meetings all started taking priority over our family game nights. What was the point of spending weeks (or months) working on a game that would rarely be played? This thought sparked the idea for the next Christmas Game.

Would it be possible to design a game in which players could take a turn even if no one else was around? What if it was designed in a way that accounted for the fact that it might take days (or weeks) to play? I did not want a game that would monopolize the dining room table for extended periods of time, but also I did not want the hassle of continually setting it up and taking it back down again. How could I get around these issues? The answer came to me at dinnertime when I looked over at the refrigerator.

Like most family refrigerators, ours had accumulated years' worth of junk. Stuck to the door with magnets were expired pizza coupons, yellowed cartoons ripped from the newspaper, and the children's elementary school artwork. What if I cleaned off the refrigerator and used it as a game board to hold magnetic pieces? The game would be located in a prominent spot in the house (we would see it every time we ate a meal) and it would not be in anyone's way. It was the perfect gaming surface!

Now I needed a theme for the game. Rather than make a simulation game that would require a lot of artwork I opted to make a purely abstract game. I also wanted the game to have an organic feel to it, with no map grid to constrain movement. The final concept was that each player would start with a home base and grow "tendrils" out onto the playing field in an attempt to touch circular targets. The more targets you touch, the higher your score.

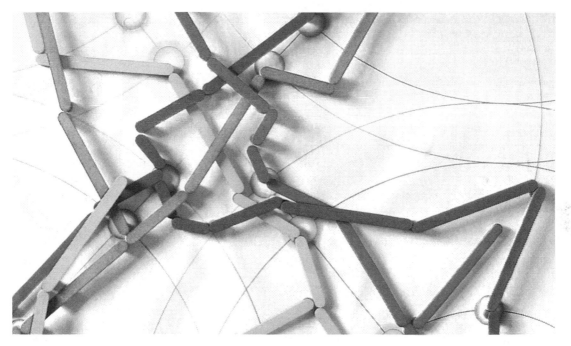

Fig. 6: Fridge pieces are magnetic and stick to the refrigerator door.

The tendrils are actually colored Popsicle sticks, painted in four different colors (one color per player). There are thirty sticks per player, ten each in three different sizes (short, medium and long). Glued onto the bottom of each stick are two round magnets that hold the stick firmly to the refrigerator door. Each player also has a resource pool of twenty extra magnets. These can be used to lift a tendril higher, which allows a player to bridge over top of an opponent's blocking tendrils instead of going around it.

Each turn a player must place a new tendril piece next to an existing tendril piece of the same color, forming an ever-growing chain that links back to the player's home base. As the game proceeds the refrigerator door slowly transforms into a work of abstract art. The brightly colored tendrils weave chaotic patterns as they reach out from the bases and head towards the targets in the center.

A key component is a special star-shaped magnet which is used to mark the current player's turn. When you finish your turn you place the marker on the next player's base to signify that your turn has ended and his turn has begun. This means that you can take your turn whenever you happen to notice the marker is on your base. You do not need to have the rest of the family in the kitchen with you; in fact, it is advantageous to take your turn when no one is watching, since you can experiment with different tendril patterns without giving away your strategy.

Fridge is surprisingly strategic and requires long-term planning, bluffing, and careful resource management. Since it never gets put in the closet it is always in play. When one game ends the next one usually starts a few days later. A full game lasts only thirty rounds (each player places one tendril piece per round and the game ends when no pieces remain) but some rounds have taken months, especially during the summer vacation period. Fridge is the perfect game for our busy family.

Nanobots

Six months before the twelfth Christmas, I started working at Maxis on the PC game *Spore*, as the lead designer of the Cell Stage. The Cell Stage is the introduction to *Spore* in which the player controls a simple life-form that grows and adapts to new challenges as it progresses up the evolutionary ladder. While working on the game I had generated a lot of art for the project and I thought it would be fun to transfer the assets over to a boardgame version.

The Cell Stage has a lot in common with *Hyperline*. In both games you start with a central body and attach new parts that provide additional functionality. Some parts are good for attacking, some provide better movement capabilities, and some are purely defensive. The kids and I love to play *Hyperline*, but the game can take two or more hours to complete so it had not been getting much play time. My idea for this year's Christmas Game was to replace the spaceship parts with cell parts (engines become flagella, scanners become eyes), remove the exploration phase, and make a fast-paced game focused on combat and survival.

I had already spent months designing the Cell Stage for *Spore*, so I felt like I had all the mechanics that I needed. In theory, the game was going to be a simple "port" from computer to paper. But problems started appearing immediately. An obvious issue was that the computer version had realtime physics calculations which allowed the cells to accelerate, rotate, and bounce through a chaotic environment. The last thing I wanted in a boardgame was for players to calculate momentum and velocity vectors. Other changes were necessary to increase gameplay variety. For example, I decided the boardgame would be more interesting with long-range attacks but these do not exist in *Spore*. To give myself more design freedom I changed the game's setting from the distant past to the far future and recast the cells as "nanobots:" manmade microscopic robots that battle it out for supremacy in a drop of water.

Despite the changes, the core theme remained intact. Each player starts with a basic nanobot body. Scattered around a hexagonal board are different types of food that the nanobots eat and convert into new mouths, limbs, eyes, and methods of propulsion. Every part has a special ability that increases the power of the nanobot and makes it unique. Ultimately, the player with the biggest nanobot dominates the battlefield and wins the game.

Nanobots was a very difficult game to produce. The hardest part was figuring out how to get the parts to connect together in a satisfying way. I tried a variety of hooks and snaps but nothing worked well enough. I started making the parts out of wood but there were too many pieces with too many intricate cuts and I soon realized it would take months to finish at the rate I was going. Fortunately, a friend of mine has a wood-milling machine and volunteered his time and garage space to help me out. We spent the next two weekends cutting and sanding approximately 100 small pieces of wood. When that was finished I stuck hand-cut illustrated stickers onto the surface of each part. The entire process required hours of repetitive and tedious production work. Looking back on it, if I had known what I was getting into I never would have started the project. In the end, the effort was worth it though because the pieces are solid, durable, and colorful, and the game has an excellent tactile feel that is unlike anything you could buy in a game store.

The kids enjoyed playing Nanobots and loved making custom battle machines. Unfortunately, the original design goal of making a fast-paced combat game was a complete failure. The game plays out slowly and requires an almost *Chess*-like thought process. Each turn takes several minutes of study before the optimal move can be determined. While it managed to capture the high-level theme of the Cell Stage it did not manage to capture any of the energy.

W.Z.D.

As the kids grew older they were spending an increasing amount of time playing videogames. Consequently, it was becoming more difficult to get them interested in card and board games. High-budget videogames offered so much more entertainment value. Why play a boardgame when there are dozens of adrenaline-filled, surround sound, action-packed shooters in the next room? How could my wood and paper creations compete?

A design technique that I have learned over the years is to concentrate on tactility, because it is the one area in which videogames are inferior. They may be better at stimulating the senses of sight and sound, but are definitely lacking when it comes to the sense of touch. When you play a videogame you are separated from the experience by a pane of glass. But when you engage in a boardgame you are touching the pieces as you play. So the trick to making a compelling boardgame is to make sure to provide pieces that begged to be touched. *RoboBall* with its plastic robots, *Kongzilla* with its giant resin monster, and Nanobots with its thick wooden components are all examples of this philosophy.

But this year I wanted to go all out and compete on theme, too. If the videogames that my kids were playing featured futuristic weapons, undead mutants, and cyborg warriors then so would this year's Christmas Game! At that point in time I did not have any ideas about the game mechanics, but I knew what pieces were needed: robots and zombies! The game, titled *W.Z.D.:Weapons of Zombie Destruction*, would feature 100 zombie enemies and the players would control high-tech robots racing against each other to wipe them all out.

My first task was to find suitable zombie figurines. It is possible to buy a cheap bag of 100 zombies but they are small and unpainted and I wanted higher quality pieces. I eventually decided to use zombies from the *Heroscape* game. Booster sets of six pre-painted plastic zombies could be purchased for about $10 a pack, but finding the seventeen packs that I needed turned out to be a challenge. I bought every pack I could find in local department stores, online game shops, and eBay auctions, and eventually obtained a full horde of 100. (Curiously, these zombie sets are now rare and sell for $35 on eBay. I like to believe that I personally caused this hyper-inflation in the zombie market.)

I have always wanted to design a game that could teach my kids basic programming concepts and this was the perfect opportunity. In the game's fiction, the players are scientists who are programming the zombie-killing robots using a deck of instruction cards. There are twelve different instructions split into three categories: Move (jet burst, strafe, stomp, flame trail); Rotate (scythe, generator, shield, memory coils); and Attack (flame thrower, ripsaw launcher, auto-turret, lightning). The robots can only carry out commands in a strict sequence and will end up shooting at walls or bumping into each other if the cards are in the wrong order. Each turn the players can add one new command or replace an existing one in an attempt to "debug" any problems in the robot's programming. The player with the best program will kill the plurality of the zombies and win the game.

From the moment that the kids opened the box on Christmas day it was clear the game was a winner. It is hard to describe the smiles on the boys' faces when they lifted the lid to reveal a large shoebox overflowing with zombies. The videogames could wait! They wanted to learn the rules and start playing *this* game immediately.

W.Z.D. is one of my favorite games and is enjoyed as much by my friends (many of them programmers) as it is by my children and their friends. Despite its grim subject matter, it is light hearted and evokes much laughter as the giant robots blast, slash, fry and electrocute all the zombies in their paths.

Soccer Bots

I was disappointed that *Nanobots* had not turned out the way I had originally intended. It had become a strategy game, not a fast-paced action game. I liked the customization and the interaction of the special part abilities, but I wanted to reduce the number of rules and prune the decision tree down in size. My desire was to shorten the game down from two hours to twenty minutes.

Both Jordan and Dylan were in robot clubs in their schools that year. Dylan was also on the school's soccer team and was constantly dribbling a ball from room to room as he walked around the house. These events inspired me to create my fourteenth Christmas Game, *Soccer Bots*. In many ways I was trying to capture the feeling of the ten-year old *RoboBall* game, while at the same time appealing to two boys that were now both in high school. (Jordan was in kindergarten when he first played *RoboBall*.)

After *Nanobots*'s lengthy production process I was not in the mood to make handcrafted parts again. I needed a faster way to make the pieces. A friend at work suggested I try Ponoko.com, which is an online laser-cutting service. You pick the material (wood, plastic, or metal), upload an outline of the image you wish to cut, and a quote appears instantly. If you like the price you can pay by credit card and sit back while you wait for the precision cut parts to arrive at your doorstep. I was instantly sold on the idea and went to work on the part design.

Since I knew that a computer controlled laser (with a .001 mm tolerance) would be doing the cutting I was excited to design the intricate pieces. It took several weeks of iteration to get the final shapes perfected but I would rather spend my time in front of the computer than doing mindless assembly line work.

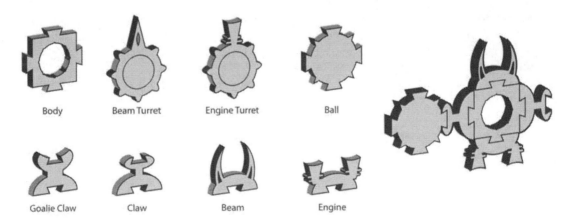

Fig. 7: The basic components needed to build a *Soccer Bot*.

I was determined to keep the game fast so I purchased a sleek digital chess clock to force the players to move quickly. As a game design technique I consider the use of a timer to be a blunt hammer solution. Given the choice, I would prefer crafting a set of rules that intrinsically encourages fast play. But in this case I justified my decision by convincing myself that real soccer has a timer, so robotic soccer should have one, too.

To win *Soccer Bots* you must score points by pushing a "ball" across the other side's goal. What makes the game interesting is that before the game starts each player secretly creates a team of four robots out of a collection of arms, engines, repulsors, and tractor beams. This leads to many different configurations and strategies. Do you want a fast team? Then put on a lot of engines. Want to control the ball? Then you will want a lot of arms. Want to shoot from a distance? Then make sure your robotic players have repulsor beam weapons. During your turn you have only thirty seconds to make as many moves as possible based on the part configurations. Then play immediately passes to your opponent.

The final game got a lot of play after Christmas and both boys quickly created dominant teams of custom robots (which, sadly, consistently beat my inferior squad). Unfortunately, they both lost interest in the game within a couple of weeks and it has not been played since, despite my prodding. I often wonder whether it was a flaw in the game itself or if the theme no longer lacked appeal. After all, why play simulated soccer on the tabletop when you could be outside kicking a real ball? Why piece together plastic robot shapes in the living room when you could be in the school workshop building real robots?

Swords

A former Blizzard co-worker, Ben Boos, had just completed his first book, *Swords*. The book features page after page of beautifully illustrated medieval weapons and armor and I instantly knew that it would be a perfect topic for a game. Ben and I began discussing the possibility of making a Facebook game based on his artwork and we agreed to move forward with the idea. While mocking up some simple ideas on paper I realized that the subject would be perfect for a Christmas card game.

The game of *Swords* started out as a simple collection game, with each card representing a different weapon. But it soon became apparent that collecting weapons was not nearly as much fun as using them. The game needed some monsters!

Dylan had been asking to play *Monster Hunter* for several months but the family could never find sufficient free time to play. With *Swords* I had the opportunity to create a faster version of *Monster Hunter*, but I did not want to resort to using a game timer. Instead I wanted to make a rules system that supported simultaneous play. My theory was that a four-player game of *Monster Hunter* would only take one quarter of the time to play if every player took their turn at the same time.

I began the design process by looking at other games with simultaneous turns. In particular I was attracted to casino games like *Craps*, *Roulette* and *Blackjack* in which an entire table of participants remains engaged in the action. These games all feature a central shared element (the dice, the wheel, the dealer's hand) that affects all of the players at the same time. Based on these ideas I made *Swords* into a type of gambling game. But instead of betting money, the players are betting the lives of their heroes and peasants.

At the beginning of the game four random monsters are placed in the center of the table. Each monster has a special ability that makes it unique. For instance, some monsters fly and can avoid melee weapons, some convert dead heroes into undead skeletons, and some breathe fire at the start of battle. Every monster comes into play with a random number of hit points and a bounty of one gold piece.

Players secretly "place a bet" on which monster they wish to attack. The more players that attack a given monster the more likely it is to die, but since the bounty is split the reward is relatively low. Conversely, attacking a monster alone is more risky, but offers a better reward. Since players do not know who is attacking which monster there is a period of discussion, negotiation, and bluffing before each player commits their army to battle.

The army is made up of small wooden people (affectionately called "meeples"). Instead of rolling dice or playing cards to resolve a battle the players toss the meeples onto the table. Meeples that fall on their heads will die, meeples on their sides do a regular attack, and meeples that land on their feet trigger special abilities (dependent on the type of sword they are carrying).

After the attack the winners split the loot and the dead monsters are replaced with new monsters. Any monster that survives has its bounty increased by 1 gold. The effect of this is that the difficult monsters gradually become more enticing the longer they are allowed to remain on the table. No one wants to risk their entire army fighting an acid-spitting dragon for only one gold, but a ten-gold reward is quite attractive.

Money is used to buy swords that convert peasants into heroes. There are a variety of different swords that have their own special properties. For instance, a paladin's shining broadsword has the power to heal other heroes in the battle, while a necromancer's unholy dagger has the power to create zombies that will join your army.

The game is fast and noisy with a lot of "oohs" and "aahs" as heroes rise and fall in the face of adversity. An entire game can be played in under an hour which makes it a good choice when time is short.

What's Next?

Over time, each of the Christmas games has become a yearly marker along the paths of my children's lives. The games are like photographs that have captured not their images, but their interests and developmental progress as they have grown from toddler to high-school graduate. In response to these changes I have had to continually adapt and evolve my designs. Each year brought a new challenge as I struggled to create a game experience that was novel, entertaining, and developmentally appropriate for the wildly different stages of their lives.

Jordan is now in college and has moved out of the house. (Our *Fridge* game continues; his last move was at the end of Christmas break and his next move will occur when he returns to visit during Spring break.) Dylan is in high school and will soon be getting his driving permit. I wonder, how many more Christmas games will there be? When both of the kids have left the house will I still have the motivation to stay up late on December nights, rushing to beat an immovable Christmas deadline?

And what new technologies will I have at my disposal? Over the last fifteen years paints and pencils have been replaced with a high-resolution laser printer. Saws and sandpaper have been replaced with a precision laser cutter. Some year in the not too distant future will I be making games with a 3D printer and programmable animatronic robots?

I know one thing for certain: I will continue making games. (Given my history that is easy to predict.) I look forward to the challenges and changes coming up in the next fifteen years. It is likely that one of those games will be a simple reindeer matching game with my first grandchild.

GAME ANALYSES

HOW *SETTLERS OF CATAN* CREATED
AN AMERICAN BOARDGAME REVOLUTION
Ian Schreiber

In 1995, the game that would become Klaus Teuber's masterpiece was shipped in Germany by distributor Kosmos. A few German-language copies trickled to the hobby market in the U.S., fueling demand that allowed Mayfair to produce an English-language version the following year. To date, it has sold more copies worldwide each year than in the previous, a trend that is the reversal of the sell-millions-in-two-weeks-or-bust sales model of big-budget videogames. To put things in perspective for any videogame fan in the audience, there are about as many copies of *Settlers of Catan* in circulation as there are copies of *Grand Theft Auto 3* and *World of Warcraft* combined.[26]

To many Americans, the marketing phrase "a boardgame that's fun for the whole family" is really code that means "a boardgame that's only fun for children, and we expect the parents to suck it up and play anyway." For many, *Catan* is the boardgame that first proved to them that well-designed games can actually be fun for children *and* adults.[27]

This raises two questions. First, what qualities does *Catan* possess that allow it to bring together players of widely varying age and skill? And second, if there were so many other pre-existing games that share these qualities, what was it about *Catan* that made it the catalyst that essentially launched a hobby game revolution in the States?

About the Game

Before tackling these questions, it is worth a quick summary of the rules of the game. What follows are not the complete rules, but it will provide enough of a picture for us to begin analyzing the gameplay.

The board consists of a set of hexagonal tiles that are set up in a random configuration. Each tile contains both a resource (one of five types: ore, lumber, clay, wheat, or wool), and a number from two to twelve (corresponding to the range of values on a roll of two dice). Players build settlements on the intersections between tiles. During the course of play they build new roads to connect their settlements, and they can build new settlements or upgrade their settlements into cities.

This game is played in turns, with turn order proceeding clockwise, as in many games. On a player's turn, three things happen:

- First, the player rolls two dice. All resource tiles with the corresponding number produce that resource, giving one of that resource to each adjacent settlement or two to each city of *any* player.

- Next, the player may trade their resources. They can trade with the bank at a rate of four for one (a terrible exchange rate by any reckoning), or they can trade with other players for any exchange rate that both players agree to. Note that the other players can only trade with the player whose turn it is.

- Finally, the player may spend resources. They can build roads expanding outward from existing roads or settlements. They can build new settlements along their roads. They can upgrade settlements to cities, which produce extra resources. And they can buy progress cards, which offer a variety of special one-use abilities.

The object of the game is to be the first player to reach ten Victory Points (VP). Players earn one VP for every settlement and two for every city that they own on the board. Players can also earn two special bonuses, one for having the longest contiguous road and one for having the greatest number of Army cards (the most common type of progress card), each worth two VP.

Game Dynamics

When we analyze the mechanics, we can see some interesting properties of *Catan*:

- Measured randomness. There are random elements in the game, such as die rolls and the shuffled deck of progress cards. However, the constraints of the randomness (odds of die rolls and distribution of progress cards) are known to the players, allowing them to strategically play the odds.

- Competitive, but not confrontational. On the one hand, players are in competition with each other; only one player can win, and it is a race to reach ten VP. On the other hand, the competition is mostly indirect. Players cannot destroy each other's cities or settlements or otherwise steal VP from each other; one player's gain is not necessarily another player's loss. Players can harm each other's standing in more direct ways (for example, there are mechanisms for stealing resources), but these tend to be limited and short-term losses. More often, players spend their time trading with one another, working out mutually beneficial exchanges. Even in a competitive game, the primary focus is on working together.

- Variety of play. The board is set up randomly each game. One game may have all of the wheat clustered together in one area, leading to some players forming a wheat oligopoly. Another game might have ore only produced on rolls of two, three and twelve, leading to massive ore shortages. Some setups have a small number of prime building locations for cities, while others have a larger number of mediocre building sites. Because of this, no two games are exactly the same, and each brings its own unique set of challenges.

- Multiple paths to victory. There are many ways to reach ten VP. You can build a large network of roads and pop up small settlements everywhere. Or, you can focus on a smaller number of settlements and upgrade them into cities. You can go after the VP bonus for building roads, or the bonus for buying progress cards, or even both. No strategy is automatically better than the others; all are theoretically viable, but their efficacy varies based on the current board and game state. Because of this, players are encouraged to modify their strategy based on circumstances, leading to a more varied play experience.

- Constrained play time. Due to the nature of the game, players are constantly advancing towards the final goal. Players can gain but never lose settlements or cities, so the game is more or less guaranteed to end within a certain time range. Games typically take between sixty and ninety minutes, pushing the upper end of a child's attention span.

- Minimal downtime. Players rarely have time when they have nothing to do. On other players' turns they are collecting resources and participating in resource trades. Even when players have nothing to do (perhaps they have no resources, or they have all they need), turns are short enough to keep the action going.

"Fun for the Whole Family"

These properties – measured randomness, competition without confrontation, variety, multiple paths to victory, constrained play time, and minimal downtime – are common in many "Eurogames," not just *Catan*. These properties do not just appear randomly in games. Game designers deliberately craft their games to have these properties, because it allows the games to appeal to a wide age range.

Measured randomness provides enough of an advantage to a lucky player to keep less skilled (typically younger) players from frustration, because a string of good die rolls can always turn the game in their favor, so they never feel like they have no chance. The randomness also lessens the sting of defeat: the losing players can conveniently blame the luck of the dice. At the same time, the ability to strategically plan based on one's understanding of the game will favor more skilled play in the long run, keeping the more skilled and competitive players engaged.

With a decreased reliance on confrontational behavior and a major focus on trading and negotiation, players are less likely to become frustrated with other players' anti-social or overly-competitive behaviors. This can prevent hurt feelings and ruffled feathers among younger children, or harshly competitive adults. It also encourages good sportsmanship and best behavior, as players are less likely to trade with or assist someone who is being unfriendly.

Variety of the game setup and the existence of multiple viable strategies give the game a much longer shelf life. Play cannot devolve into players following rote patterns or always pursuing the same strategies; the randomness of the game encourages players to have a variety of experiences. Repeat play is important, as it allows the game to be played regularly as a family activity that does not get boring or stale for a long time.

Constrained play time and reduced downtime cater to young players with relatively low attention spans, helping them to stay engaged. The game is also long enough to offer a satisfyingly complete experience to older and more patient players.

Not a perfect game

As with any game, *Catan* has its share of flaws. These generally seem minor to first-time players, but may wear on an individual after repeated play (by which time, that individual has likely discovered other Eurogames). For example:

- Uneven starting positions. Depending on the board setup, certain seats may be more or less advantageous than others. For example, on a board where certain key resources are clustered together (say, there is a Wheat hex with the number six, but all other Wheat hexes have infrequent numbers like two or twelve), there may be one single position on the board that is better than all the others. This would give an advantage to the first player, who gets to place their initial settlement first. Conversely, other board setups may have three or four prime building locations, giving the first player a disadvantage: they gain little if any advantage from first placement, but they place last when placing their second settlement during game setup, meaning that their second settlement may be in a less valuable location than the other players. To be fair, uneven starting positions do encourage players to trade and cooperate, since everyone starts with access to different kinds of resources; but the starting positions can also give some players the negative perception that they are at an inherent disadvantage from the beginning.

- A positive feedback loop. Near the end of the game, players have expended their network of settlements and cities to the point where those in the lead are gaining large amounts of resources each turn, and the game typically ends quickly once it reaches a certain point. By contrast, the beginning game can sometimes feel slow, particularly if the dice roll numbers for resources that few players have built on, or if a lot of sevens are rolled (which allow players to steal resources from one another, rather than generating net wealth for everyone on the board). A player who falls behind in the early game because their numbers refuse to come up on the dice can feel frustrated for the rest of the game. Even in the end game, a player with six VP may feel they have no chance to win when other players have eight or nine.

- Unbalanced progress cards. The progress cards vary from being a net loss (gain two resources of your choice, but it already cost you three resources to buy the card) to marginally useful (a free Victory Point) to a huge swing in the game state (force all opponents to hand over to you all of their resources of a type of your choice). The unpredictability of the cards stops them from being a consistent strategy. On the other hand, the few cards that can unbalance the game allow sudden swings that come from a single event – making the cards feel more arbitrary than exciting.

Not the only Eurogame

Catan is not the only game, or even the first game, to embody Eurogame characteristics (measured randomness, competition without confrontation, variety, multiple paths to victory, constrained play time, and minimal downtime). Indeed, players new to *Catan* often quickly find their way to other Eurogames, sometimes newer and sometimes older.

Consider *Can't Stop*, released in 1980. This is a dice game in which players attempt to move their pieces to the end of tracks labeled with the numbers two through twelve. Players roll four dice, then split them into two sets of two dice, and advance their pieces on the corresponding tracks. Players can only advance up to three tracks per turn, but can continue rolling to advance along those tracks as much as they desire. However, a roll that cannot advance at least one track causes all gains on that turn to be wiped out, leading to a series of push-your-luck decisions of risk-versus-reward. This game has measured randomness, as the risk/reward calculations are pure mathematics, but a player can still have a lucky (or unlucky) roll. There is competition in trying to reach the ends of each track first, but very little confrontation, as players cannot directly set back their opponents. There is variety, in that certain numbers become unavailable as play progresses, making each game play a little different than the others. There are multiple paths to victory, both in terms of which numbers to go for, and in how risky or safe a player chooses to be on their turns. Play generally lasts about half an hour, and since turns always end in either some progress or none (but never a net loss) the game is always approaching completion. Player turns go quickly, so players generally don't have to wait long between turns.

Or consider *Bohnanza*, released in 1997. As a game with the core mechanic of trading with other players, it could be thought of as a heavily streamlined version of *Catan*. Players are dealt a hand of cards of different kinds of beans, and they are trying to collect up to two or three different kinds of beans (the rest are of much lower value to them). Players can trade freely with each other to plant their beans and harvest them for points. There are no upgrades or special cards to buy as there are in *Catan*, nor is there a game board that affords any kind of starting advantage, nor any kind of positive feedback loop; players draw a set number of cards each turn, and continue playing until the deck empties three times.

Bohnanza offers measured randomness (cards are dealt randomly, but each card displays how many matching cards exist in the deck, so players have the opportunity to do card-counting and probability calculations at the table). There is competition but not confrontation (players mainly get ahead by making good trades, after all, so it is in everyone's best interest to be friendly to their opponents). There is variety during play (since players receive different sets of cards from game to game). There are multiple paths to victory (players can try to collect small sets of beans for marginal but steady gains, or large sets for larger but more infrequent scoring; they may try for rare beans or more common ones; and they may collect beans that everyone else is neglecting, or compete with opponents for the same bean type). Play time is constrained (players draw cards every turn, so the game is guaranteed to last for a set number of turns). Downtime is minimized (since players are always trading with each other, even when it's not their turn).

The rules of both *Can't Stop* and *Bohnanza* are simpler than *Catan*, and the games play faster. As each is easier to play and easier to teach, both games are accessible to a slightly younger audience while keeping many of the same positive qualities of *Catan*. Keep in mind that these are merely two examples out of dozens, perhaps hundreds of games that offer similar qualities. And yet, more often than not for those being introduced to Eurogames for the first time, it is *Catan* that is the gateway to these other games and not the other way around.

Why *Catan* and not some other game?

All of the characteristics that make *Catan* so compelling can be found in many games. What was it about *Catan* in particular that made it such an international sensation, if the gameplay is not unique?

In fact, some Eurogames did come to the States in the 1980s and were commercially disappointing.[28] The success of *Catan*, then, relies as much on its historical context as its game mechanics.

Before Eurogames could reach a certain level of success, they needed a market of enthusiastic hobby gamers. For that to happen, a few other events had to happen first.

For the first half of the 20th century, boardgames were not considered a hobby in mainstream American culture. Games were a pastime, perhaps. They were a family bonding activity. They were a way to pass a rainy afternoon. But with few exceptions, people did not think of games as part of their identity or part of their regular weekly schedule. This began to change in the 1960s with the rise in popularity of historical wargames (this period also saw a rise in American-designed boardgames, many of which were published by the same companies that produced wargames). The audience expanded considerably in the early 1970s with the release of *Dungeons & Dragons* (itself derived from the fantasy-based wargame *Chainmail*). With the rising popularity of tabletop wargaming and later tabletop roleplaying, players were encouraged to form groups and meet on a regular basis to play the latest wargame release or to continue their roleplaying campaigns. For the first time, games were not just a one-off activity, but an ongoing and regular hobby. With the success of these new genres of tabletop game, a hobby market for games emerged and expanded.

However, there was another condition required for any hobby game to reach the level of popularity that *Catan* eventually did, and that was the ability to spread virally throughout the hobby game community. In the 1960s and 70s, the internet was still a military project and not the mainstream online social community that it is today. Tabletop game conventions existed, but drew crowds of thousands, not the tens of thousands of today. Particularly with roleplaying games, players tended to play with the same group over time; even if a new game was introduced into a group, there was not necessarily a large cross-pollination with other groups, so the spread of new games was limited. While there were some retail stores that were dedicated to hobby games and some of these served as local gaming community centers, the hobby itself was still small enough that it could not support the kinds of sales numbers that *Catan* eventually saw. For a breakout hit with multi-million-unit sales, another game would first need to be released to expand the market and form larger, more fluid communities. The year this happened was 1993, and the game was *Magic: the Gathering*.

Magic was practically an overnight sensation. With its open-ended business model that allowed players to spend however much they wanted, it became profitable enough that some stores were able to exclusively support themselves with trading-card game products. While *D&D* mostly required players to form a single closed group, the short play time and competitive nature of *Magic* allowed players to play with friends or strangers. *Magic* tournaments were organized, bringing together gamers who might not have had occasion to play together otherwise. The success of *Magic* also significantly boosted attendance at game conventions, with 1995 being a record high attendance at both Gen Con and Dragon Con. As a result, local, national, and global communities organized around the game, often with game stores themselves serving as cultural centers for players to meet and play.

When *Catan* came along with its near-universal appeal, distribution and sales channels were available. Additionally, hobbyist game groups and communities had already formed around games that could be individually played in a short time span; integrating a new board or card game into an afternoon's *Magic* play session was an easy transition.

Summary

In this chapter, we explored the success of the boardgame *Settlers of Catan*. In part, this is because *Catan* catered to a previously unserved market of game players that were looking for a family game with broad age appeal. The appeal of the game comes from its mix of mechanics. Children and casual players are satisfied by the game's relatively simple rules, limited play time, lack of downtime, and sufficient random events that allow small victories and a chance of winning even to players who are unskilled. Sophisticated gamers can enjoy the complex player interactions and strategic depth. While these properties are true of many games (and in fact, many games arguably serve these needs better than *Catan*), this particular game came along at just the right time historically, allowing it to reach a broad market.

---

[26] As of 2009, there have been more than 18 million copies of *Settlers of Catan* sold worldwide (this is just the base set in its various incarnations, not counting expansion sets, spin-offs, and digital versions). By contrast, there were about 8 million units of *Grand Theft Auto 3* sold and 11 million *World of Warcraft* subscribers.

[27] Germany, meanwhile, had a backlog of decades of excellent games, which provided plenty of fuel for the Euro-game market in America once it became established.

[28] Examples include *Ghosts!* (1980), *Scotland Yard* (1983), and *The aMAZEing Labyrinth* (1986). Many games from the 80s were reprinted after *Catan* opened the distribution channels, and have done well in the post-*Catan* hobby game market.

CONQUEST
by David Parlett

It's funny how some people like games to be "about" something while others have no such desire. The former go for games that might be described as thematic or representational, like *Monopoly* or *Settlers of Catan*; the latter prefer abstracts like *Chess*, *Checkers* and *Othello*. I'm one of the latter. For me, a game doesn't have to be about anything other than itself. I think of thematic games as being theatrical: the players seem to be wanting not only to play a game but also to play a role in a dramatic representation of some aspect of real life. Personally I'm quite happy with being who I am, and who I am is somebody who enjoys rising to the challenge of problem-solving in spatial and mathematical relationships. It's obviously a personality thing: I don't much care for drama as such, and hardly ever go to the theater (though I enjoy movies - so long as they're not too dramatic!).

I'm one of the older generation of games enthusiasts. A games inventor since childhood, I first started writing and reviewing for the late *Games & Puzzles* magazine in 1972, and invented my first published boardgame, *Hare & Tortoise*, the following year. Immediately before coming up with that solitary success, I spent several months vainly playing about with the idea of basing a game on dice - not rolling them so they fall at random, but flipping or tumbling them by their edges from square to square so that you work out where they would finish up and with which side uppermost. My first experiment was to place letters on their sides and move them around in such a way as to form words. This didn't work very well, so I tried the next and perhaps more obvious device of keeping to the traditional arrangement of spots and decreeing that you could roll a cube over as many squares as indicated by the number on top at the start of your move. There was, if I remember rightly, a 10x10 squared board and you each started with ten dice on your back row. The obvious objective was to get one or all of your dice over to the far edge. But, despite much playing around with possible ideas, I couldn't get anywhere satisfactory with it, and moved on to something completely different.

Two years later we received for review at the *Games & Puzzles* office a dice-rolling game called *Conquest*, published by Denys Fisher Games and invented by Geoffrey Hayes (as we now know, though in those unenlightened days inventors were not credited anywhere on the published product). I pounced on this game immediately, played it with delight, and asked to review it. My review appeared in *Games & Puzzles* #48, dated May 1976, and I am still playing with the review copy.

To my chagrin, but equal admiration, Hayes had come up with a solution that had consistently eluded me. I quote the following description more or less verbatim from my review.

Each player takes eight large plastic dice of a distinctive color and places them on their nine-long back rank of a 9 x 8 checkered board. The middle or 'key' square of the row is occupied by a piece awkwardly referred to as a 'key-dice', which may be regarded as the equivalent of a *Chess* king. The key-piece, marked with a single spot on every face, moves one square at a time, and the object is to move it across the board so as to occupy the opposing key square. An alternative win is achieved by capturing your opponent's key-piece.

The point of the play lies in the way the dice-pieces are used. Each one is rolled (or 'flipped' or 'tumbled') from square to square so that each succeeding face is turned uppermost as it crosses the ridge on to an adjacent square - all moves being orthogonal, of course. The distance it moves is determined by the number of spots shown on the top face at the start of a turn. It must move in a straight line, but may make one (only) right-angled turn at any point in the course of it. It may not pass over another piece, but may capture an enemy piece by replacement if its legitimate move brings it on to a square so occupied. And that's all!

The basic strategy of the game is, of course, to get your pieces working together like an army or bodyguard to protect the passage of your key-piece across the board, while attacking and removing enemy pieces where possible in order to prevent your opponent from achieving the same objective. Alternatively you may concentrate less on advancing your key-piece and more on moving your army out to capture your opponent's. In either case, skill depends entirely upon the ability to position pieces correctly and move them in such a way as to ensure that they finish with a suitable number uppermost. What that is, of course, depends on the position: in an open game sixes are strongest; in a close game threes and fours are best; ones are nearly always positive weaknesses.

One's first reaction to the game may well be of bewilderment - at first sight it seems impossible to quickly think your way around a three-dimensional piece in order to work out where it can land up and in what orientation. In fact, however, it is a knack that can be learned in the course of your first few games. Once achieved, the game becomes one of pure skill, though before you reach that stage the progress of the game does tend to be a bit - er - dicey.

Presentation and durability are superb. I particularly admire the way the squares are defined by ridges while the pieces have grooved edges to key them in as they roll over, though I wish the surfaces were not so slippery. The rules are not bad, but for a game so simple to describe, they ought to be better. I assume, for example, that once you have got your key-piece on to your opponent's key square you win immediately, but it would have been helpful of the rules to confirm that your opponent cannot then snatch away your victory by capturing it at once. It is a point which, without clarification, could lead to argument.

The world today is so full of two-player abstract boardgames, most of which are *Draughts* (*Checkers*, for Americans) with knobs on, that it is refreshing to come across one whose concept is so original that it can be explained in a few words. For this reason, and for its intrinsic depth, *Conquest* deserves a solid future. I rated it six out of six.

So ended my review. *Conquest* did indeed go on to enjoy a future of sorts, albeit a rather piecemeal and scrappy one. To my disgust, it was soon after rebranded for the UK market as *"The George vs. Mildred Dice Game"*, in reference to a then popular TV domestic sitcom. It has appeared in various countries and under various titles, including also *Alea*, *Tactix*, and, in Germany, *Duell*. (Further details from BoardGameGeek.)

My brother and I have taken it up again recently, and my ten-year-old grandson enjoys it. Which just goes to confirm, in my view, that a preference for abstract games is a personality thing, and that personalities tend to run in families.

I'll just end by adding a few regulatory refinements that don't appear in the original rules (I haven't seen any later ones) but which we have found useful and desirable:

- To decide who plays which color and who begins: One player holds out a dice of each color concealed in each hand. The other announces a color, for example "Red", and points to a hand. The chooser then plays the color actually revealed, and moves first if (and only if) they correctly predicted that color.

- Having selected which dice to tumble, you should first announce its topmost number so that your opponent can monitor and correct any mistake in movement.

- You may retract a move but only so long as you have kept in physical contact with the dice you moved.

- As in Chess, you should announce "Check!" upon placing your opponent's king *en prise*. (There's no fun in winning a game by your opponent's lack of observation.) If you don't, you can't take it on your next move. You can announce the check later, but can't take it till the move after that, if still possible.

- Most importantly of all (in our opinion): to win, it is not enough to merely move your king on to your opponent's king square - it must not then be immediately captured, otherwise you lose.

FAIR ISN'T FUNNY! THE DESIGN OF *COSMIC ENCOUNTER*®
by Peter Olotka

Cosmic Encounter has been acknowledged among game designers for its ground breaking design. We called it a simultaneous-revelation-social-interaction-game. What's intriguing, is that unlike the vast army of boardgames in existence, *Cosmic Encounter* has not been the victim of copycat products. At the time of this printing, *Cosmic* has entered its fourth decade at 38 years old and counting, with a new 2008 version from Fantasy Flight Games and an Expansion set, *Cosmic Incursion* from FFG hitting the shelves in 2010.

A 2009 Boardgame Geek review from Nate Owens, a first time player, sums up the game's appeal as well as anything written in the previous four decades "…This is no museum piece. Even if it's a 32-year-old design, *Cosmic Encounter* feels as thrilling and cutting edge as anything I've ever played."

Disclosure: Nate is not a relative and I have never met him. Anyway, the $$ I sent him was a small sum, relatively speaking.

Creative people are always being asked: "How did you come up with the idea?" So let's talk about inspiration. As with lots of new designs (in any field), it's nice to have no clue about what you are doing. Preconception of what a game is can often be a debilitating factor among many designers. "Hey let's get some monsters and give them some stuff, and then they can go beat up some other monsters. And my innovation is to make a sword that is worth a gazillion flimbats. Oh and, the graphics will be really cool."

Yawn.

New Alien: The Snob - power to yawn

It would be able to swat away intruders with the back of its hand - as long as its card was the lowest.

Anyway, when I am asked, it makes me think of the five second elevator pitch: *Risk* meets the *Godfather Game* in 1971. My partners-to-be and I used to play epic games of *Risk*. Over time, the incessant clatter of dice (see my *Risk* essay in James Lowder's *Family Games Best 100*) cultivated a desire to have a diceless game. Just about then, I saw a picture of the 1971 *Godfather Game* ensconced in a violin case. I never played it, but was taken with the idea that it was marketed, literally, outside the box. I was formally bitten by the game design bug, and have suffered from it lo these many years.

In retrospect here are some of the influences on *Cosmic's* design:

- *Chess* was weighed in strategically because the pieces had their own unique movement.

- *Poker* had a hand because it was the ultimate bluffing game.

- Star Trek of the sixties scripted *Cosmic's* flavor with its self-deprecating stars lurching around the set.

- Science fiction authors Asimov, Herbert, Niven and Pohl suspended our disbelief, and we never recovered it.

As long as we are discussing the game, here is a brief retrospective of the team's cosmic journey. The *Cosmic Encounter* design journey started in 1971 with Bill Eberle and myself, and expanded to four by the time Eon Products, Inc. was founded. We called ourselves *Future Pastimes* as a design team. One of the keys to *Cosmic's* design was the collaboration and clash sparked by the personalities and skill sets of the designers. We did everything by unanimous agreement. Think about that for a minute. Were we mad? Most definitely. But we produced a cascading rush of rule breaking. "If you can do that than I can do this."

"Oh yeah? Then I will...."

I brought the idea of doing a game that was different and science fiction based. Bill Eberle contributed seeing everything from unexpected perspectives. Jack Kittredge carried the torch for logic and rationalism and precision. Bill Norton tossed in offbeat humor and whimsy and then on a whim, sold out for cash. Three way split.

If you are new to design you might want to experiment with thinking in the abstract about how to theme your game.

Theme is more than window dressing, and less than fanatical immersion. To be true to theme, a design should strive to capture the essence of the setting or construct by creating a system in which players naturally adopt behaviors that fit their circumstances. Success is when a player is surprised to act in a way that is not in keeping with their real life personality, as though it were normal.

In our case, we wanted a science fiction game because we couldn't find any in 1971. Science Fiction has no restrictions. We were free! The Moody Blues played "Days of Future Passed." So we were *Future Pastimes*. Note: Alert gamer Greg Costikyan has cited the *Lensman* boardgame made in 1969 by Philip N. Pritchard. Glad we missed it lest we had fallen in love with it.

Since we are starting from the abstract and moving to the specific, let's play the name game. Game names are tough to come by. Our first take was *The Universe Game*. We went through a collection of "not quite" names before settling on *Cosmic Encounter*. I think it still needs work. It evokes longhaired hippies sitting under crystal pyramids. Of course the designers were longhaired hippies, who hated rules. So there you go.

And now that we have named it, we have to explain/sell it with a tagline which is very useful for games which have bad names.

Cosmic Encounter has had in no particular order:

- The science fiction game for everyone

- A quantum leap in games

- The game that breaks it own rules

- Always Different, Always Fun

- A Game of Infinite Possibilities

There are probably even more taglines in the non-English version.

Crafting underlying principles is an important place for the designer to start. I mean, really start here. Draw up a list of principles to follow and /or elements for your game to have. Then design with them in mind. Here were ours:

- No dice allowed

- Everyone had to be different

- Play would offer compromise and conflict

- No one would be eliminated

- Players could win together

- Each game would be different (re-playability)

- License to cheat. Pretty much all players in all games would just love to be able to peek. Just a little. Woot!

- Almost all the early *Cosmic* aliens were hatched from a player wishing "If only …"

    - I could see what she has (Mind)

    - I could get a do-over (Chronos)

    - I could get rid of this junk (Philanthropist)

    - I couldn't die (Zombie)

I think it can be profoundly liberating to make a list of things you want your game to be and to not be, and then stick to them. Think about your likes and dislikes in the games you've played, and then try to settle on what you want your game to feel like.

A major subsection of crafting your game's principles has to do with for whom you are designing. Who is your audience? If you were scoring attendance at a game convention; the score was Males 90 – Females 10. We all know why. Too many games were humorless exercises in mayhem. It's still true today. The gorier and war-ier, the bloodier and fouler, the better. Footnote: If you were in the 90% and were just trying to score, the odds were against you.

When *Cosmic Encounter* was introduced at the cons, despite the 90 - 10 audience, the *Cosmic* players would be 50% female. We figured that the boys should notice. Good design is inclusive. Over the years *Cosmic Encounter* has been praised by many publications, from The Gifted Children's Newsletter to *The Playboy Winner's Guide to Board Games*, which just shows the range. Social interaction is an inclusive characteristic for a game.

When you get to mocking up your game for the first time, a whole bunch of surprises spill out of the physical design. We call this "Cutting the Plant's Vines." In our very first tinker toy-cottage cheese container-erector set-egg carton *Cosmic* prototype, we had a Plant Alien with actual foam rubber vines. Each alien was festooned with egg carton cups serving as planets. If the plant vine could reach your planet it could get a base. The machine had some wire tendrils that were used in the event that it had to duplicate the plant's power. We had a dodecahedron the size of a tennis ball with two each of six colors on its twelve sides. If you rolled your own color you had to roll again...and...again...and again...

These fussy and annoying mechanisms stopped the developmental progress of *Cosmic* for more than a year. But suffice it to say that when we fast talked our way into Parker Brothers and forced them to play our game, all they could do was roll their own color over and over.

Exit us, in round one of "What do we do now?"

Months later we unceremoniously cut the vines from the Plant and sent the dodecahedron to the archives. The result was a flood of new aliens and new ideas, which birthed the current incarnation of our game. The moral of the story is to let go early and often.

New Alien: The Preacher - power to moralize

It could offer to let you on to a planet of its choice anywhere in the game.

I like funny games. Games can create a social structure that operates under its own constitution. Most games labor under rules that are designed to be fair. Otherwise why bother playing? Right? Here's the problem: Fair is not funny.

Let me put it this way: If you play a game for three hours and follow a complex set of perfectly balanced rules which feel fair to all, and you eliminate your four opponents one by one until you are the last one left, it's not all that funny. And it's particularly not all that fun for the losers. Many players and some publishers have railed that things which happen in *Cosmic* are *"not fair."* In *Cosmic Encounter*, we give you that rail and allow you to stick it up your opponent's.... Especially if said opponent is whining that his alien has no such rail with which to stick you. This whole process led to the design of the Sniveler, who has the power to whine. Now that's funny.

A component of "Not Fair" is "The Gloat."

When a player makes a stunning upset from a hopeless position, or totally dominates, or sets up an air-tight strategy, or finds a new wrinkle in an alien power, it introduces the gloat factor. We would often measure new features which we added to *Cosmic* by their gloat factor. The more gloat, the merrier (or the infuriating), depending on whose gloat is being factored.

Game development often gets short shrift, but it is the guts of design. Playtest. A lot. Don't be afraid to get rid of things that don't work. Don't grow attached to anything in the game. Be ruthless. And, painful as it always is, we really do need others to weigh in. Listen to the ones who make a good case for their proposed changes. And never reject any criticism out of hand. If you do reject it out of hand, sleep on it. The flip side of accepting the critics' complaints is to design what you like despite the skeptics. Ultimately I suppose it's a blend.

Since *Cosmic Encounter*, despite its longevity, has never had blockbuster sales, here are four cosmic measuring sticks which you can adopt for your low selling but brilliant game.

Losing Can Be Fun

When you hear that the players who lost start out by saying, "I lost but I didn't care because it was so much fun," it's a reminder that *in multiplayer games most people lose*. So if you can make losing fun......

I Lost My Game In The Divorce

Here we have the ultimate designer compliment. I mean, you know, the house, the car, the dog, the *Cosmic Encounter* set! Footnote: The records of any divorces due to a momentous spouse-to-spouse *Cosmic* Gloat have been sealed for the protection of the *Cosmic* designers.

Surprising The Designers

If, after you are well past the design phase, and you've been playing for a while, you are still surprised by what happens in your very own game, I'd say you have a winner. It means that your design creates situations that are not planned, but rather are generated by the unique circumstances of any given game. While I was writing this I surprised myself by thinking of two new aliens and decided to leave them in here. Just for fun.

The Retelling

This is a measure of a game's appeal. If it gets a lot of this then it's a success. (See "Not Fair" and "The Gloat".)

Final thoughts.

We in the biz like to think of ourselves as professionals. And I suppose we are. But if you are reading this book there is a good chance that you might not quite have professional status just yet. I say good! Focus on creating games that are unique. It's very crowded out there in copycat gamer land. Work hard at defining your own space. For most game designers, once bitten by the design bug, there is no choice about your career. You just have to do it, so you might as well do it well.

THE GREATEST GIFT
by Ray Mazza

Let me introduce myself – I'm Ray Mazza, a recovering traditional game designer. I've been afflicted with a game for more than six years now. This is the story of how I (kind of) published that game, and the words of wisdom I can speak from the experience, with a primary focus on the creative thought process during the earliest stages of design.

The Beginning: A Brief Word on Games

Rewind to the year 1979. I'm only a few months old, lying in a crib, looking up at my mom. She smiles, holding a blanket. And then, just like that, she disappears. *Poof!* Gone. I look around and don't see her. Then, suddenly, she's back. I'm astonished! *Holy crap!* And then she does it again. I can't help but giggle when I see her reappear with her wide green eyes and a jubilant smile. "Tada!" she exclaims.

For me, this is my first game. My mom is playing *Peek-a-Boo* with me by hiding behind a blanket.

On to the year 1986. I'm seven. My mom, dad, sister, and I crowd around a table every Wednesday for family game night, and play *Yahtzee, Uno, Sorry, Careers, Fireball Island, Clue, Scrabble,* and *Rummy,* to name just a few. I also sometimes wake up at 5:00 am so that I can sneak some *Super Mario Brothers* on my Nintendo.

I am now conscious of the fact that games are *really fun.* Although I probably said I wanted to be a dinosaur when I grew up, I think I subconsciously wanted to make games. Kids do it all the time – they play with toys and engage in make believe and fabricate elaborate scenarios and situations and rule sets for what you can and cannot do when you're playing:

this fallen tree trunk over here is the star-destroyer-battleship and that tire in the sandpit over there is the escape pod, and the escape pod is immune to laser fire but not immune to this stick which is the "magical sword of destroying escape pods."

Many of you grew up with similar experiences, as games have been part of our lives since the earliest moments of our comprehension. They're not just a thing we do on occasion for fun – they're ineffably etched into the way we live our lives.

Why Games are Important

For many people, games are the most natural form of social group interaction. If a party doesn't have at least one game, I dock it points. Games give an event context. There's no need to stand around and dig for conversation – a game creates it, and helps you get to know people, or get to know them better – even friends and family.

Games are so social that by the end, you really learn who the other players are on a level that you might not have reached so quickly had you been standing around having conversations like:

Guy: *So where are you from?*

Girl: *Oregon.*

Guy: *That's a beautiful state.*

Girl: *Yeah, the coastline is amazing. I hear you're an English major, huh? What do you think about Chaucer's short poems?*

Guy: *A bit whiny, actually.*

Girl: *Mmhm. Some people say Chaucer first associated Valentine's Day with romance.*

Guy: *Oh yeah? I read that the greeting card industry popularized Valentine's Day.*

This conversation is okay, but you aren't really learning who the other person is. You aren't experiencing something with them, and that's what games do. People lower their barriers and reveal their true personalities when they play games. You find out that Grant giggles like a schoolgirl when someone pantomimes being a banana. You get to experience the terror of Paul when you don't support his proposed trade embargo. Somehow it comes up that Ira can solve a Rubik's Cube in 12 seconds, and that Natalie wants nothing more in the entire world than a pair of roller skates, but for some reason she just doesn't go out and buy a pair.

This is why games are important. Because as adults, we no longer just make them up when we're standing around. We need these games to help us play, socialize, and experience each other.

Let the Games Begin: Brainstorming

One of the first games I designed was an interesting and informative exercise, as simple as it was, so I'll share it. At the time, I was enrolled in a Game Design course taught by Jesse Schell at Carnegie Mellon's Entertainment Technology Center graduate program. Assignment number 1? *Design a new version of Hopscotch.* One should learn to be creative with a small game before attempting something momentous. Whether you're designing a board-game, videogame, or a child's playground game like *Hopscotch*, many of the same principles apply.

Step 1: Quiet brainstorm time. I find it wildly productive to tie myself to a desk chair and list out as many ideas around the game or topic as possible. For the first sitting, this is all I do, and I do it until I wear myself out.

I noted anything and everything that seemed remotely interesting, different, novel, fun, etc. Thanks to computers (wave of the future) I still have the list. From the mundane to the insane, here's a snippet:

- Use eggs as landmines or obstacles on each square. Combine with losing shoes.

- Different height squares

- Throw something that moves instead of a stone

- Hop on the beats of music

- *Hopscotch* Joust

- Build the course as you go. You toss your stone, and where it lands becomes a square.

- Each turn you can move remove a line from a square or add one (to join or split squares).

- Dodgescotch (your opponent may throw one large kickball at you during your turn).

- Put huge, strong fans blowing adjacent to the board. They randomly come on. Wear big flowing clothing and pinwheel hats.

- Add a monkey.

- High stakes *Hopscotch* (on the edge of a bridge or tall building... then it could become a great spectator sport).

- Football *Hopscotch*. You have to play on the fifty yard-line during Monday-night football. Whoever has won the most *Hopscotch* games by the end of the football game wins. Players must pretend they don't see the football game.

- You get to make a rule every time you get two successful points in a row.

- Play on ice.

- Dizzy-*Hopscotch*. Add way for opponents to have an opportunity to spin you before you hop.

- All players play at the same time on a wide board. It's a race.

- Each player has an apple. If you toss your stone and miss your square, take a bite of the apple. If you finish the apple, you get to advance one square. Get a new apple.

- Gambling. Play with quarters instead of a rock. All quarters remain where they lie, i.e. – each toss costs you a quarter. Winner gets to keep the money on the ground/floor.

- When hopping, hop to the far end with an empty glass, stand on one foot and fill it from a punch bowl, and hop back. If the turn is successful, your opponent has to drink whatever is left in the glass.

- Infinite-*Hopscotch*. Draw the *Hopscotch* board in a gigantic loop. Everyone hops around the board at once, spread out, some in the opposite direction. Jumpers have hard hats with a ball Velcroed to the top. Have one or two kids riding bikes around with plastic bats. If they swing and hit the ball off your hat, you're out.

In the end, I had 61 ideas spread across 3 pages of bullet points. That felt about right for *Hopscotch*. Larger games could fill far more pages of ideas.

And yes, some of the ideas are unrealistic. It's important to put everything interesting that comes to mind down on paper, regardless of how insane it may be. Otherwise, you're cutting your imagination off. Ludicrous ideas can lead to some excellent, perfectly reasonable ones.

Recursive Brainstorming and Lists!

Designing a game is a recursive and iterative process. Once I had a list of ideas, I picked the four most promising ones, and developed them by generating lists of rules and mechanics.

From those, I picked the single idea I liked best, called *Burdensome Hopscotch*, which came from the brainstorm idea, *Make it difficult for your opponent to hop by dressing them up in crazy gear*. It appealed to me most because it had the opportunity for players to creatively prepare for the game based on their own personalities, and the gameplay had huge opportunities to be downright hilarious. The varying equipment would also change the physical mechanics from game to game, resulting in a very replayable experience.

Now that I'd chosen *Burdensome Hopscotch*, I went through its potential rules and mechanics and drilled down again and brainstormed around each one of those.

This process may sound obvious, but a common design pitfall is running with the first feasible idea you think up. Don't shortchange yourself at any step of the way.

Burdensome Hopscotch

The gist of *Burdensome Hopscotch* is that before the game, each player rounds up ten items that can be worn or held, and everyone tosses them into a heap. They should be things that would make playing difficult when used. (The items most fun in playtests were: cleats, a backpack of rocks, giant sunglasses, big mittens, snowboarding boots, winter jackets, a staff, and a tennis racket, among other things.)

Each board square has a smaller target inside it. If a player lands their marker on the target, they get to draw a slip of paper from a hat, and put the indicated item on another player. Players must wear the items until the game is over. The game ends when only one person is left. Everyone else is a winner.

The game often breaks down into hilarity as people try to jump around loaded with burdensome gear. Hence the name, *Burdensome Hopscotch*.

Like any new design, shortcomings came to light as we playtested, and I made adjustments on the spot or between rounds:

- The targets were too difficult to hit, so I increased their size.

- When you did hit a target, getting to take your turn and put a burdensome item on another player was too much of an advantage. A more balanced mechanic was to end your turn, but let you put a crazy item on an opponent, which was reward enough.

- Originally, the winner was the first person to finish, but then you missed out on watching some of the most burdened players duke it out (the best part!).

Any worthwhile playtest will lead to some opportunities for re-design. During playtests, watch players for signs of frustration or boredom. If someone says, "This is fun," and you didn't already know that just by watching, then something is off. Your game isn't as fun as it needs to be. Get a dialog going to figure it out. Reflect on your mechanics and/or balance. It can also be extremely helpful to run a test where players vocalize their thought processes as they're playing.

Hopscotch **Graduate**

One of the most important takeaways for me was that much of designing a good game comes from establishing a solid thought process for brainstorming and reflecting on features. What follows is an exploration into my experience designing a card game called *The Greatest Gift*, which delves further into this process.

Defining Goals

A great starting point is to define goals so you don't lose sight of what's important to you. For *The Greatest Gift*, they were:

- Keep everyone as happy as possible at all times.
- Keep everyone as involved as possible at all times.
- The game should be socially meaningful.
- Include humor or opportunities for humor.
- The game should have lasting replay value.
- The game should be very fun.

Let's look at each of these goals individually and why I chose them.

Keep everyone as happy as possible at all times.

Many games have a tendency to punish players. *Go to jail! Lose a turn! Pay each player 3 resources! Lose the game and sit sulking in the corner while you watch everyone else have fun for the next half hour!* Those may be fun mechanics for everyone else, but they are lousy for at least one player. They're often used to insert randomness into the game to even out chances for those less skilled, but that can be accomplished with positive events instead. Rather than lose a turn, try gain a turn. Instead of *pay each player*, try *collect from each player*. The happier everyone is, the less likely they'll never want to play again.

Keep everyone as involved as possible at all times.

I can't tell you how many times I sit down to "play" a game with four or five people, only to spend 80% of the time waiting for my turn. Maybe that's okay for a cerebral game where you need 10 minutes of super-cranial brainpower to compute the optimal next move, but how many of those players will finish the game and say it was an incredible experience? (Hint: often just two – the ones duking it out at the end.) The less downtime players have, the less time they have to think about what else they'd rather be doing. If players are getting up to go to the bathroom or get drinks (and they're not jogging), or if they're futzing with their phone, there's too much down time. (If you want to make a game with downtime, consider making a fully asynchronous game.)

The game should be socially meaningful.

If you can craft a game that affects people's lives through their interactions, then it creates an emotional bond. Here's an example: you're playing *Mafia* (also known as *Werewolf*) and people are dying left and right; it's not until too late that you realize Jen – who's quiet and unassuming in everyday life – is *Mafia*, and she's been telling bold-faced lies and ruthlessly killing the entire time. A great, memorable moment like this forges such a bond, which can be a powerful force in word-of-mouth promotion, and will instill a desire to play again or make a purchase. Some questions to ask yourself about your design:

Will people learn things they didn't know about each other? Will they form connections they didn't have before? Can they learn to work together? Can they experience something memorable while playing?

Include humor or opportunities for humor.

I personally have the most fun in games where I realize I'm laughing a lot. Whether it's from scenarios created in the game, the content, or conversations, the more laughter, the better.

The game should have lasting replay value.

The more replayable a game is, the greater value it has to its players. And because it's being played more often, there are more chances for players to decide they'd like to go and pick up their own copy. On the minimal level, a game will remain fun and interesting over a long period of time (e.g. – *Apples to Apples*). On the higher level, a player's perception of the game and its strategies will actually evolve in such a way that it may even feel like a different game (e.g. – *Chess*).

The game should be very fun.

Well, at least it's easy to declare. If only it were as easy to deliver on. Entire books have been written about what 'fun' is.[29] It isn't a single rule or play style or theme… it's all aspects of a game combined in an elegant way. You can't just sit down, decide to make something fun, and do it. So what is one to do? From playing loads of games and reflecting on fun experiences, you have both a wealth of examples of things that are fun and an arsenal of ideas you want to try. You can break these down, build upon them, use them as inspiration – and with imagination – mold them into something unique that fits together.

Starting with a Mechanic

There are plenty of ways to begin. One approach is to brainstorm game mechanics, hoping to find one that you really like. Some games are built entirely around a single mechanic that works very well, and it's a great approach to developing a game.

Hungry Hungry Hippos – the key mechanic is eat marbles. Simple. Nailed it. Kids love it. *Pictionary* – the key mechanic is *your partner has to guess what you're quickly drawing.* Another simple concept constructed into a wildly successful game. *Trivial Pursuit* – the mechanic: *guess the answers to insignificant questions.* The pies and the board could have been designed a hundred different functional ways, and it would barely matter because the central mechanic of answering trivia questions is such a strong focus. *Magic: The Gathering* – the mechanic: *construct a deck from spells you find, by chance, in booster packs, then face off with other players.* The game has many details, but the overarching mechanic has rendered it one of the most successful games of all time.

The game market is saturated with mechanics, and it's only getting more saturated over time. Games aren't un-inventing themselves. Because of this, many are merely old mechanics mixed in a new way or with a new theme slapped on them. Such games can certainly be fun and successful, but will have a harder time of it. So if you can come up with a mechanic that is both fun and novel, you should *strongly* consider developing it. That is one of the surest ways to create a unique game that has a chance of standing out amongst the crowd. It's one of the holy grails of game design.

Starting with Theme

Another point to start from is to brainstorm themes. *Lost in the desert. The revolutionary war. Space travel. Prom night. Cliff jumping. Baking. Quitting work. Antarctic excavation of lost civilizations. Bedwetting. Espionage and explosives.* Et cetera, et cetera.

Then choose one that appeals enough. Say you picked Antarctic excavation of lost civilizations. Now it's time to go nuts and brainstorm a list of possible mechanics and other game elements. You'll find they come a lot easier in the context of a theme:

- "Chunks" of ice on the board that stack. Chunks start randomly distributed around the board with various depths. Turns might consist of getting to move (dig) a random number of chunks to an adjacent square to find pieces of alien technology underneath. Stacks can be pushed and collapse on players.

- Can fall through thin ice.

- Can we have a frosty board surface and technology items scattered underneath, so lights can be activated by your character to illuminate under the ice a bit?

- Cooperative game? A way players can help each other when spread out? Goal: find the weak spots in the ice shelf and all activate explosives at once to unearth the technology before it destroys Earth?

- Possibly have characters connect circuits that light up areas between them.

- Find breaks in the surface ("dive spots") and can dive under the board. Shortcuts to other dive spots on the board. Maybe the board is raised so your character can actually go under it, and stick to it with magnets.

And so on, for a few pages or more. You'll know you have enough when you're feeling a mixture of satisfaction, excitement, and exhaustion.

Starting with Play Style

A third way to begin (and the last I'll discuss, though there are more) is with appealing play styles and game elements. This was my starting point for *The Greatest Gift*.

I had been inspired by *Apples to Apples* because it keeps everyone engaged at all moments, involves an element of self-expression, and has no punishing mechanics. Based on my goals and this inspiration, I made some structural decisions to start the game off:

- *It will be a card game.* At the time, I had just made a boardgame, and wanted to try something different. The elegance and expandability of card-centric games were alluring.

- *Every player will make a "play" of some sort each turn.* I believe in the power of this so strongly that I will attempt to include it in any tabletop game I ever design. It can practically eliminate downtime.

- *The outcome of a round will be determined by the opinion of the player whose turn it is.* I admired this aspect of *Apples to Apples* because it makes people's personalities an aspect of gameplay, and makes the game vastly diverse with different players.

Now, you may be thinking, *Wait a minute! That's a lot of "inspiration" to take from another game.* True. But that's fine. So many masterpieces in this world are inspired by other great creations. Don't hesitate to build off portions of other designs that work! But when you do, make sure to find what it is that makes your game unique and fun and gives it its own voice. Look for that holy grail.

The Drawing Board: Going Back to It.

I had a few false starts when I moved on to brainstorming mechanics. I'd even gotten on to the point of playtesting a battle-themed version, and it failed miserably. It happens – make sure to recognize it. I returned to the drawing board with my goals and three ground rules, and decided to brainstorm themes to see where that might get me.

Now, I didn't just sit down and start listing things. I gave myself direction with a single question: *I need to come up with a theme… Well, what kinds of things do people like?* This is notable for two reasons.

1. It became the concept of my game, though I didn't know it yet, and

2. it demonstrates a very powerful design technique that I use relentlessly: *asking yourself questions.*

The Power of Asking Questions

Any time you find yourself stuck on a game design problem or needing fresh ideas, start asking yourself related questions. Try and answer them. That may require asking further and deeper, more specific questions that demand their own answers. The more questions you can raise, the more you will end up exploring the problem space and the more likely you'll find something you're happy with.

Doing this will feel like a recursive conversation with yourself. Humans inherently think this way[30], but you can harness its strength by making it an explicit exercise.

Here's an example from a fictional board game where the designer finds the pawns tedious:

- Pawns not working (*Why not?*)
  - Not satisfying to move the pawn around (*How so?*)
    - Too little choice
    - Resulting movement doesn't matter much in the short-term
  - Turns are long because of the pawn movement (*How can I fix it?*)
    - Can we make pawns faster?
    - Possibly remove pawns altogether? (*What could satisfy their purpose instead?*)
      - Need a way to determine a player's allowed play during a turn that has both an element of randomness and choice. (*What are the possibilities?*)
        - Use a die roll plus the castle types player has to determine allowed plays (*rather than the space the pawn lands on*).
        - Or players build up a set of cards as a personal toolkit of possible plays, and draw one from here each turn?

Quite often my thinking, brainstorming, and questioning all ends up in tiered, bulleted-list form. This is exactly what I did when brainstorming themes for *The Greatest Gift*: *What sort of theme do I want? Well, what kinds of things do people like? Let's see… Wealth. Fame. Romance. Being smart or skilled. Superpowers.*

My list of potential themes looked something like this:
- Wealth
  - Diamonds
  - Pirate's Booty
  - Winning the lotto
  - Owning an Island
  - No debt
  - (etc…)
- Fame
  - Rock Star
  - Famous Athlete
  - Part of the Mob
  - On TV
  - (etc…)
- Romance
- Smarts/Skills
- Superpowers
- (etc…)

Once I had a large list, I looked it over trying to decide if any of the themes would lend themselves to a game with fun mechanics and ample humor. Then, I had an epiphany that I attribute to the exercise of listing out ideas exhaustively – *All these themes are fun… why don't I make a game about all of them?* And thus, *The Greatest Gift* was born. Each potential theme became a card in the game.

The Greatest Gift

I went through eight iterations of various rule sets and mechanics. Here's the basic idea for the final version:
- There are hundreds of cards, each with a unique skill, item, or other desirable thing pictured and described on it.
- Each player gets a hand of 7 cards which they refill each round.
- Each round, it's one player's turn to receive gifts. The other players pick something from their hands they think this person would like most *in real life*, and put it face-down in a pile.
- The gift receiver flips over these gifts and decides which one he or she likes best, and keeps it in a personal collection of loot on the table (these are points).
- The player that gave the best gift gets rewarded from a central collection of stuff for their own loot collection, thus also scoring a point for a gift-well-given.

Based on mechanics, playtests, and feedback, let's look at how it stacked up against my original goals.

Keep everyone as happy as possible at all times.

The game has no punishing mechanics and the theme is about kindness, life aspirations, and getting wonderful things. In practice, players never appear upset or frustrated.

Keep everyone as involved as possible at all times.

This goal is satisfied by the play style of having everyone make a move and provide input on every turn, and turns being quick.

Try to make the game socially meaningful.

As predicted, basing the outcome of each turn on a player's opinion means you learn about that player. As players choose gifts, you're learning what they want and value in life, and you're also finding out what other players *think* you want and value in life – times when these don't align are often the most exciting. (One of the most memorable turns for me was when a girl named Natalie was playing, and narrowed her gift choice down to *Own your own Island* and a pair of *Roller Skates*. Natalie chose roller skates, and meant it; an impassioned explosion of conversation ensued.)

In an effort to cater to this goal, I developed cards that would create morally difficult choices when compared to cards grounded in materialism. These include *Cure Cancer, End World Hunger*, and *Save a Life*. One card, *Avoid Apocalypse*, describes a scenario where the world will be obliterated in 263 years – long after you're dead – but you have the power to stop it. So do you choose that, or one of the other gifts that someone has offered you, like being *Fluent in All Languages*? For some players, these are difficult decisions, and everyone can go home with new insight into the personalities of their friends and family.

Include humor or opportunities for humor.

I included a small number of cards that catered to both silly and sarcastic players (too much and the game starts losing social significance because it can't be taken seriously) and I took care to make the text entertaining when possible. For example, gifts like Tofu or A Girlfriend let players rag on each other, while some class-clown types are drawn to presents like Really Big Hands because they can rationalize what would be awesome about having hands the size of large frying pans.

The game should have lasting replay value.

I believe this is the game's weakness. *The Greatest Gift* does well in that it feels fresh each time you play it with a new grouping of people, and that each combination of gifts feels different than the last. But once everybody knows the cards, the game loses some of its novelty. If I were convinced the game needed it, a fix would be to add a mechanic that randomly changes a player's mind set each game. For example, this could be accomplished by having each player draw a "personality card" which would affect their decisions. Bob could draw *Evil CEO of a Mega Corporation*, and for that game, Bob would choose his gifts as if he imagined himself to have turned into that character – which is interesting because different players would take on those characters uniquely. Another way to increase shelf-life is to release expansions, which is appealing because the game is so easily extendable.

The game should be very fun.

I'll let anyone who plays make up their own mind about this!

Promise Cards

One interested publisher tried the game, and sent it back with a note saying, *We like it, though it needs something else, but we're not sure what.*

Deep down, I agreed. I realized I wanted *The Greatest Gift* to be more surprising, and for it to more strongly affect people's lives. That's asking a lot, but I began to think about games I consider very memorable and surprising.

Two that came to mind were *Truth or Dare* and *Spin the Bottle*. What fascinating games! Merely by making something a "rule" of the game, human beings will take actions that are normally far outside their realm of comfort. *Now I have to kiss Evelyn? Okay, if that's the rule… Or, What? You're daring me to eat this crate of jalapeños and then call my boss and quit? Well… okay, but only because it's my turn. I wouldn't normally do this!*

These games contain powerful moments that people remember their whole lives. That's the essence I wanted to design into *The Greatest Gift*. So I asked the drastic question, *How could I make players kiss? And how can I do it such that it fits with the game rather than overpowering it?*

It felt natural as a gift, like any other card. *A Kiss* – except this gift was different because if you offered it to someone and they chose it, they got a real kiss from you rather than an imaginary thing. And it was surprising, because the person choosing amongst the gifts could only speculate who had offered it! It was a totally new type of gift, dubbed a *Promise Card*. This felt like the missing element, so I added more: *A Hug, A Dollar, A Free Meal, A Massage, A Date, Servant for a Day, Snacks,* and so on.

In testing, promise cards proved to be a success and created some potent moments. They were a hit even when they weren't picked above other offerings. Merely their presence in the set of gifts upped the stakes and caused more chatter and excitement than usual.

Know Your Audience

Some playtesters wanted more strategy, and I tried a few versions with additional cards that would change rules, augment a player's abilities, or thwart others (counter to one of my goals, it's worth noting; a moment of weakness on my part). In all cases, the changes only made gameplay more choppy, complicated the rules, and diluted the essence of *The Greatest Gift*.

It took me a while to realize a game doesn't have to satisfy everyone, it just has to be an amazing game to the audience you're targeting. *Know your audience.* I couldn't please the entire *Settlers of Catan* contingent because they look for distinctly different characteristics from the games they play.

Once I was able to step back and realize this, I became as satisfied with *The Greatest Gift* as I expected I could get. The audience I was after was the casual mass market audience of families, friends, and party gamers looking for a short and social experience; as long as they enjoyed the game, then it was what it needed to be, and the rest would be icing. (Though the best designers are never truly satisfied; it's what pushes them to constantly evolve new and better concepts.)

The World of Publication

Now, it's one thing to design a game you're satisfied with, and it's an entirely different world to try to publish it. There are different approaches, and the first question you have to ask yourself is, *Do I want to self-publish, or try to license to a publisher?* One informing factor should be how much time you are willing to spend working for your game. Self-publication can become a full-time job. It also has higher monetary risks, but higher rewards, too.

For deep insight into how publishing works and deciding which path to take, I highly recommend reading *The Game Inventor's Guidebook*,[31] written by a selection of industry leaders. It proved vastly informative for me, and helped me decide that I didn't have the time nor the money to self-publish.

Publishing and My Next Six Years

I can quickly sum up the six years following my decision to find a publisher. I found an agent that wanted to represent me, and had plenty of industry contacts. My agent found an interested publisher and we sent off a prototype for the publisher to work from. What a wonderful feeling! Then, *years* of waiting – with large publishers, you cannot count on anything. Sometimes they are black holes where games go to die. Other times, the publisher can have a game out in multiple continents within the year and promote it like it's the best thing to happen to gaming since dice.

My publisher tweaked gameplay, added hundreds more cards, and named it *The Perfect Present* (I've been referring to it in this piece as *The Greatest Gift*... if you read on, you'll see why). In 2007 it finally showed up on the Amazon and Barnes and Noble websites, though I was waiting for the day when I could stroll down an aisle and see it on store shelves. More waiting and delays. Then scads of toys manufactured in China went through recalls, and the publisher developed major financial issues and needed to make cutbacks. Somewhere in there, I was told, they shut down their games division.

This is why I say I "kind of" published it. There are ten thousand copies floating around out there, but there aren't likely to be more until the game finds a new publisher.

Today

This leaves me back where I sat before finding my agent and publisher. I can't use any of the changes the publisher made to the game after receiving it because I don't have the intellectual rights. Luckily, I was only attached to the name they came up with – *The Perfect Present* – and not much else. I've already renamed it to *The Greatest Gift*.

On the brighter side, I'm a free agent now. I have not begun to send *The Greatest Gift* around to publishers again, but when I do, the process will be easier with the advent of print-on-demand gaming resources. One such website is called *The Game Crafter* (thegamecrafter. com). It makes prototyping easy by providing plenty of options for game pieces, and I've found the cost in printing to be less expensive than going to a printing service. There are currently tradeoffs in print quality, but I'm pleased with the ease and convenience. (*The Greatest Gift* is available there if you want to check it out.)

Some Advice about Agents and Publishers

It was wildly exciting to go through the process of finding an agent and licensing *The Greatest Gift* to a publisher. It felt like a honeymoon phase. In retrospect, I can say in actuality I made some poor decisions with respect to both parties, partly due to my naiveté and general lack of communication.

I'd like to share some lessons with you so hopefully you won't get tripped up in the same way I did.

Namely, if you do find an agent, make sure you know how much they are willing to support you and what level of input and communication you'll have with potential publishers. See if you can be included in the development process to give feedback a couple times along the way, since you, the designer, will have valuable insight. Where my relationship broke down with my agent was that they only served to insulate the publisher from me, when they should have been supporting me and the game. I should have raised this as something that was important to me when settling on terms for representation.

Later, when I finally had the published version of the game in hand, I noticed problems that could have been avoided had there been any communication allowed. Here were the worst offenders:

- The text was too small. Older players would not be able to read it. (You must always consider readability! Use legible fonts and sizes.)

- The category name was too prominent at the top of the card, which some players thought was the name of the gift (the real gift name ran along the left side of the card). This was a problem that I'd *found in playtests and fixed before sending to the publisher.* The best arrangement had the name of the gift both along the left side and at the top of the card, with the category occupying a smaller space in the corner relative to its lesser significance.

- The *Promise* card category had disappeared, and those gifts were mixed into another category such that their function was obscured and lost.

So make sure you know what your Agent-Publisher-Designer relationship will be before signing any contracts. And you don't necessarily need an agent. Many smaller publishers have instructions on their websites for submitting games directly.

In the case where you do get a publisher but they aren't willing to work with you directly, the hardest thing about getting your game published is letting go of control. You'd expect it would be one of the happiest days of your life when you receive a freshly-boxed copy of your very own game. Opening the packaging and looking at the pieces and setting it up should be a momentous occasion. Hopefully it will be! But it's no guarantee. For me, it was the opposite. It's extremely difficult to see what someone has done to your idea. A creative director once told me: "One of the hardest things about becoming a creative director is having to watch people less talented than you implement designs that you could do better." Sometimes you just have to let go.

Now What? Tips!

Okay, you've heard my story. Now, I have a few final tips to pass on before I release you back into the wild of game design.

Keep a Game Journal

This is relevant no matter your choice of creative medium: experience as much diversity in it as possible, and keep a journal with your salient thoughts about those experiences. For games, this translates to: play as many different games as possible, and write your thoughts on them!

I make sure I have my journal with me when I play a new game, because I know I won't remember half my revelations and feelings afterwards. I have to jot notes as I'm playing.

I write anywhere from 2-15 bullet points per game (total), even if I play often. The sorts of things to write down are...

- Moments that surprised you, and why.

- Mechanics that work well. Maybe you can build on them.

- Ideas for ways to improve an aspect of the game. Any time you don't like something, don't just complain about it, ask yourself how you'd improve it! If you ever make a similar game, wouldn't it be great to already have notes on how to do better?

- Amazing game moments. Did something make everyone laugh? Argue light-heartedly? Gasp in surprise? Write it down. These are moments to strive for in your own games, and dissecting them can help you understand how to potentially work them into your designs.

Here are some examples:

- *Cosmic Encounter* – The alien power card you choose at the start of the game gives you unique powers and makes it different each time you play. Wonderful mechanic; always feel like you have something special nobody else does.

- *Magic, The Gathering* – Buying and opening a pack is like gambling. (*Will I get good cards? Will I get that rare I need? If I buy enough I'm sure to get it…*) No wonder this game is so addictive.

- *Magic, The Gathering* – The number of possibilities when creating combos with cards is staggering. And almost all cards feel useful in certain occasions and against specific decks. I could sit here and build a deck forever.

- *Shadows over Camelot* – Still can't decide whether the grail quest is worthwhile without Arthur, since it's difficult to get enough grail cards in there in time and it wastes turns to go and come back. (Later I made a firm conclusion, but it's a sign of good game balance that I wasn't sure if our time was better spent on this quest or others. It prodded us to try various strategies.)

Why keep a journal? Two reasons. First, you'll find that you're thinking more critically about the game as you play it, and you'll make observations your conscious mind may otherwise miss. It will help you think more insightfully about your own games as well.

Second, it's brain fuel. When you need a boost in creativity, flip to a random page in your journal and start reading. Since you're poring over all the most interesting moments and salient aspects from all the games you've played, it jumpstarts your brain to thinking about what truly makes a game good or bad, and the variety of your notes will help energize your creativity.

A Resource – Stock Photography

Now, a tip about a great prototyping resource. When I designed *The Greatest Gift*, it had roughly 200 cards, each different. I love art, and I knew that if each card had unique imagery, it would not only make them more interesting to look at, but would often enhance the meaning of the card. Images can be suggestive, they can be humorous, and they can also set a mood for your game.

There was no way I could afford to pay an artist to produce the needed imagery – that would cost tens of thousands of dollars. The solution lied in stock photography. I used a website (istockphoto.com) that had a huge database of photography (and some art) and only cost a couple dollars per download.

Ask Drastic Questions

Here's a tip for when you're thinking about your game on a high level or realize there's a problem around a central aspect of your game: Sometimes it helps to not only ask yourself questions around your design, but also to ask *drastic questions* – questions that address the very nature of your design and could cause you to rethink it, even in its entirety.

For example: *Would a different kind of die better suit my game? Do I need a game board? What would happen if the players didn't have pawns?* Often, the answers to these questions are what you'd expect – *of course my players need pawns!* But, on occasion, they lead to an epiphany.

Here's a list of questions to ask yourself about your game designs. There are a multitude for you to come up with on your own, but this should get you started:

- What would happen if I removed mechanic x from the game? Was it necessary? What would I replace it with?

- How can I make people laugh? Cry? Get excited? Be eager for their turn?

- How can I make players think about the game a day or a week after playing?

- Is there anything in my design that has never been seen in a game before? How would I add that?

- What if this were cooperative and not competitive?

- What aspect of this game will make someone excited to buy it when they're reading the back of the box? (What's the hook?)

- How can I get players to learn about each other?

- How will this game be fun while playing the 100th time?

- What if gameplay had to be half as long as it is now? What would that look like?

- What if there couldn't be any dice? Pawns? Board? Cards?

If you want a ton of great questions to ask about your game to get your creativity flowing, check out Jesse Schell's *The Art of Game Design: A Deck of Lenses*[32] – a deck of cards full of such questions.

What's Next? You.

Now it's time for you. There's a reason you're reading this book: you have a deep desire to do great things in the world of gaming. You can, and you will. All you need to do is get out there and make a game, or finish up and polish the one you're working on. Coalesce those ideas that have been swimming around in your head. Whether you make it for yourself, your family, your friends, or for the world, a game is more than just a piece of entertainment. Games may only appear to be a few plastic pieces and a board, but they're much more than that. With your ingenuity, those items can become an elegant unification of mechanics and theme that can help us learn about each other and really spend our time together in a meaningful way.

Define evocative goals, then stick to them, and let them guide you. Find a starting point that works for you – from theme, mechanic, play style, or another angle. Brainstorm the hell out of all aspects of your design. Ask yourself questions to explore your work, and build on your observations from other great games. Make sure your game finds its own unique voice. And establish a thorough thought process and use it each step of the way. If you do these things, great designs will be within your reach.

So go out there, and make this world a more fun, interesting, and connected place. Help us get to know ourselves, our families, and each other.

It's important.

29 Raph Koster, *A Theory of Fun for Game Design* (Paraglyph Press)

30 John Allen Paulos, "Human Consciousness, Its Fractal Nature," in Beyond Numeracy (New York: Vintage Books, 1992) p. 107

31 Brian Tinsman, *The Game Inventor's Guidebook* (KP Books)

32 Jesse Schell, *The Art of Game Design: A Deck of Lenses* (Schell Games)

I LOVE *PANDEMIC* (AND I DESPAIR FOR SERIOUS GAMES)
by John Sharp

I.

I really like Matt Leacock's *Pandemic*, a boardgame in which players work together to protect humanity from four world-devouring viruses. The game ranks up there with *Settlers of Catan* as a sure-fire "gateway drug" to German-style boardgames; it is thoughtfully designed, deeply polished, and has just the right amount of story world. Most everything about the game suits my idea of 'fun': strategic thinking, a healthy dose of variability from play session to play session, emergent complexity, cooperative play and thoughtful communication design.

Rather than rambling on about how much I like the game, I would like to use it as a lens for thinking about serious games.[33] There is an increasing gold rush to serious games — the Apps for Healthy Kids initiative, an ever-growing number of conferences and festivals, the incredible amounts of foundation and grant money supporting their creation and study, and on and on. We are looking to games to solve societal problems, to free people from ignorance, to proverbially solve world hunger. But more often, we are doing a disservice to ourselves, to the causes we embrace and to games alike. We need to stop and reflect on whether or not games are really the best solution to the issues we fight for, and if they are, we need to do the real work to make the right games.

During his first *Pandemic* play session, Eric Zimmerman said something along the lines of "*Pandemic* is my new favorite serious game." His comment made a great deal of sense to me— the game embodies many of the best qualities of serious games. It gives an abstracted overview of the process by which the Centers for Disease Control and Prevention address epidemics. It encourages important collaboration and active listening skills. It provides a meaningful context for thinking about probability. The space of possibility of the game requires the development of strategies, learning the lessons of focusing on short-term issues at risk of allowing long-term problems to fester. These are all qualities that most any serious game designer would love to embed in their creations. Sadly, few manage to get anywhere close to this level of success.

I would like to use *Pandemic* as a vehicle for considering the four flawed assumptions made about serious games that alternately irk and depress me— first, that games are a form of media; second, that games can deliver messages; third, that games are simulations; and fourth, that videogames are the most suitable form of games for serious games to take.

II.

Pandemic is a boardgame in which two to four[34] players cooperatively work to eradicate a group of four viruses spreading around the world before any one virus hits a tipping point or before there are eight virus outbreaks. The map comprises cities connected by travel routes overlaid with a ball and stick graph around which the players travel. Players move though four zones, each with their own color-coded virus — the blue of North America and Europe; the yellow of Central America and South America; the black of India, the Middle East, Eastern Europe and Russia; and the red of Asia.

Player cards and Infection cards are the two card types in the game. Player cards are composed of three distinct card types— City cards that are used to cure the four viruses and facilitate movement on the board; Epidemic cards that cause the infection engine of the game to speed up; and Special Event cards that grant players one-time actions that facilitate their quest to cure the four diseases.

The Infection cards function as the "engine" that spreads disease around the board. The Infection cards begin their work before the game even starts; the cities represented by the first three cards atop the shuffled Infection deck are assigned three virus cubes each, the cities on the next three cards are assigned two virus cubes each, and the next three are assigned one virus cube each. The nine used Infection cards are then placed in the Infection discard pile where they await the first epidemic.

The game begins with all player tokens on Atlanta, the home of the CDC. On their turn, each player can do four actions selected from a list of eight— move from their current city to an adjacent city; clear a virus unit from the city they occupy; expend a Player card to take a direct flight to the city represented on that card; build a Research Station on a location they occupy and for which they hold the corresponding Player card; move from one Research Station to another; cure a virus by playing five city cards of that virus' color while in a city of that color; and finally, give a Player card to another player when both players are on the same city and the active player holds that city's Player card.

Each player takes on a randomly selected role from a set of five— Dispatcher, Medic, Operations Expert, Researcher and Scientist. Each role provides a unique "special skill" for dealing with the containment and eradication of the viruses. For example, the Medic role can clear all virus units on a city at the cost of one action, and the Researcher can cure a virus with only four city cards (all other players must have five) of the corresponding color. In order to have a chance at winning, the players must cooperatively apply the unique strengths of their roles in order to maximize their ability to successfully eradicate all four viruses.

Once a player has completed her four actions for a turn, she does two things: draws two Player cards from the top of the Player card deck to add to her hand (and immediately discards as many cards as it takes to get down to a hand of seven), and then draws two, three or four Infection cards[35] from the Infection deck to indicate which cities get an additional virus cube.

Any given city can hold no more than three virus units of any type. If, through the draw of an Epidemic card or through actions triggered by the Infection Cards, a city is assigned more than three virus units of one type, an Outbreak occurs. All adjacent cities gain an additional unit of that virus type. If any of these already have three of that virus unit color, then they too have an Outbreak.

Drawing from the Player deck is always fraught with anxiety, as interlaced with the City and Special Event cards are Epidemic cards. The Epidemic cards cause viruses to spread on the player's current location, and tightens the loop on the occurrence of new virus cubes popping up on the already-infected cities by virtue of the shuffling of the already-played Infection cards in the discard pile.

The game is won when the players can cure all four viruses. The game ends when eight of these outbreaks have occurred. The game is lost when the entire deck of Player cards is used, when all of one color of virus cube are placed on the board, or when eight Outbreaks have occurred.

III.

Since the industrial revolution and the commodity culture it brought to bear, games have increasingly been treated as media products like books, movies and songs. The business models and patterns of consumption relating to books, magazines, movies and music are all based on a short cycle of release, consume and move on. It is into this model of consumer culture that videogames have positioned themselves, and in the process became a form of ephemera– quickly consumed with little or no expectation of lasting effect. But games are ever-changing, culturally-shaped practices that have more in common with square dancing, and, as Frank Lantz has pointed out, butterfly collecting[36] than they do with passively-consumed entertainment products. And so the more we try to treat games like media, the less game-like they are.

This is a real issue for serious games — if we approach them like leisure products with the associated 'empty calorie' expectations, we are destined to fail. For the systemic exploration of a phenomenon to really sink in, we need our players to spend more time with our games. Most serious games are positioned in such an overtly didactic manner derived from linear media without a real consideration of the necessary design considerations of games as practices. This leads to the treatment of serious games as pamphlets or documentary films that serve up a productized point of view.

Yes, *Pandemic* is a product— a shrink-wrapped German-style boardgame— no getting around that. But like most German-style boardgames, it is designed as a serially revisited play space primed for replay. Purchasing *Pandemic* is more like buying a social practice than buying a sugary snack or taking a bitter pill that is eaten and quickly forgotten. *Pandemic* is the kind of game that provides a space for spending time with people, and a structure for players to get to know one another. The very rules of the game require players to engage with one another socially and intellectually in order to come up with the best possible approach to contain the four viruses before they destroy the world. Players learn from one another, give one another advice and work as a team to contain the viruses on the board, collect the cards necessary to cure the viruses and generally make the most of their roles and turns.[37]

A rhythm quickly emerges as players struggle against the four viruses, in large part due to the cooperative nature of the game. The player roles provide just enough distinction to give everyone a feeling of importance. At the same time, everyone is swept up in the cause — working together, suggesting strategies for using one another's capabilities, collectively thinking through each player's options, sometimes even planning a round or more ahead for all players.[38]

Pandemic is a game, through and through. It is not another consumer media product— it is a game that encourages repeated play sessions that are all very similar and yet made distinct by the ways play unfold around and through the mechanics and rules. For me, this is what a game is— a space to return to again and again to test myself, to engage with others, to have opportunity to do things that daily life does not permit. The average serious game lacks this depth, in large part due to the emphasis on content, and the product-oriented conception of games as medium and not a practice.

IV.

In his critique of *Bioshock*, Clint Hocking stated, "*Bioshock* seems to suffer from a powerful dissonance between what it is about as a game, and what it is about as a story."[39] He coined the phrase ludonarrative dissonance to describe this— what happens when the narrative mapped onto a game does not work in concert with the game's mechanics and goals. Hocking goes on to discuss the two 'contracts' a game makes with its player: the ludic contract, and the narrative contract. At first glance, these seem compatible with one another — game-wise, *Bioshock* is a first person shooter in which you are given the opportunity to engage with a Randian Objectivist exploration of the limits of self-interest threaded through with a narrative that explores a dystopian vision of a Randian Objectivist world gone rancid. The player's role in the gameworld as enacted through the mechanics and goals, however, contradicts the Objectivist agenda of the narrative— the player is asked to help out Atlas, a character who rails against the Randian vision. This creates a dissonant, confusing play experience, as players looking for the optimal way to 'beat' the game will bump into the tension between the games mechanics, goals, theme and narrative.

Pandemic does a good job of pairing the relationship between the gameplay (using an action economy centered on movement, virus removal and card collection in order to cure the four viruses while working against the game's Infection engine) and the theme of the game (a team of CDC professionals combat four simultaneous pandemics). The Infection engine drives the experience, with players carefully watching the spread of virus cubes via the Infection deck, players cringing with each draw of an Epidemic card, and the players' strategizing to contain and eradicate the four diseases.

Within the flow of the game, a narrative unfolds, but not one that follows any strict predetermined, nuanced arc. Still, the bewildering array of possible play experiences all lead to one of two possible conclusions to the story arc — either the viruses overtake the world, or the players successfully cure the four viruses. Getting from the starting point with nine infected cities to one of these outcomes happens in very different ways from play session to play session. It is in this space of possibility that a rich player-driven experience unfolds.

Serious games have their own version of ludonarrative dissonance — what I will call ludopedagogical dissonance. There is often a disconnect between the theme of a serious game and the actual play experience and the assumed knowledge and experience it transfers to the player. Perhaps through a lack of understanding of games and their strengths, many people create games that attempt to use the form as yet another medium through which a point of view is disseminated. Games are not a secret language through which we can communicate with youth to make them understand the important things we have to tell them. Nor are they the newest multimedia spin on the old chocolate-coated cod liver oil trick that makes something 'good for you' seem 'fun for you.' The fact is games are not going to be good at explaining a single position or a set of facts in the same way a documentary film or a pamphlet or a poster might.

Paraphrasing James Paul Gee, games are excellent tools for preparing for future learning. I interpret this to mean that games can and do educate, but not in the ways traditional media do. And so a game intended to teach about the environmental impact of plastic wrap may really provide players with improved hand-eye coordination and spatial awareness. Or a game about immigration may really make players better at answering multiple choice questions and optimizing their test-taking skills.

Consider *Pandemic* in this light. The game avoids ludopedagogical dissonance because it was designed to be a game rather than as a ludic pamphlet or a play-powered film strip. The premise of the game is containing and curing four virulent diseases by taking on the roles of five CDC employees. One might say the subject of the game is the methods by which the CDC controls and prevents disease, or the incredible complexities of containing disease.

Leacock does not seem to view the game as a tool for teaching players how to eradicate the next plague. Though the game does impart a logically consistent high-level abstraction of the CDC's methods, that is not really the point. If you listen to Leacock discuss the game, he focuses not on the narrative conceit, but on the design of the mechanics, the balance of the roles and the tuning of the difficulty in achieving the win condition. These are all things relating to the play experience. Leacock seems to view the pandemic containment premise as the scaffolding players use to grasp the game's goal and the mechanics enacted in its pursuit and as a tool for expressing the internal logic of the game system. The game still provides many insights and strengthens player skills — collective problem solving, probability analysis, decision-making within a tight choice space, and of course a high-level understanding of the way the CDC approaches pandemics.

Pandemic supports the idea that games have a premise and not a subject. This may seem like a subtle distinction, but it is an important point. A premise is something akin to the set up of an improvisational theater piece, and not a strict plot to be followed from beat to beat. In the course of following *Pandemic*'s premise, the players are, on the surface, wrestling with the containment and cure of a set of diseases. But they are really doing something else altogether. The players are exploring and working to navigate a ball and stick diagram overlaying a map and two sets of randomized cards with their only tools to fight back being an economy of eight shared actions and a set of unique, per-role actions.

V.

A friend of mine, the stop-motion animator M.T. Maloney, speaks of stop-motion animation being to film what poetry is to prose. Games are more like stop-motion animation or poetry than film. To strive for high-fidelity themes, to perfectly model a phenomenon, denies the potential of games, and in particular their expressive power; games need the freedom to take liberties, to bend and break the known models of the world. This is necessary to create a space of possibility within which play can unfold.

If you look under the hood, games are systems populated by objects with certain attributes that interact within a specified environment. While this might sound like the recipe for simulations, it is more than that in the case of games. With serious games, we can certainly attempt to accurately model our world and its phenomenon so that our audiences can grok them. But unless you have lots of time, money and expertise, games are not good at providing high fidelity models of phenomena. And even then, the role of the player pushes back on pure simulation. How can the player accurately model their role in the simulation without losing most of their agency and freedom?

In the case of *Pandemic*, there is a nominal amount of understanding developed around the fighting of pandemics by the CDC. The roles assumed by players roughly model the kinds of people working on containing and eradicating disease; the general process by which they go about the task— responding to the local spread of disease, tamping down hotspots, responding to unforeseen epidemics, developing strategies for containing and ultimately curing disease— is represented in a highly abstracted form. The genius mechanic for shuffling the played Infection cards and putting them at the top of the Infector draw pile every time an Epidemic card is played seems to approximate the likelihood of an already-infected region having additional outbreaks. But beyond this surface level detail embedded in the thematic skin of the game, there isn't really that much in *Pandemic* to accurately model the process by which the CDC addresses virulent disease. If the CDC were ever to use the game as a training tool, I imagine Leacock would be horrified.

VI.

A big part of the problem with serious games is the assumption that videogames are the best approach. The reasons for this are complicated and are difficult to fully unwind, but there are a few core reasons: many of the funders of this sort of work are particularly interested in computing as a platform for enacting change; many of the people involved in making the games are involved in the videogame industry and videogame education; the target audience of most serious games is K-12 and college students, who are believed to live in a digital world. But objectively, none of these should obligate the creation of serious videogames. As much as computation can and has done to augment human intellect, the solution to every problem is not a serious videogame. Non-digital games are still a viable, sometimes more appropriate solution.

In the case of *Pandemic*, the game and the play experience it affords as a boardgame would suffer greatly from transposition to a videogame. The procedural characteristics of videogames would mask and obscure the most tangible and important contact points with the game's systems. The interaction with the Infection and City cards as physical objects give a much more palpable engagement with the probabilities of epidemic outbreaks and the placement of virus cubes and the movement of player pawns create a direct connection to the gameworld. All of this would be stripped away and automated in a digital form. Sometimes we do not need or benefit from the advantages computation affords. Sometimes computation subtracts or reduces rather than augments. *Pandemic* is such a case.

VII.

Serious games can learn a good deal from Leacock's game and other German-style board games: that games are practices, not products or media; that games are not a didactic form; that games are more than simulations; and that games are often better off in non-digital form. The bigger point is that Leacock approached the design project as a game. He wasn't seeking to convince anyone of how or why the CDC should do their job. He was designing a board game that happens to lead to a number of different learning outcomes. If only serious games were approached the same way more often.

[33] The term 'serious games' is increasingly viewed with suspicion with not completely satisfying alternatives including newsgames and applied games. For the purposes of this essay, I will stick with serious games.

[34] Up to six if you add the expansion. *Pandemic: On the Brink*. I focus on the basic game in this essay.

[35] The number depends on how many epidemics have occurred so far in the game.

[36] Frank Lantz, "Doorknobs and Butterflies: Games After Art." Art History of Games symposium, February 5, 2010. The High Museum of Art, Atlanta, Georgia.

[37] Most games I have played that end in a loss are immediately followed by another attempt to defeat the four viruses. It is hard to walk away from *Pandemic* without winning.

[38] One criticism leveled against the game is that it can become a single player game even when four people are participating. It is true that a particularly strong-willed and vocal player can dominate the strategizing and decision making.

[39] Clint Hocking. Ludonarrative Dissonance in *Bioshock*." *Clicknothing* blog. October 7, 2007. http://clicknothing. typepad.com/click_nothing/2007/10/ludonarrative-d.html. (Accessed June 12, 2010). Tom Bissell has a good discussion in the chapter, "Far Cries," in his book Extra Lives.

DESIGN LESSONS FROM POKER
by Richard Garfield

Historically games were less designed than evolved. Not many of these games are credited with a designer, and for those games that are, the contribution of the "designer" is usually a small variation of an existing game. It is often worth going back to these traditional games and looking at their characteristics, what made them work in their time and culture, or for those that have survived to the current day, what makes them work across the times and cultures in which they were popular. *Poker* is an interesting case from which I have learned a lot.

Poker has Luck and Skill

One of *Poker*'s distinctions is how much luck it has. Anyone can win a hand of *Poker*. Yet there is a lot of skill to the game. This betrays one of the popular myths in game design – that skill and luck are opposites. They are better considered as two axes.

As a game designer it is important to consider how much chance you want in your game. I believe game designers in general have a bias toward reducing chance in a game, perhaps because they tend to be excellent game players and the games with less luck tend to showcase their talent.

One of the most important things about a game with a little more luck is that a larger breadth of players can play it. This is not as important for

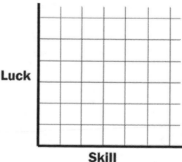

computer games, where you can draw on the player base of the world to find an opponent, but for analog games – you are often stuck with the folk who are currently in your living room. Those people will not always be happy sitting down to a *Chess* tournament, or a *Starcraft* game. They are much more likely to play a game like *Poker*, with a little more luck, a game where a player can always come back from behind.

Poker is Quick

An excellent characteristic for a game with a lot of luck is a short playtime. No one wants to invest hours in a game and then have it lost on a coin toss. With *Poker* each hand only lasts a few minutes – so having a lot of skill will – probabilistically – show itself within a fairly short time, even if not in every hand.

An additional feature of a game with a short length like *Poker* is that it can fit into any schedule – you can play *Poker* for a few minutes, or hours on end. You can link the hands into a tournament, or have people flow in and out of the game, or even do what some pals of mine at Adobe do – keeping track of the game over the course of years.

Poker has a Simple and Flexible Framework

It is easy to learn *Poker*, but when you learn it you have learned much more than a single game. You have learned an operating system for a family of games. Going from *5 Card Draw* to *7 Card Stud* to *Texas Hold'em* to *Omaha* to *Dyslexic Blind Anaconda* is easy once you know the rank of the hands and the general play pattern. A couple of ways this idea can be applied to game design are *Magic: The Gathering* or *Dominion*, where the rules are modified only by the components, or the *Mystery Rummy* Series by Mike Fitzgerald, where the rules change from game to game – but the general structure is the same. This idea can also be used simply by leveraging the rules for different games the players already know – for example, role playing games often use elements like levels and experience, saving their innovation for different parts of the game. Every unusual rule in a game has a cost to the new player, and a designer should make sure that the cost is worth the benefit.

Poker is Customizable

Poker is extremely customizable. There are many different types of *Poker* and many different styles of game. *Dealer's Choice Poker* even takes this to the extreme, with the dealer choosing the game to be played when they deal. The concept of players really taking ownership of their play experience in this way is unusual, it is much more common for players to look to the game rules or the game publisher for "the right" way to play. As a designer, one can explore different ways to play one's game and present some of these to the players, with an invitation for them to customize the play for the tastes of their playgroup.

Poker has Hidden Information

When one player knows something that another player doesn't a world of game opportunity opens up. This opens the door to game theory – where there is bluffing and misdirection, and the play of the game can leap from the dry statistics of the rules into things like reading the opponents and smelling fear. At its best it allows a heady mix of intuition and reason that is hard to match. Hidden information is not appropriate for all games, but I never design any game without considering it long and hard.

Like luck in games, hidden information can increase the breadth of players that will play it. Whenever I learn a new game with no hidden (or inconsequential) information I know there are some players in my playgroup that will make that game a misery to play. They are not doing it to be abusive – but they can't help themselves when the optimum line of play is there to be calculated. Even the luck of dice may not reduce their calculation – because they can always seek the probabilistically best move. But if there is meaningful hidden information they can't overcalculate because they know that other people might be misleading them. And they also can make more arbitrary moves because they know that this may mislead the opponent.

Poker is not Very Political

It is difficult to pick on a player in *Poker*. For very casual players this is not so important; given the opportunity to pick on another player in a game like *Risk*, for example, they will always pick on the leader or take the most obviously advantageous move that they see. With more sophisticated players however, the politics can easily become the central feature of the game: alliances will form and players will be picked on not for their position but for their allegiance or lack of allegiance. In itself, this is not a bad thing – there are many excellent games that focus on this (most notably *Diplomacy*), but it is a characteristic of the game that will dominate all other parts of the game if the politics becomes too pronounced.

Poker has Stakes

Typically *Poker* is played for money. Most players find that unless it is played for money it is pointless. If you experiment a bit, however, for some playgroups one may find that there are some ways around this – for example, playing a tournament where you can't buy back into the game. In this case the stakes are elimination from the game. My pals from Adobe have another solution as mentioned above, they keep track of the results over the course of years – and players value their "score" because it is being recorded. The score is a measure of game honor.

Playing for stakes has an interesting effect on a game, whether or not the stakes are money or honor. The stakes make it so that players are playing for more than just first place, they are competing every hand to win and it means something to them even if they are still in dead last. I have used this mindset to completely alter the nature of a *Hearts* league I played in, where we played as if we were playing for money and kept track of the results. It is amazing how that change alters the play of good players!

Ways this might be leveraged in an original game design might be to link together small game scores into a larger metagame that takes place over hours or even months. When the metagame is nearing the end, players will start playing in a different way as they begin to worry more about their rank relative to the other players and less about their particular score. You can see this happen in games like *Hearts*, in which players start off just worrying about their score, then later in the game the person in the lead is simply trying to get points on the person furthest behind to end the game.

Last Thought

Several years ago I saw a panel of distinguished computer game designers which included Nolan Bushnell, the founder of Atari. They were asked what games they drew inspiration from – and while his copanelists mentioned computer games which were occasionally so recent they couldn't really have had much formative impact – Nolan said "Golf." It was long enough ago I am sure my memory embellishes this – but I imagine a giggle running through the audience simply because my experience has been that so few people really pay attention to the truly classic games like *Golf*, or *Poker* with regard to what makes them well "designed" games that have endured over a century. To lose sight of that not only costs a designer a rich supply of ideas, but more tragically, cuts them off from our heritage of games which extends back not twenty-five or fifty years but millennia.

APPLYING DESIGN CONCEPTS FROM *RA* TO DIGITAL GAMES
by Brian Magerko

My interest in boardgames used to be solidly focused on playing *Chess*. My notion of other boardgames was that they were either boring versions of *Candyland* or party games, neither of which held my attention very long. The only exception to this view was my experience with Eberle et al.'s *Cosmic Encounter* in graduate school, a fantastic game experience that I enjoyed but never took as any indication that there was a plethora of other game design innovations out there to discover. It was not until a friend in Chicago introduced me to his boardgame group that I discovered, quite embarrassingly late in my career as a researcher in digital games, that boardgames were not only played often by adults, but also that a renaissance of boardgame design had taken place. Instead of games that involved simple die rolls and moving around a board or trading card games like *Magic*, which did not interest me, there was an entire spectrum of new kind of games to experience that provided a deep, intricate, often elegant experience with game mechanics that did not overly rely on chance nor have obvious strategies. My first and most memorable such experience was with the Reiner Knizia game, *Ra*.

Ra is about playing through the major historical epochs of ancient Egypt (the Old Kingdom, the Middle Kingdom, and the New Kingdom) and collecting fame points through the acquisition of different valued tiles at auction. This game represents a wholly unique experience, especially for a newcomer to modern boardgames. The board is hardly significant. As opposed to focusing on moving game pieces around a board, this three-to-five player game is essentially a competitive auction. Unlike *Chess*, in which materiel and position contribute heavily to a single goal of capturing the opposing king, *Ra* creates an experience where there are multiple possible goals to pursue, and what a player decides to follow can change from game to game and within a single game. Playing *Ra* felt more like playing a game like the digital game *Starcraft* in which players have multi-dimensional goals to consider in a strategy, than a boardgame like I was used to playing. I was hooked.

This chapter will briefly explore the main mechanics of the game, though I highly recommend playing it. It will then discuss what makes this game unique. Finally, it will follow through the exercise that the *Digital Tabletop* project (digitaltabletop.org) typically undergoes – a comparison between the interesting mechanics present in a boardgame (in this case, *Ra*) with what is / isn't done in modern digital games. The purpose of this comparison is to better inform game design in both domains as a practice.

The Game

The game mechanics of *Ra* are fairly simply. A game lasts three rounds (called epochs). Players take turns choosing among a) drawing a tile from a bag and placing it on the 'auction block' on the board, b) starting a voluntary auction to set off a round of bidding on the items on the auction block, or c) discarding a God tile to grab a tile off of the auction block (see below). Tiles drawn are either: Gods (worth +2 at the end of an epoch or can be used as an action to grab one tile off of the auction block), Niles and Floods (Niles are worth +1 if you have a flood), *Civilization* (-5 if you don't have any at the end of a epoch, worth points if you have multiple Civilizations of different types), Monuments (worth multiple points at the end of the game), Gold (worth +3 at the end of a round), and the *Ra* tile, which instantly starts an involuntary auction when a player draws it from the bag.

An auction involves each player getting exactly one bid on all of the tiles on the auction block. Highest bid wins. When a player wins an auction, they pick up all of the tiles on the auction block and exchange the single Sun used for winning the auction. The next auction winner then exchanges for that Sun, etc. The Sun obtained by the winner is theirs and turned face down, to be used in the next epoch.

Once a certain number of *Ra* tiles have been drawn, then the epoch is over. Players add up their points for that epoch, which are affected by the tiles they currently hold or don't hold, and begin the next epoch with the same Suns that they held in the previous epoch. If they have some Suns still face up (i.e. they didn't use them to buy anything during this epoch), then they were simply not used. This is common when players hold onto high value Suns and then the epoch suddenly ends.

Why Is It So Compelling?

The use of *Ra* tiles to count down each epoch is of particular interest. *Ra* tiles serve as a probabilistic device for reaching the end of an epoch. It is possible that players will never draw a *Ra* tile, but will instead go through all of the valuable tiles in succession. It is also possible that players will draw *Ra* tiles until the end of an epoch without ever drawing a tile of value. It is much more likely that a combination of both will be drawn, but this is a core feature of *Ra* that makes it so fascinating – players always have to keep in mind the likelihood of the epoch ending at a certain time. As discussed below, this likelihood plays prominently into how tiles are valued, player long-term and short-term strategy, and buying decisions.

The complexity of the evaluation function that players attempt to use during nearly every single tile draw is part of what makes this game so compelling. For each player at the table, there is likely a very different evaluation going on. Even if an auction doesn't happen, when a new value tile (i.e. not a *Ra* tile) is drawn, players are constantly reconsidering their current strategies, considering the value of the current auction set to the other players, and pondering the use of a God tile if they have one. When an auction does occur, a player's evaluation of how much they should bid is dependent on a wide array of factors, and the influence of those factors depend on the player's strategy for winning, what epoch the game is in, and how many *Ra* tiles are out on the board (i.e. how probable it is that the game will end soon).

A key unifying feature of the game is that the values and probabilities (of tiles and Suns) change with each new non-*Ra* tile drawn; with each new *Ra* drawn, signifying that an epoch is getting closer to ending; and with each new epoch, which means that the game as a whole is closer to the end. If an epoch is one *Ra* away from ending, players are faced with spending that precious twelve Sun on what earlier in the epoch would have been bought with possibly a four or a five.

The relationship between decision-making and drawing tiles is connected to the fact that the likelihood of drawing a certain tile at any given time is dependent on the previous draws. Players are drawing from a fixed and continually decreasing resource. Just as in *Scrabble*, there are n tiles in the bag and once a tile is drawn, the bag has n-1 tiles remaining. In other words, if there are multiple civilizations that are drawn early in the game, players may note that civilizations will be a scarce resource in later epochs.

The fact that there isn't a clear mapping, as pointed out above, from early or mid-game state to player success, makes it all the more interesting when trying to make decisions as a player. A large part of the experience of a player is trying to figure out how much an auction is worth to them versus forcing another player to spend more than they would want to. All the players are on a journey of trying to mentally summarize how well everyone is doing, how well everyone is likely to do given the game history to this point, and what to do at this moment (do I start an auction? what should I bid right now?). The factors for deciding if / what to bid are:

- What tiles the player and everyone else has

    - Their absolute value

    - Their relative value

    - What sets are desired for this epoch (e.g. wanting one more Civilization to get extra points)

    - What tiles are desired for the last epoch (e.g. wanting more Monuments to get extra points)

- What numbered tiles players are primed to start with next epoch

- What the current epoch is

- How many *Ra* tiles are on the board

- How many *Ra* tiles have been discarded in previous epochs

- How full the auction row currently is

- How many of each tile have been previously drawn

- What bids are on the table for the current auction, if any

- How many Suns each player has left

- Everyone's projected score

- What Sun would be gained with the current auction

As mentioned above, there is a ton to compute. It is immeasurably difficult for even an interme-diate player (I cannot say much for experts, since I am not one nor know any) to say with certainty what a winning strategy will be in the first two epochs of any given game. The actual leader of the game does not generally materialize until at least the last half of the second epoch, if not later.

Comparison to Digital Games

My academic research is mainly involved with the design and development of game-based experiences that have AI as a core component. It has led me to think about the design of digi-tal games, give lectures on design to undergraduate and graduate students, and think about the affordances that different approaches to AI can bring to a digital game experience. When the floodgates to boardgames opened with my introduction to *Ra*, I was suddenly exposed to a wealth of game experiences that I really hadn't considered before. Boardgames had their own set of game mechanic clichés and innovations that had some overlap in the digital realm, but was definitely separate. I co-founded the *Digital Tabletop* (thedigitaltabletop.org) as a means of collaboratively exploring the relationship between digital games and boardgames. As stated in the mission on the project website, the purpose of the group is to engage in "...discussing the game mechanics used in designer boardgames & other tabletop games, their relationship or pos-sible influence on digital games, and a meta-level discussion about the intersection of non-digital games and digital games within the context of academic game studies."

Ra was truly the catalyst for the creation of this group and the first boardgame studied. Our main finding was that the main experience in gameplay – the auctioning of non-replenishing resources with the value of both the currency and the resources changing over time - has no obvious parallel in the digital (or even the non-digital, to the best of my knowledge) game world. Basic auctioning mechanisms occur in MMO's for example, but they are more of the traditional type rather than the kind seen in *Ra*. The key feature here is that *the value of any given set of tiles or resources is highly contextual*. This goes beyond the concept of picking a strategy to best match your opponent's (e.g. catapults in some *Civilization* games may be less useful if nearby oppos-ing cities have knights that have multiple movements per turn). The decision to obtain more resources for auctioning (i.e. drawing from the tile bag) has a direct effect on the value of those resources (i.e. you may draw a *Ra* tile, making the end of the epoch that much sooner).

Considering the auctioning mechanism in *Ra* could lead to some interesting interactions in existing games. For example, *Counterstrike: Source* allows you to purchase weaponry and armor before each battle. One could imagine a *Ra*-style auctioning mechanism that blends battle success (e.g. if you kill someone, you swap your lowest sun with their second-highest) with between-bat-tle auctioning. In other words, more thought would need to go into who you attacked (similar to which auction you decide to start or bid on) based on how it would affect future attacks (similar to what Sun you wind up with when you win an auction). The addition of having fixed resources could also be expanded in games (e.g. only some percentage of civilizations in *Civilization* can learn any given technology or only so many sniper rifles exist for purchase in a round of *Counter-Strike: Source*) with an inclusion of a *Ra* tile-esque component that, when it appears, counts down a timer that will effect which resources are accessible (e.g. temples are unavailable in *Civilization* after a certain number of ticks on the timer go by). This would lead to the kind of game theoretic situations that occur in *Ra*, where players not only reason about the absolute value of obtaining resources but also the relative value according to how much of that resource is left and how much longer it will be available.

The approach of conducting a transmedia comparison of mechanics across digital games and boardgames has been an interesting design path to travel. It has lead to multiple novel concepts for digital games via the discussions on the *Digital Tabletop* blog. However, like any design ideas, the real test of how these ideas would work out is in implementing the ideas in actual playable games. The examples provided above are not so much obvious amazing improvements to the games discussed, but more so thoughtful attempts at how we as designers of digital games can learn from the rich mechanics in boardgames like *Ra* when considering new game designs or updating takes on standard digital game genres.

TRAIN: FROM BLACK BOX TO WHITE CUBE
Simon Ferrari

Train is part three of Brenda Brathwaite's "The Mechanic is the Message" project.[40] It is a game about one of modern history's most traumatic events, meant to teach through interaction rather than narrative. *Train* is a work of fevered inspiration, declared a work of Torah by a respected rabbi.[41] It is undeniably the work of an artist, though it is unclear exactly what the term means in an era when many consider the very concept of art to be dead. Brathwaite brings *Train* with her around the country, like a circuit preacher, carrying the precious cargo in her transport of choice: a German sports car. Clad in leather and one of her many pairs of fabulous shoes, she summons the work into a space and then walks away as people begin to play it.

Presenting at an academic conference on the art history of games, Brathwaite stood before a crowd of jaded intellectuals and stated, "I'm an artist, and I'm sensitive about my shit."[42] It's difficult to separate *Train* from Brathwaite's charismatic persona. This means that judgments of the game almost always collapse into judgments of Brathwaite herself. People take *Train* personally. Either they instantly see how the game works and why it's so effective for them, or they question the depth of its design and intent, or they lash out in disbelief at Brathwaite's nerve and poor taste: "She made a game about the Holocaust?" Or is it "out of the Holocaust?"

Of course, many people make these same judgments about *Train* and its creator, positive and negative, without even playing it. Discourse around the game is fragmentary to say the least. In order to avoid retreading old ground and the common pitfalls plaguing many articles on *Train*, I'd like to begin with a question that I haven't seen asked before: "Why trains?" If the purpose of the game is to remind us of the brutality of the Holocaust, or to make us think about it in a way that we haven't before, why would this one aspect be singled out? Although we can point to a few examples of games that focus on the development and traversal of railway, the answer, I think, lies in the wider tradition of tabletop train play outside the history of formal game design.

Many children desire at some point to be a train conductor or engineer, in much the same way that they go through periods of wanting to be a fireman, an astronaut, or even a garbage collector.[43] The vehicles coupled to these professions wear their functions on their sleeves, so it's easy for children to comprehend their purposes and aspire to controlling them. This impulse is actively marketed to, so there are miniature trains for every age range imaginable—from a child's first wooden Brio set to the intricate models of adult hobbyists. Typically arranged in a loop and surrounded by miniatures of small town civilization, toy and model trains don't "go" anywhere. They're based on a nostalgic picture of how local rail works, a larger than life, sexy contrast to the contemporary reality of subway systems.

Most importantly, train sets create a spatial form of storytelling: passengers go in the carriages, the engineer in the engine, and the cargo in the freight cars. Ask any child about the trains they're playing with, and they'll be able to describe, in detail, the daily life of the town ands its people that surround the track. And when Brathwaite was testing *Train* to make sure that its mechanics made for enjoyable play without its infamous reveal moment, she told her daughters that the train was headed to Disney World.[44] It is our failure to remember this storytelling function of train sets that *Train* exploits.

Adult train play is more about the machine than about the people who ride it. When I was younger, my father and I volunteered to run a model train competition at a local train show. This competition—a sort of logistics race—focused solely on the procedural aspects of train operation. Three players were tasked with linking a series of freight cars to an engine they controlled. This required driving the engine forward, switching a junction, and then reversing slowly to catch a latch between the engine and the target freight car. Once three freight cars were attached in the proper sequence, the players proceeded to the end of a linear course, stopping only to reconnect cars if they became detached.

As one can expect, nobody asked where the trains were headed or what they were carrying. The freight and the track's terminus had nothing to do with the task at hand.

Train as game

Looking at *Train*, any game designer or convinced ludologist probably asks at some point: "Is *Train* a good game? Why would I play it instead of any other game about trains?"

Anyone with an iDevice need not travel across the country to play a well-designed railroad game. *Trainyard*, a puzzle game by Mark Rix, performed remarkably well in the iDevice App Store in late 2010, even in the face of overwhelming competition from the far more popular genre of simple physics games.[45] Players trace tracks into existence with their fingers, connecting starting hubs to endpoints while avoiding collisions. The game layers obstacles and mechanics steadily, requiring players to navigate around rocks or combine two trains of different color before they can enter an endpoint. Mid-level play requires a basic understanding of track switching, and the game affords easy track erasing and editing for fluid testing and execution. Like the model train competition mentioned above, *Trainyard* has no fiction, though each puzzle does bear the name of a city.

We don't even need to look outside the tabletop to find other examples. *Ticket to Ride*, a German-style boardgame designed by Alan Moon in 2004, tasks competing players with connecting real-world cities by claiming routes along a network of predetermined, color-coded tracks.[46] The game is remarkably minimalist, allowing players to take only one of three actions per turn: draw two color-coded train cars, choose (at least one of three randomly-drawn) destination cards linking one city to another, or claim one section of track. Strategy here is a combination of cost-benefit analysis—measuring one's ability to connect two locations and claim destination points against the likelihood of failing to do so (and thus losing points at the end of the game)—and underhanded sabotage—purposefully claiming tracks that one's opponents need to complete their own destination cards.

Both of these games focus on the creation of tracks, their destinations predetermined. They make no mention of what the trains are carrying, their common color-coded designs creating challenge rather than denoting anything special about the trains themselves. *Trainyard* and *Ticket to Ride* possess a number of qualities we associate with good design: they are mechanically elegant, allowing players to do a lot without having to memorize too many rules; thus they're easy to pick up, yet difficult to master; and they provide ample amounts of replayability, the former through an exhaustive puzzle list and the latter by way of a large possibility space and optional expansions.

In contrast, *Train* can be awkward to play. Players have to constantly refer back to the rules, which are sometimes purposefully vague and difficult to read on account of their printing method. And, after playing *Train*, few players seem to want to come back for a second helping. Even if they desired to replay the game, they'd have to travel to the one place where it's currently on display to do so. So why was *Train* quickly canonized as a premiere example of the expressive power of games? What does it have that other railroad games don't?

There's an austere beauty to *Train*'s board, pieces, and instructions: muted browns and steely grays predominate, striking a powerful contrast with the bright yellow of the "people" pieces. The little yellow people are almost weightless, especially compared to the heft of *Train*'s cardboard action cards. This imbues fragility to the people pieces and gravity to one's choices. Surrounding the track board are two fetish objects: an antique typewriter, which Brathwaite uses to produce the game's rulebook, and a broken window pane that the players are encouraged to smash with a hammer at the beginning of the game. Even if players don't immediately recognize the significance of these objects, they are presented in a straightforward and solemn way that informs how they should be interacted with.

The rules don't try to explain what *Train* is "about"; they simply tell players their allowed actions and the order of play. Each of three players controls a train car on its own track, which is staggered against the other two. Each turn, a player takes one of four actions: load her train car, move her car, draw an action card, or play an action card. The actions cards allow a player to accelerate her car, damage a track, repair a track, join her car with another, or derail a train to make it lose half its passengers. Players are told that they get "100,000" for each of the 60 tiny yellow game pieces they bring to the end of a railway. Once a car reaches the end of a track, the player must remove its pieces and place them on a Terminus card. "*Train*," the final rule reads, "is over when it ends."

This ruleset and the tracks are designed for genuine tactical complexity: it is fun to try to stymie the efforts of other players to reach their Terminus, to break their tracks, to pack as many tiny yellow people into the cars as one possibly can. And then the game makes a major reversal once the first Terminus is reached. The Terminus cards reveal to what concentration camp a train car has arrived. Each of the 60 yellow pieces represents 100,000 human lives, totaling the 6 million lost during the Holocaust. This is a snap contextualization, a kind of narrative twist called anagnorisis—realizing that Bruce Willis was a ghost all along in *The*

Sixth Sense or that Oedipus is the son of Jocasta and Laius.[47] Players now realize the meaning of the two fetish objects: the typewriter was manufactured for use by the *Schutzstaffel* (SS), while the broken window was meant to invoke *Kristallnacht*.

According to Brathwaite, all but a few games of *Train* have ended once the first Terminus card has been drawn. To those who have not seen or experienced *Train*, it might seem that the game relies too heavily on this realization for its strength, that "the Holocaust is not a twist ending." The game's greatest defense comes from Ian Bogost, who argues that it is a "game of gestures."[48] Players modify their attitude toward the game and its pieces, according to Bogost, once they realize what's happening. For instance, he observed that a number of players made it a personal rule to always organize the yellow game people into neat little groups after every turn. After the Terminus reveal, this ordering retroactively becomes a signifier of crowd control. A contextualization such as this takes on greater meaning in a game than it could in any other dramatic medium.

Brathwaite does not intercede at any point during the game, and she won't comment on its meaning. Bogost himself holds that the game "never makes an argument about the Holocaust."[49] Yet surely it simulates something: first the mind of a strategic mass murderer who has mentally converted human beings into numbers, second the sobering process of realization experienced by the German people after the fall of Berlin. This goes far beyond creating a feeling of complicity in the player. Complicity only exists within a specific legal context, and morality is a social construction. In the cultural logic of Nazi rule, players have committed no crime or moral violation. Instead, *Train* is a game about the banality of evil. It's about what happens when we accept the rules and instructions handed down to us by a higher authority. *Train* is a game about playing games.

One under-discussed aspect of the game's re-contextualization is the meaning of the competition between players. Perhaps the players were Nazi commanders vying against each other for a promotion. Or maybe it's an indictment of organizational politics in general. What's clear from all our examples of competitive train-based games is that an agonistic relationship between players leads to less discussion about fictive context. This is something that most "pure" game designers actively desire: why waste time discussing where the trains are going when there are tactics to master and opponents to best?

Jean Lave has argued that task-oriented cognition is better understood as the setting of expectations, or "potential resolution shapes," rather than the planning of explicit goals.[50] In competitive games, goals and expectations are clearly more conflated than they are in everyday cognition. One expects only that, in satisfying the win conditions, one will be duly recognized as the best player of the lot. We don't expect our in-game actions to signify anything outside the "magic circle" of play, except perhaps producing some small amount of pride for being generally clever enough to have won. *Train* thus foregrounds the subdued cognitive formation of expectations characteristic of competitive play.

Our hypothetical ludologist or pure game designer may now re-emerge to ask one final question: "Why should I play *Train* once I already know how it ends?" One measure of a game is not what designers and critics think about it, but what players do with it.

As with any well-designed game, there's more than one way to play *Train*. During some play sessions, the players have openly discussed how the game works. Some have used the "derail" card to free as many yellow pieces as possible, interpreting the loss of half the car's passengers as them escaping from their captors. But this interpretation is messy; we all know what happens when a train derails—people die. For my play session, I devised a different strategy. In the wake of common knowledge about its context, players consciously bear the role of a Nazi officer; therefore, they may revel in their brutality, to see how it feels. Their efforts to be the best at delivering human beings to slaughter emulate the openly competitive nature of a military hierarchy.

But if a player of *Train* foregoes the two mechanics of loading and moving trains, it frees up a considerable amount of turns for accruing and spending resource cards.[51] The pool of cards is limited, so this player will eventually be able to collect every "repair" card within the deck. Once she has done so, she has only got to break each of the three train tracks to end the game in a stalemate ("*Train* is over when it ends"). If one balances the collection of cards with stalling tactics, it is possible to finish a game of *Train* without any tiny yellow people reaching a Terminus. The game becomes even more exciting once the players filling the roles of dutiful Nazis realize the strategy: they will begin racing to a Terminus or trying to pull a repair card in an effort to prevent their own failure. Instead of competing against each other for a higher score, the Nazi players cooperate to quash their shared enemy. *Train* effectively becomes a simulation of wartime resistance.

It is *Train*'s spatial simplification of the German transportation system that makes this alternate play style possible. The design expresses universality to a series of population displacements that in fact occurred quite distantly (spatially and temporally) from each other. In the dominant reading of the game first discussed, this placement of the tracks next to each other helps simulate the mentality of the Nazi officer who has turned people into numbers and their displacement into a uniform process. But because the entirety of the nation's rail network is reduced to three contiguous tracks, and because the three Termini exist alongside each other, one is able to bottleneck movement in a way that wouldn't be feasible during the actual conflict.

Train's value is best understood not as a laundry list of traditionally desirable features but as an aesthetic experience uniquely rendered by the manipulation of a now-dead rule system. In *Newsgames: Journalism at Play*, my co-authors and I discern three categories of realism in "documentary games," or games that recreate historical events.[52] The weakest realism is spatial, the reconstruction of a historical space for casual, unguided exploration. The middle ground is operational reality, guiding the player through a historical problem space by the establishment of a specific role and a series of tasks. The most promising category of documentary reality is procedural; it models a historical rule system to expose "the behaviors underlying a situation, rather than merely telling stories of their effects."[53] And it is this truest form of ludic documentary work that *Train* exemplifies.

Train as art

Many contemporary games raise questions about the relationship between games and art, but few actually help answer these questions. *Train* comes at a time when many game designers struggle for popular recognition of their work as art, as the building blocks of a new expressive medium. The reasons for this are many, but the primary motivation may come from two fundamental misunderstandings—first, that games lack some form of legitimacy, and second, that artistic merit is the highest measure of cultural value. Games predate humanity, narrative, and art. Nothing so old and integral as play need ask for cultural legitimacy. Nevertheless, attaining the recognized status of art grants one's work notoriety, increased chances for funding, and a guarantee of archival preservation.

Train has now been played at game industry conferences and academic symposia, in galleries and the Strong Museum of Play. It fits traditional display contexts, with its strong visual rhetoric of the yellow people pieces standing out against the somber tones of the rest of the board. Yet, alongside other recent examples of "gallery games," its place in these formerly hallowed places becomes problematic. When I played *Train* at the Kai Lin Art Gallery, alcohol was served. Although those in attendance were expected to drink only a polite amount, things tend to get rowdy when games are involved. A few feet away, crowds were laughing and shouting during a heated game of *Sixteen Tons*.[54] Grinning as he sauntered up to the table bearing *Train*, one of my soon-to-be opponents made an exclamatory, drunken joke about how we were "gonna kill some Jews."

It wouldn't make sense to demand that visitors to a gallery featuring games be completely quiet, serious, and contemplative. Why clip the wings of a form that inspires exuberance, roughhousing, and trashtalking when so few pieces of art are able to muster such behavior? Even the flippant bigotry of my *Train* opponent has to be accommodated in some way for the spirit of play to remain alive inside art's white cube. The Dutch historian Johan Huizinga noted that games were set apart as not-seriousness because of their separation from the real world and its concerns, yet also that games were able to inspire absolute seriousness during play.[55] One of *Train*'s strengths is its ability to contrast with the space around in it, in much the same way that it conceptually contrasts with the mainstream game industry. Passersby watch *Train* in play, a public context that adds to the game's sense of unease and trepidation.

We can select three broad lenses from aesthetic theory and the philosophy of art to understand why *Train* succeeds so well as an artgame: the Enlightenment aesthetics of Immanuel Kant, the sociopolitical aesthetics of the Frankfurt School, and the contemporary philosophy of art after Wittgenstein.

In The *Critique of Judgment*, Kant argues that there are necessary and sufficient conditions, or "rules," by which we can identify an artifact as belonging to the class of objects we call "artistic." Yet, these rules cannot be "determinate," or derived a priori from a rational concept. This presents a problem that, for Kant, can only be solved by a "genius":

> ... *fine art cannot itself devise the rule by which it is to bring about its product. Since, however, a product can never be called art unless it is preceded by a rule, it must be nature in the subject (and through the attunement of his powers) that gives the rule to art; in other words, fine art is possible only as the product of genius.*[56]

This artist-genius "deriv[es] the rule from the particular" a form of aesthetic judgment called the "reflective" mode.[57] Fine art is thus the production of rules outside those of nature, a practice to which game designers can surely relate. Kant's genius figure is characterized by originality, the ability to create "exemplary" rather than derivative works.

If all of this highfalutin philosophical jargon sounds strangely familiar, this is because it's an early form of the "auteur theory" that informs most naïve contemporary notions of art. Brathwaite embraces this early modern conception of the artist unironically when she admits that much of her design process occurs within what her friends call the "black box" of her mind.[58] Kant himself wrote of this black box as a *sine qua non* characteristic of the genius, who "does not know how he came by the ideas for [the work]; nor is it in his power to devise such products at his pleasure, or by following a plan."[59] Brathwaite's possible status as a genius aside, in what ways does *Train* itself crystallize Kant's notions of originality and exemplary status?

There is only one physical copy of *Train*, while even the oldest folk boardgames, *Senet* and the *Royal Game of Ur*, were reproduced and played by all social classes. Even one-of-a-kind archeological finds like *The Stanway Game* were, in all likelihood, not always one-of-a-kind. Both as social practices and economic products, games seek wide audiences. Only in the history of fine art do we see one-copy games like Brathwaite's, such as the prepared gameboards of the Fluxus movement. Yoko Ono's *All White Chess Set* (1966), for example, is a modified game of *Chess* wherein all the black pieces of the board are switched out for a second white set.[60] The game is theoretically playable, but its political message is just as easily communicated through a short conceptual exercise.

Like *White Chess*, *Train* works on the level of concept art. In reply to a prospective player who saw *Train* and openly stated that she didn't want to play, Brathwaite replied: "you just did."[61] Yet, unlike a concept piece, *Train* does not end with its concept. The game has been refined for playability. Although all but a few games of *Train* have ended with the revelation of the first Terminus card, we've seen that it's nevertheless possible to keep playing, or play the game for score, or even set alternative goals for oneself. *Train* is thus distinct from the Fluxus games in its simultaneous refinement of high concept and actual play, as good an argument for its exemplary status as any.

But are these Enlightenment notions of art relevant today? *Train*'s existence as an individual, non-reproducible artifact opens it up to further scrutiny by the neo-Marxist political philosophy of the Frankfurt School. In the 1930s, Walter Benjamin described the effects of mass production on the status of art. Historically, so long as works of art remained singular and were stored primarily in museums and estates, they retained an "aura," or "unique phenomenon of distance."[62] Reproduction diminishes that aura, troubles the notion of originality, and brings a piece of art closer to an idealized "public." *Train* retains its aura after the age of mechanical reproduction, during an even more turbulent time for the popular idea of authenticity: the age of digital reproduction.

For Benjamin, this reduction in aura was a good thing: "for the first time in world history, mechanical reproduction emancipates the work of art from its parasitical dependence on ritual."[63] That which retains an aura inspires fear and hatred in the masses but garners critical acclaim, while in a mechanically reproduced medium, such as film, critical and popular receptions align. This holds true for *Train*: it is critically acclaimed and popularly reviled. Games and ritual have a special relationship with one another: *Train* and its space of play retain much of the secrecy and separateness that characterize folk games and religious rites alike for Huizinga.[64] Perhaps one way that artgames set themselves apart from the rest of the medium is by playing with these notions of aura and ritual.

Of course, all the "The Mechanic is the Message" games share this aura. The reason *Train* justifies additional concern is that it deals directly with the same political situation that the Frankfurt School was reacting against. The cult of the Fuhrer in Nazy Germany had "aestheticized politics," while Marxism hoped to politicize art.[65] Benjamin reacted favorably to the constructivist art and Soviet montage cinema of the early revolution, but after WWII the political climate changed. From 1949 to 1956, the USSR enforced a state art doctrine known as "socialist realism," which denied the basic truths of life and labor in the Soviet system. Instead it showed workers a vision of the future that was promised if they remained true to the Party through its many stages of revolution.

Writing later in the Frankfurt tradition, Theodor Adorno's aesthetic theory was an argument against this twisted form of politicized art. This school of art's greatest offense, to Adorno, was that its works contained false social content rather than formally reflecting the social conditions of their creation:

> *Art becomes something social through its in-itself, and it becomes in-itself by means*
> *of the social force of production effective in it. The dialectic of the social and of the*
> *in-itself of the artwork is the dialectic of its own constitution to the extent that it*
> *tolerates nothing interior that does not externalize itself, nothing external that is not*
> *the bearer of the inward, the truth content.*[66]

Train proves the sociopolitical value of procedural reality embodied by the "The Mechanic is the Message" series, a dialectic between a player's actions and the cultural dimensions they take on through simulation—the "proceduralist style" is itself a working argument about the ludic medium's form. *Night and Fog's* long, slow tracks through Auschwitz and Majdanek, required viewing in many middle schools throughout the United States, have somehow distanced us over time from the horrors of the Holocaust.[67] Films such as this disconnect the results of the Final Solution from its causes. But people already know to be in the lookout for openly homicidal impulses; *Train*, on the other hand, has the ability to approximate the hidden, mental source of genocide. It examines the historical period not by indirect reference or mummified audiovisuals but through direct ludic experience and player interaction.

Finally we're ready to tackle the contemporary situation of art that *Train* engages. Noel Carroll characterizes much of the mid-20th century philosophy of art as "neo-Wittgensteinian."[68] That is, for a short time, philosophers gave up on trying to provide a definition or set of necessary and sufficient conditions for art. Morris Weitz provided two convincing arguments against the definability of art, the "open concept" and "family resemblance." The open concept argument claims that art cannot be defined because new artworks are constantly being created, and no definition could ever hope to predict what we might accept as art in the future. The family resemblance argument holds that we cannot identify all the things called "art" by common features; rather, we accept something as art through disconnected "strands of similarities" relevant to each medium.[69]

Carroll exposes the critical flaw in these arguments when he asks, "What does that have to do with the conditions requisite for the status of artwork?" (emphasis added).[70] Perhaps paradoxically, even if art is a dead concept, this doesn't prevent us from identifying works of art. According to Carroll, in a preliminary version of the argument in "The Artworld," Arthur Danto held that at least one necessary condition for the artwork is that it be "enfranchised by art theories."[71] *Train* thus comes at a privileged time, having the chance to help forge the very theories of game art that will allow us to categorize and critique the artgames of the future. None of these theories need break radically with the continuum of art history, so long as they remain mindful of the medium's defining qualities: procedural rhetoric, configurative play, the donning of roles, and the creation or demarcation of a space.

At the Art History of Games symposium, Brian Schrank and Jay Bolter presented a model for the avant-garde in games, distinguishing between the *formal* and the *political* avant-garde in art history.[72] The formal avant-garde questions the assumptions of mainstream art, while the political avant-garde confronts the place of art in society. Schrank holds the mods of Jodi. org, an art collective known for deconstructing famous games until they are unrecognizable, as the ideal of formal avant-garde games that work by manipulating the player's flow state. The political avant-garde in gaming is represented by virtual world griefers and alternate-reality games, which call into question the magic circle that divides the "real" world from the games we play.

Train seems to straddle these two avant-gardes. The game's "reveal" moment, when the Terminus card is turned over, has been proven over the game's short life to cause a game-ending shift in flow. If flow is the avoidance of both frustration and boredom, then *Train's* reveal pushes the player so deep into frustration as to cause a feeling of futility. On the other hand, *Train* troubles the notion of the magic circle in a number of ways. Even if we hold that games aren't inherently ethical systems, we can observe that some residue of historical guilt sneaks into *Train*'s circle of play. And, although the "The Mechanic is the Message" games stand on their own, we must nevertheless recognize their instrumental value—especially since we know that Brathwaite was inspired to begin the series when she saw that her daughters weren't receiving a satisfactory historical education at school.[73]

Conclusion

Charles Pratt, in his short review of *Train*, concludes that, "Perhaps it's best to see *Train* not as a game, but as move in a larger game played between the cultural forces of 'fine art' and 'games.'"[74] He seeks to move the discussion beyond a question of whether or not it's a successful game design. With this piece, I hoped to show that the concepts of fine art and games are in no way mutually exclusive; further, I wanted to find *Train*'s roots in the histories of unstructured play and formal game design to see how and why it works as a game divorced from its artistic aspirations.

Of course, it is unclear as of yet whether games will find a home in the artworld as members of an existing contemporary art movement, such as Nicolas Bourriaud's "relational aesthetics," or whether a new breed of ludic curators will have to gradually prove their worth to buyers and critics alike.[75] We also don't yet know whether the theories of art espoused by curators of games will adhere to or differ greatly from the ludological theories of game studies academics. What's important to remember is that the many cultural spheres at play here don't need to completely overlap: the artworld, the academy, and the industry can and should all have their own unique valuations and judgments of game art. This is how it's always been, yet our current analysis takes place in a strange time when many seem to desire for all three discourses to eventually align.

I'd like to end now with a word of caution.

Train instills fear in me. It works on so many levels, answering so many questions about the potential of games as design and art, that it threatens to dominate any and all discussion of those questions. We must always remember that *Train*'s methods and goals are not the only methods and goals worthy of our best designers and their work. Not every game needs to command our respect, to make us reflect on history, or to make us cry in order to be worthy of aesthetic appreciation. Games are a mess, "a strew of inconvenient and sometimes repellent things," and we should strive to keep them that way.[76]

---

40 Brenda Brathwaite, *Train* (Savannah, GA: Self-published, 2009).

41 Brenda Brathwaite, "How I Dumped Electricity and Learned to Love Design," Game Developer's Conference, San Francisco, CA, March 2010.

42 Brenda Brathwaite, "One Falls For Each Of Us: The Prototyping of Tragedy," Art History of Games Symposium, Atlanta, GA, 6 February 2010.

43 Ian Bogost, *Alien Phenomenology* (In press, 2011), 122.

44 Brenda Brathwaite, email to Simon Ferrari, Ian Schreiber, and John Romero, 29 April 2010.

45 Matt Rix, *Trainyard* (Mississauga, Canada: Self-published, 2010).

46 Alan R. Moon, *Ticket to Ride* (Paris, France: Days of Wonder, 2004).

[47] Malcolm Heath, trans., *Poetics* by Aristotle (London: Penguin, 1996), 52a, 18-19.

[48] Ian Bogost, "Gestures as Meaning," Gamasutra, 30 June 2009, http://www.gamasutra.com/view/feature/4064/persuasive_games_gestures_as_.php?print=1.

[49] Bogost, "Gestures as Meaning."

50 Jean Lave, *Cognition in Practice* (Cambridge, England: Cambridge University Press, 1988), 184-185.

[51] Simon Ferrari, "The Judgment of Procedural Rhetoric" (Master's thesis, Georgia Institute of Technology, 2010), 9.

[52] Ian Bogost, Simon Ferrari, and Bobby Schweizer, *Newsgames: Journalism at Play* (Cambridge, Mass.: MIT Press, 2010), 64.

[53] *Newsgames* 64.

[54] Nathalie Pozzi and Eric Zimmerman, *Sixteen Tons* (Atlanta, GA: Art History of Games Symposium, 2010).

[55] Johan Huizinga, *Homo Ludens* (London: Routledge, 2002), 8.

[56] Werner S. Pluhar, trans., *Critique of Judgment* by Immanuel Kant (Indianapolis: Hackett, 1987), §46, 175.

[57] Hannah Arendt and Ronald Beiner, ed., *Lectures on Kant's Political Philosophy* (Chicago: University of Chicago Press, 1997), 83.

[58] Brenda Brathwaite, email to Simon Ferrari, Ian Schreiber, and John Romero, 29 April 2010.

[59] Kant, §46, 175.

[60] Mary Flanagan, *Critical Play: Radical Game Design* (Cambridge, Mass.: MIT Press, 2009), 112-113.

[61] Brathwaite, "How I Dumped Electricity and Learned to Love Design."

[62] Walter Benjamin, "The Work of Art in the Age of Mechanical Reproduction," in *Film Theory and Criticism: Introductory Readings*, ed. Leo Braudy and Marshall Cohen (New York: Oxford University Press, 2004), 795.

[63] Benjamin 796.

[64] Huizinga 77.

[65] Benjamin 811.

[66] Theodor Adorno, *Aesthetic Theory*, translated by Robert Hullot-Kentor (Minneapolis: University of Minnesota Press, 1997), 248.

[67] Alain Resnais, *Nuit et brouillard* (Paris, France: Argos Films, 1955).

[68] Noel Carroll, "Introduction," in *Theories of Art Today*, ed. Noel Carroll (Madison, Wisconsin: University of Wisconsin Press, 2000), 3.

[69] Morris Weitz, "The Role of Theory in Aesthetics," in *Contemporary Philosophy of Art: Readings in Analytic Aesthetics*, ed. John W. Bender and H. Gene Blocker (Englewood Cliffs, N.J.: Prentice Hall, 1993), 195, cited in Carroll 8.

[70] Carroll 9.

[71] Arthur C. Danto, "The Artworld," *Journal of Philosophy* 61 (1964): 571-84, cited in Carroll 3.

[72] Jay Bolter and Brian Schrank, "Videogames & the Two Avant-Gardes." Art History of Games Symposium, Atlanta, GA, 5 February 2010.

[73] Brathwaite, "One Falls For Each Of Us: The Prototyping of Tragedy."

[74] Charles Pratt, "300 Word Review - Train," *Game Design Advance*, 22 April 2010, http://gamedesignadvance.com/?p=2155.

[75] Nicolas Bourriaud, *Relational Aesthetics* (Dijon, France: Les presses du reel, 2002).

[76] Ian Bogost, "Videogames are a Mess," Keynote, Digital Games Research Association conference, Uxbridge, UK, September 2-5, 2009.

TWILIGHT STRUGGLE AND CARD-DRIVEN HISTORICITY
Pat Harrigan and Noah Wardrip-Fruin

Mark Herman's *We the People* (1994) is generally regarded as the first wargame to use a truly Card-Driven System (CDS). Many previous wargames had incorporated card decks into their design, but *We the People* was the first system to put the cards at the center of gameplay. Cards in *WtP* are used for player movement, combat, and combat results, as well as other events; in most earlier wargame designs, these mechanics would have been handled through die rolls and a series of charts. Certain other design choices, such as the incorporation of a point-to-point map instead of the traditional hex-based maps, helped to smooth gameplay and reduce play time, resulting in a highly successful product for publisher Avalon Hill. Designers quickly adapted the CDS to other subjects; Avalon Hill shortly published two more card-driven games by other designers, Mark Simonitch's *Hannibal: Rome vs. Carthage* (1996) and Simonitch and Richard Berg's *Successors* (1997). Since then many wargames have been designed around some variation of the CDS, including Herman's *For the People* (1998) and *Washington's War* (2010; a comprehensive redesign of his earlier *We the People*), Ted Raicer's *Paths of Glory* (1999), Herman and Stephen Newberg's *Empire of the Sun* (2005; the first CDS game to use the more traditional hex map), Chad Jensen's *Combat Commander* series (2006-on), and Ananda Gupta and Jason Matthews's *Twilight Struggle* (2005), among many others.

Gupta and Matthews's design differs from many earlier CDS games in that it is not, strictly speaking, a military simulation. Depending on one's definition, it is not even a wargame.[77] While *Paths of Glory*, for instance, models large-scale military operations in World War I Europe and the Near East, and the *Combat Commander* games model small-scale tactical engagements in various theaters of World War II, *Twilight Struggle* takes as its subject the Cold War between the United States and the Soviet Union, covering the period 1945-1989.

Twilight Struggle, by simulating a global non-military conflict, demonstrates the flexibility of CDS game design. Although eminently playable and highly competitive, it adopts a more linear style of gameplay than many other CDS games, striking an intriguing balance between historical predictability and robust gameplay.[78]

For all its effectiveness as a historical simulation, Gupta and Matthews are clear that the game reflects a certain perception of history, not history itself. In the first place, "winning" is truly an option, unlike the murky outcomes of the real Cold War. Nor does the game reflect any ideological differences within nations or their leadership, except as the limited effects of certain card events, which do not meaningfully realign the geopolitical goals of either side. Ideology, communist or capitalist, is unimportant, as are the local politics of nations except insofar as they affect the wider game struggle. At the same time, one of the most compelling features of *Twilight Struggle* is how it places players in a collage Cold War mindset, in which competing historical ideologies are literally true and have definable in-game effects.

The game is played over a map of the globe, with individual nations represented as small boxes connected to each other by lines. Nations are further grouped into political Regions: Europe, Asia, Central America, South America, Africa, and the Middle East.[79] This style of "point-to-point" representation of map areas is common to many modern wargames, and can be seen in *We the People, For the People, Paths of Glory* and many others. In CDS games, it has largely though not completely supplanted the previously-standard "hex-based" style of wargame maps.[80] (Province/area movement is also common in CDS games, but this is topologically equivalent to point-to-point movement.)

Twilight Struggle, however, uses the point-to-point representation differently from these other games. In military simulations such as *Paths of Glory*, a path between points (e.g., Liege and Sedan) represents a possible line for armies to move and attack, as well as the path along which an army can trace a supply route. By contrast, in *Twilight Struggle* those lines represent instead a sort of geopolitical affinity that channels certain player actions. For example, a player's Influence markers can usually only be placed in nations adjacent (connected by a path) to ones in which he already has Influence. Further, when a player attempts a "Realignment roll" for a particular nation, the rolling player receives a bonus to his roll for any adjacent country he controls. In other words, if a player controls a nation near the target nation, it is easier to realign the target or increase one's influence there. This gameplay mechanic specifically simulates the famous "domino theory" of Cold War geopolitics. Although essentially discredited as a theory among real-world scholars, the domino theory is absolutely true within the internal logic of *Twilight Struggle*. For Gupta and Matthews, the domino theory is one part of a wider series of design decisions:

> *Also important for players to understand is that the game has a very definite point of view. Twilight Struggle basically accepts all of the internal logic of the Cold War as true—even those parts of it that are demonstrably false. Therefore, the only relationships that matter in this game are those between a nation and the superpowers. The world provides a convenient chess board for US and Soviet ambitions, but all other nations are merely pawns (with perhaps the occasional bishop) in that game. Even China is abstracted down to a card that is passed between the two countries. Furthermore, not only does the domino theory work, it is a prerequisite for extending influence into a region. Historians would rightly dispute all of these assumptions, but in keeping with the design philosophy, we think they make a better game* (Gupta and Matthews 2005).[81]

This literalization of the domino theory could be seen as politically hawkish, but dovish attitudes are detectable in the treatment of the game's DEFCON track. The game rules require each player to perform a certain number of military actions each turn or suffer a penalty. But doing so raises tensions between the superpowers and risks degrading the DEF-CON track further toward possible nuclear war. Any player who degrades the DEFCON track to "1" triggers a nuclear war; that player immediately loses the game.

What would this gameplay look like in the real world? It presumes that the actors in the game are constrained by the logic of the Cold War to constantly flex their military muscles, even when doing so necessarily brings the globe closer to a nuclear holocaust. It implies that the logic of mutually assured destruction is inescapable: the superpowers have limited control over their own nuclear arsenals, and must respond in kind to any escalation of the nuclear threat by the other side. Finally, it is inarguable that no rational actor would deliberately start such a war, in which the only guaranteed loser is himself, and which would immediately end the Cold War game and begin some much grimmer game of simple survival.

These attitudes are inherited from the anti-nuclear movements of the 1960s-1980s and reflect their pessimistic logic. *Twilight Struggle* is, in fact, structurally more pessimistic than any real-world anti-nuclear activist in that the logic of deterrence is hard-wired into the very rules of the game. There is no way to escape the military-nuclear treadmill and still correctly play the game.[82]

Twilight Struggle's view of the Cold War is thus one formed from a modern sensibility, by designers who grew up during the period described, but can now reflect on it with something like nostalgia.

Nostalgia, or something like it, permeates the game. *Twilight Struggle* simulates and recreates the major events of the Cold War; it does not attempt to speculate on or generate an alternate Cold War history. In no possible *Twilight Struggle* scenario, for instance, can China take the place of the US or the USSR as a primary superpower; nor is it possible for a popular revolution to bring down the US or Soviet governments. (In earlier versions of the design, Matthews and Gupta permitted a much more extreme range of outcomes for China. As with many elements, this led to ahistorical gameplay, as players vastly overcommitted to influencing China.)

Insofar as *Twilight Struggle* deviates from history, it does so by abstracting or avoiding real events, not generating an alternate global history. It is true that the ultimate historical outcome can diverge, as when a game ends with the USSR winning, or the world being destroyed by nuclear war, but these are logical progressions from real-world historical events, not science fictional ones. In recreating this real-world history so closely, Gupta and Matthews have necessarily limited certain strategic decisions available to the players. They have done so by utilizing the CDS in specific ways.

To see exactly how they have done this, we can compare *Twilight Struggle* to the tactical combat game *Combat Commander: Europe* (*CC:E*) for maximum contrast.

In *CC:E*, Allied and Axis players battle each other in one of a number of pregenerated scenarios, modeled on actual historical WWII combat engagements in the European theater.[83] Unlike *Twilight Struggle*, games of *CC:E* are well-known for their unpredictability. In a game of *CC:E*, several elements combine to limit a player's possible opening moves. From most to least constraining, they are:

- *Game rules.* Hard-wired rules constraints specify how many units can be placed in a hex at a given time, how fast units can move, how far weapons can shoot, etc. To break this constraint would be to play the game incorrectly.

- *Optimal strategic choices.* Often at the beginning of a scenario, there are clearly evident good and bad choices that channel events into a small number of possible paths. It is possible in Scenario 1 ("Fat Lipki"), for instance, for the German forces to reach a particular building on turn 1, and take advantage of its cover, only if they follow a strictly optimized sequence of moves. To delay in this instance means that Russian forces can advance far enough to make it very difficult for the Germans to take control of the building, with severe consequences for the remainder of the game. This constraint relaxes as a game moves from the initial stages, and unpredicted actions and events, as well as strategic choices, proliferate.

- *Historical accuracy.* Each scenario is faithful to the geography of the terrain over which the battle occurred, and forests, roads, buildings, etc., exist where they did historically. In addition, the setup conditions of each scenario specify what troops and materiel are available to the Allied and Axis players, and where they can be initially deployed. This is a design constraint, not a gameplay one; gameplay will likely deviate from history within the first move or so.

As a game of *CC:E* progresses, the series of player choices, along with a large number of random and unforeseeable events (a notable feature of the *Combat Commander* rules system), make it so that a vast number of outcomes become possible. *Twilight Struggle* does not operate in this way. While it is true that no one can predict, before the game begins, who will win, there are a number of things that can be said in advance of any game of *Twilight Struggle*, as a direct result of how Gupta and Matthews opted to utilize the CDS.

Twilight Struggle's single card deck contrasts with certain other CDS games, such as *Paths of Glory* or the *Combat Commander* series, which give each player a dedicated deck of cards. Neither is there a separate "battle deck," as in Hannibal, which players draw from to perform tactical military operations.[84] Instead, the single set of event cards used in *Twilight Struggle* is drawn from by both the US and USSR player. The cards are divided into three sub-decks: Early, Mid, and Late War. Players begin by using only the Early War deck; the later decks are added at pre-established points in the game. This ensures that the game generally follows a rough chronology—that the Korean War happens before the Vietnam War, for example. Furthermore, the playing of certain cards is a prerequisite for the playing of certain later ones: the card "NATO" can only be played after either "Marshall Plan" or "Warsaw Pact." Finally, certain cards prevent the playing of later ones, as with "Camp David Accords," which prevents the play of the card "Arab-Israeli War."

But these are exceptions. For the most part, history in *Twilight Struggle* is modular, with few cause-and-effect chains. In the logic of *Twilight Struggle*, the revolution in Cuba does not lead to the Cuban Missile Crisis, but are both discrete cards ("Fidel" and "Cuban Missile Crisis"), which can happen, or not happen, independently from one another. This is illustrative of *Twilight Struggle's* approach to historicity: for playability, historical events are detached from wider national and global concerns and their Cold War essence extracted, as it were, in order to form a single playable Event.

Each card Event is beneficial for either the US or the USSR (or in some cases, both or either). In addition to their Event, any card can be played for its Operations Point value. Therefore, if the US player holds a card that shows a beneficial Event for himself, he has the difficult choice of using it to trigger that Event, or to play it for the card's more-flexible Operations points.[85] However, a US player holding a card beneficial to the USSR has an even more difficult choice, since playing the card for Operations points *will still trigger the Event for the other player*. The choice then becomes when to play that particular Event card.

For example, the "Marshall Plan" card is worth four Operations Points, and can be used as such by either the US or USSR player. But the card effect is helpful only to the US player, allowing that player to add one Influence marker to each of seven non-USSR controlled nations in Western Europe, as well as allowing future play of the extremely useful "NATO" card. If the USSR player held this card, he would never choose to play it for its effect, and would likely choose to play it instead for its Operations Point value. But doing so will still trigger the event: the US player will place his Influence, and the future play of the "NATO" card is now allowable.

Because players must play nearly all of the cards in hand every turn, they are regularly triggering these sorts of deleterious events. It is true that to a limited degree a player can delay the play of a suboptimal card (by holding onto it until the next turn), or potentially defuse its effects (by using it as a resource for the Space Race), but in most cases, a player will find that he has a hand of cards composed of very few good choices.

The game contains 36 Early War cards, and as eight cards are dealt to each player each turn, all of the Early War cards will have passed through the players' hands at least once by the third turn. Specific rules enforce the playing of the Europe Scoring, Asia Scoring, and Middle East Scoring cards, so any experienced player will know that these cards will all be played at least once during the first three turns.[86] There are 46 Mid War cards, and—due to a rule increasing to nine the number of cards dealt out to each player on a turn—they will all be dealt out by turn six. The 21 Late War cards will also all see play in the following three turns, and so every card in the game will have been dealt out at least once should the game reach the final, tenth, turn.[87] *Twilight Struggle* therefore is designed such that players will have the opportunity to play most of the historical Events if they choose to do so.[88]

Since players have very limited ability to discard cards from their hand—*CC:E*, by contrast, allows for rapid card-cycling—and since the play of a card for Operations points will often trigger an event beneficial to one's opponents, any play of *Twilight Struggle* will see many, if not most, of the card events triggered.

The rules that govern Event triggers are therefore modeled along a particular idea of Cold War logic: that each action taken by one side will provoke a potentially more damaging counter-action by the other side. Yet, agonizingly, the cards must be played.

The number and distribution of Victory points also provide incentives for players to be active in all regions and indicate the emphasis each player should put on each region. Further, the value of a particular region often changes as the players move through the Early, Mid and Late War decks. In this way the game inclines the players once again toward a realistic Cold War chronology: the game begins with Europe as the hot spot, but gradually the importance shifts to Central America, the Middle East and Southeast Asia, before spreading into Africa in the late war.

We can see that the three initial gameplay constraints we identified for *CC:E* are here present for the entirety of a *Twilight Struggle* play: Rules and limited strategic choices governing Event triggers combine to ensure a roughly-accurate historical experience; within this framework of bad and suboptimal choices, one player will eventually squeak out a victory. In a game of *CC:E*, we cannot know in advance who will win or much of what will happen along the way. In *Twilight Struggle*, we can predict much of the action, but not the eventual winner.

Finally, however, it is the very fact that one side or another will win—and do so based on gameplay actions such as military operations, coups, realignments, controlling regions of the world, and moving forward in the space race—that is both *Twilight Struggle's* largest deviation from history and its most necessary design element for placing players in a Cold War mindset. Though it is certainly true that the US was the only superpower left standing at the end of the Cold War, to play out how this actually occurred would require a radical restructuring of the rules of the game, one that would compromise *Twilight Struggle's* most powerful accomplishment: drawing players through a recapitulation of most of the Cold War's dramatic events, in which they behave according to its internal historical logics.

References

1960: The Making of a President. Christian Leonhard and Jason Matthews; Z-Man Games. 2007.

1989: Dawn of Freedom. Jason Matthews and Ted Torgerson; GMT Games. 2010.

Balance of Power. Chris Crawford; Mindscape. 1985.

Campaign Manager 2008. Christian Leonhard and Jason Matthews; Z-Man Games. 2009.

Combat Commander: Europe. Chad Jensen; GMT Games. 2006.

Empire of the Sun. Mark Herman and Stephen Newberg; GMT Games. 2005.

For the People. Mark Herman; Avalon Hill. 1998.

Founding Fathers. Christian Leonhard and Jason Matthews; Jolly Roger Games. 2010.

Hannibal: Rome vs. Carthage. Mark Simonitch; Avalon Hill. 1996.

History of the World. Gary Dicken and Steve Kendall; Avalon Hill. 1991.

Paths of Glory. Ted Raicer; GMT Games. 1999.

Settlers of Catan. Klaus Teuber; Kosmos. 1995.

Successors. Mark Simonitch and Richard Berg; Avalon Hill. 1997.

Supremacy. Robert J. Simpson; Supremacy Games. 1984.

Tigers in the Mist. Ray Freeman; GMT Games. 1999.

Tigris and Euphrates. Reiner Knizia; Hans im Glück. 1997

Twilight Struggle. Ananda Gupta and Jason Matthews; GMT Games. 2005.

Washington's War. Mark Herman; GMT Games. 2010.

We the People. Mark Herman; Avalon Hill. 1994.

Pat and Noah would like to thank Ananda Gupta and Jason Matthews for their comments on this chapter.

[77] In some respects, *Twilight Struggle* resembles a modern-style Eurogame more than a wargame. Like *Settlers of Catan*, *Tigris and Euphrates* and countless other Eurogames, *Twilight Struggle* offers multiple scoring paths: Victory points can be acquired through area control (Europe, South America, etc.), scored at irregular times during gameplay; via the Space Race and military operations tracks; and as the direct result of card events.

Matthews has said that the primary design influences on *Twilight Struggle* were Chris Crawford's seminal computer game *Balance of Power* (for the futility of nuclear war); Gary Dicken and Steve Kendall's board game *History of the World* (for "presence," "domination" and "control"); and many Euro-style games, in particular the games of Alan Moon, for whom "scoring cards" are something of a trademark.

According to Gupta, *Twilight Struggle's* military-nuclear treadmill derives in part from Robert J. Simpson's 1984 abstract modern-era geopolitical game *Supremacy*. In this lengthy game, player activity involves conquest with conventional forces and includes a fairly strong strategic warfare component (e.g., nuclear weapons, anti-nuclear technology, boomer subs, and chemical and biological weapons). But the game allowed for defeated players to launch final strikes with their entire arsenals—causing everyone to lose. This game option was modified for *Twilight Struggle*, in which only the player who triggers a nuclear war is the loser.

Finally, Gupta adds that a major influence on *Twilight Struggle*'s domino theory mechanic was Mark Herman's *For the People*. In that game, the Union capital of Washington is much easier for the Confederate army to capture than it would have been in real life. This is because *For the People* playtesters discovered that a historically accurate defensive capability for Washington led to distorted force allocations, as the Union player lacked the sense of urgency to defend the city that the real Union high command could not ignore. For Herman and later for Gupta and Matthews, an unrealistic rule led to a better, more authentic mindset for the players, and thus to a more immersive game.

[78] Much of what is written here can also be applied to Christian Leonhard and Jason Matthews' board game *1960: The Making of a President* (2007, Z-Man Games), which simulates the electoral battle between John Kennedy and Richard Nixon. In this later design, *Twilight Struggle*'s nations are replaced with the states of the Union, and electoral votes take the place of victory points. These and other rules refinements ensure that *1960*'s design reflects its subject matter. Matthews and other collaborators have further repurposed the basic *Twilight Struggle* design in the games *Campaign Manager 2008*; *1989: Dawn of Freedom*; and *Founding Fathers*.

[79] China, as a powerful geopolitical entity that does not fit into the simplified gameplay duality of USA/USSR, is broadly abstracted as a single physical card, the "China Card," which provides certain advantages to the player who holds it.

[80] Notable exceptions are Mark Herman and Stephen Newberg's *Empire of the Sun*, and Chad Jensen's *Combat Commander* series, the particularities of which are more suited to the use of old-style hex maps.

[81] Compare with *Combat Commander: Europe*: "CC was born of a desire to make a game about WWII tactical infantry warfare that had more feeling and flavor to it than pedantic historical detail. That is not to say the game is unrealistic; just realistic in a broader, more visceral manner while abstracting things like caliber, rate of fire and muzzle velocity into a more streamlined presentation (Jensen 2006)." Jensen explicitly compares *CC:E* to Ray Freeman's *Tigers in the Mist*, about which Freeman has said that the design considerations were, first, a fun, playable, challenging game; second, historical accuracy; and third, realism.

[82] Though it is worth noting that nuclear war does not result in both players losing, which would be the antinuclear position. However, as in *Supremacy*, this would provide an inappropriate outlet for players in a bad strategic position, allowing them to turn a likely individual loss into an assured shared loss, simply by pursuing the maximal nuclear escalation that the current rules deter.

[83] To increase gameplay possibilities, *CC:E* also includes rules for randomly-generated scenarios. Except for historical fidelity, the same gameplay constraints apply to these.

[84] *Combat Commander*'s card deck consists of generic tactical actions (Move, Fire, Advance, etc.), and can be seen as an expanded version of *Hannibal*'s battle deck. Even *CC*'s less-generic card Actions and Events are all tactical in nature.

[85] Operations Points can be used in four ways: "To place Influence markers, to make Realignment rolls, to attempt Coups, or to attempt advancement in the Space Race" (Gupta and Matthews 2005). The first three of these are functionally different in the game rules, but can be thought of in real-world terms as a range of international intervention activities ranging from propaganda and political pressure to overt or covert military actions. The Space Race functions as a sort of sub-game in *Twilight Struggle*, allowing players to use Operations points for a chance at gaining Victory Points and other special benefits.

[86] This semi-predictable scoring also serves to model Cold War paranoia. Players begin to wonder why their opponent is focusing his attention on a particular region—is it because he has the scoring card for that region? The player then responds by focusing his own resources on that region, which begins a mutually reinforcing feedback loop, with both players escalating their attention on a region that might well have very little value to either side.

[87] Unpredictability is still present via the "Wargames" card, which lets a player win the game abruptly if he has

a sufficient margin of victory. This makes it impossible to play entirely for the endgame position with its arbitrary time limit (unless, of course, "Wargames" is in the discard pile—expert players will often hold the card to keep opponents in the dark about when the game might end).

88 *Paths of Glory* also approximates historical chronology in this way, by further dividing its two decks of Allied and Central Powers Strategy cards into Mobilization, Limited War and Total War decks, most of which will see play in any reasonably lengthy game. However, Events are less likely to be played than in *Twilight Struggle*, since in addition to an Event, each card has values for Operations Points, Replacement Points and Strategic Redeployment points, and a player must decide which of these he will use with each card play. All of this, as well as the wealth of strategic options presented by possible movements of units on the board, make each player's every turn an agony of difficult decisions. There is always too much to do, and too few resources. This models the difficulty of WWI military command in a way similar to how *Twilight Struggle* models its Cold War logic.

THE STUDY OF TABLETOP GAMES

UNDERSTANDING STRATEGIC BOARDGAMES AS COMPUTATIONAL-THINKING TRAINING MACHINES
Matthew Berland

Playing strategic tabletop games requires that individuals think like a computer. It requires that players follow a set of relatively uncomplicated rules with a few (relatively circumscribed) decision points for which players have voluminous data. However, humans have a difficult time writing succinct rules, understanding rules, and/or enacting the rules of these games (Berland & Lee, 2010). As game designers and players know, writing effective instructions is a key (often overlooked) challenge of game production. Even with effective instructions, novice players of almost any strategic boardgame will undoubtedly make several rule errors, (mis)communicate their idiosyncratic understandings, and generally create a mess of even a very well designed game.

This essay details the ways in which the thinking involved in playing strategic boardgames relates to computational thinking, both in terms of the algorithms that players must learn, and the types of bugs they generate and fix. These parallels suggest that players of boardgames are engaged in computational thinking, without ever touching a computer. I therefore posit that strategic tabletop games are a productive way for humans to learn the basic elements of computational thinking—that tabletop games can be computational-thinking training machines.

Computation With Or Without Computers: Computational Literacy
The ability to use computation as a 'lens' for thinking and learning is called 'computational' or 'procedural' literacy.[89] Papert (1980) used the term procedural literacy to propose that all students be taught to program and to use computer programming as a means to think and learn about math, science, and even literature. More recently, Bogost (2007) and Mateas (2008) have taken up the mantle of procedural literacy as a way to express how stu-

dents learn to think with videogames, by virtually inhabiting their rule-based worlds. This work builds upon that work by adapting it to an analog space. Both the work on procedural literacy and this work stem, in part, from work by constructionists such as diSessa (2001); diSessa argues that computational literacy can be understood in terms of three core components: the social, the cognitive, and the material. Material computational literacy is being able to use the tools of computer science and computation to solve problems. At this point, boardgames are unhelpful in teaching material computational literacy – no boardgame on the market will teach you computer programming or modeling. However, games are much better suited to social and cognitive computational literacies. Cognitive computational literacy is being able to think computationally. Social computational literacy is being able to communicate about computation. This essay explores the ways that strategic tabletop games engender the cognitive and social aspects of computational (or procedural) literacy.

Cognitive Computational Literacy: Computational Thinking

Cognitive computation focuses on creating, understanding, following and debugging rules. It is fundamentally about the enactment of explicit sets of instructions in a specified order. We call these instruction sets algorithms. An example of an algorithm might be:

- Roll the dice
- If you roll a seven, move the robber and enact the robber rules.
- Otherwise, deal resources matching the rolled number to the appropriate player
- The player who rolled can now enact one of three rule sets: building, trading, or playing cards.

These, not coincidentally, are the rules for *Settlers of Catan* (Teuber, 1995) phrased in a computer code idiom.[90] In this example, at least five different computational concepts are required for understanding and following these instructions. Table 1 exemplifies these concepts by depicting the rules in both pseudocode ('human readable program code') and the rules of the game.

Computational Concept	Description	Pseudocode	Game Instructions (summarized)
Primitives	A primitive is a basic action that the computer/game knows how to enact.	dice_roll();	Roll the dice.
Branching Logic	If some specified set of logic is true, enact branch A, otherwise enact branch B	result = dice_roll(); if (result == 7): robber(); else: deal_resourcs(result);	If you roll a 7, move the robber and enact the robber rules; otherwise, deal resources matching the rolled number to the appropriate player.

Computational Concept	Description	Pseudocode	Game Instructions (summarized)
Functions	Encapsulated and internally consistent set of instructions for a particular task.	function deal_resources(result): foreach player: foreach property of player: if(number_value_of (property) == result): give_resource(resource_value_of (property), player);	To deal rsources, give each player the appropriate resoure(s) of any tile on which they have a property.
Imperative Ordering	In both computer programming and tabletop games, the order of instructions is paramount.	(see any of the example above.)	1. Roll the dice 2. If you roll a 7, move the robber and enact the robber rules.
Looping	Do some specified sub-set of the instructions repeatedly, until some end condition is met.	while not done: foreach player: enact_turn();	Go player by player, allowing each one a turn until the game is done.

However, it can be difficult for humans to enact these rules. In earlier work (Berland & Lee, 2010; Berland, Lee, & DuMont, 2010), we showed how novices playing a game of *Pandemic* (Leacock, 2008) encountered several fundamentally computational problems, and how they solved those problems using debugging techniques relatively similar to those in computer programming. These bugs shed light on how players understand the game. The table below presents potential bugs resulting from the active player rolling a seven in *Settlers of Catan*:

Action	Problem	Rule in game (summarized)
Robber is placed back on the 'desert' title.	Misapprehension of a (sub-) rule	The robber must be moved upon rolling a 7, but it cannot be placed on the desert tile.
Players with 9 cards keep 5, rather than 4	"Off by one" -- a common error in computer programming.	Any player with more than 7 cards can only keep half, rounded down.
Players who did not roll are trading.	Not following rules that seem unnecessarily runitive or "un-fun."	The active player must be involved in any trade on his/her turn.

The problems are inherent to the context; humans are not explicitly rule-comprehension or rule-following machines. The main reason that a human would work to follow a rule without error when playing a game for fun is if s/he believes that the game will be more fun when the rules are perfectly followed. If this is not the case, players will change or ignore the rules. These are (perhaps paradoxically) the core strengths of the environment:

- Computational thinking is socially reinforced.

- Rule modification (or 'computer programming') is socially reinforced

The following section describes the ways that boardgames socially reinforce computational thinking by all players.

Social Computational Thinking: Boardgames As A Socially-Mediated, Collaborative Computational-Learning Environment

Not only do tabletop boardgames encourage or require that players engage in computational thinking, but they require that players talk about their computational thinking and engage in the social aspects of computational literacy. In fact, boardgames, rather than being self-learning environments, can be excellent collaborative learning environments (Berland & Lee, 2010; Zagal, Rick, & Hsi, 2006). They share myriad characteristics with environments that "foster communities of learners" (Brown, 1992); such environments have been shown to be an effective way to support learning complex content. That is, they:

- Engage a group of learners in solving a joint task

- Encourage learners to share information to move towards a unified goal

- Engage in a consequential independent task serving the unified goal

- Engage learners in reflection about the viability of their contribution

Furthermore, the experiences around strategic tabletop games share many characteristics with the types of discussion boards that we see around multiplayer online games. (Steinkuehler & Duncan, 2008) detail the literacy benefits and the scientific argumentation styles that occur with frequency on videogame message boards. Boardgames have a feature that much of the literature on games and learning has not addressed in significant depth: this collaboration is happening in real-time, face-to-face, and it is self-motivated.

In a game of *Red November* (Faidutti & Gontier, 2008) that I observed recently, there existed an exchange in which:

1. A player proposed a problem with a specific rule.

2. Another player proposed a resolution.

3. The third player commenced reading the rules through the instruction booklet, pausing for collective analysis, in which:

   - She read a variable number of words, pausing on any complex construction.

   - Each person offered an interpretation of those words, based on prior evidence.

   - The reader summarized the collective decision of the meaning of those words, often revisiting prior rule understanding decisions.

This looks remarkably similar to the exploratory talk described by Mercer (1996) "in which partners engage critically but constructively with each other's ideas..." (p. 98) while making their knowledge public and working toward agreement. This is one of the ideal ways that participants can engage in collaborative knowledge construction.

Not coincidentally, it also looks like a hardware resource conflict resolution algorithm (i.e., how a computer decides which resources need addressing). When motivated by problems requiring an algorithm to solve, humans can spontaneously generate algorithmic resolutions to those problems.

Learning & Implications

Much of the games or informal learning environment research has, contained within itself, a question that appeals to learning scientists: how much of what people learn in an experience can they take away from it? So, what are people taking away from these experiences? What do they learn when playing tabletop games that they can use in other aspects of their lives?

- Players are not only learning to think computationally, but they are learning tools with which to communicate computational concepts. Social and cognitive computational literacy skills are most likely an effective "preparation for future learning" of material computational literacy (Bransford & Schwartz, 1999). That is, while students may not be able to program upon gaining boardgame skills, they have a framework on which to build those skills, and; as such, will likely do so more robustly.

- Expert boardgamers become boardgame designers. Harel & Papert (1990) show that when engaging students/players as teachers/designers, the students learn much more effectively. They are forced to think through their design decisions and the implications of rule changes. I suggest that strategic tabletop games encourage this type of decision-making. In fact, expert boardgamers often edit the rules of a game fluidly, communicate those changes to other expert gamers, and understand how to best implement those changes. As there is no overhead to changing a boardgame's rules – you simply say the changes aloud – it has become very common among expert gamers. In an informal survey of frequent gamers, most of them adapt the rules – if sometimes only slightly – of every single strategic boardgame that they routinely play. As such, boardgamers routinely trend towards game design, which is itself a key mode of learning computational literacy.

Conclusions

Though I have no evidence for it, I would suggest that the spread of the modern strategic boardgame in the US became possible only after the spread of broadband access and computer use. All material technology for these games has existed for upwards of two hundred years at a relatively low cost; it is the form of cognition that was not immediately available. These games only became fun to Americans when they became better prepared to "think like computers," if only at a surface level.

This essay has shown how playing through tabletop boardgames can turn us into more expert computational thinkers, and how it can make us more computationally literate (without ever touching a computer). The benefit of deeper computational thinking is relatively clear: it gives us a new way to think about hard problems. Having these new ways to think about data, to work through problems, and to understand the world is undoubtedly important; learning to think in this way by enjoying oneself could only be positive.

References

Berland, M., & Lee, V. L. (2010). Collaborative Strategic Boardgames as a Site for Distributed Computational Thinking. *International Journal of Game-Based Learning.*

Berland, M., Lee, V. L., & DuMont, M. (2010). Small Groups, Big Mistakes: The Emergence of Faulty Rules During a Collaborative Boardgame. *Proceedings of the International Conference of the Learning Sciences* (ICLS-10).

Bogost, I. (2007). *Persuasive games : the expressive power of videogames*. Cambridge MA: MIT Press.

Bransford, J. D., & Schwartz, D. L. (1999). Rethinking transfer: A simple proposal with multiple implications. *Review of research in education*, 24(1), 61.

Brown, A. L. (1992). Design Experiments: Theoretical and Methodological Challenges in Creating Complex Interventions in Classroom Settings. *The Journal of the Learning Sciences*, 2(2), 141-178.

DiSessa, A. A. (2001). *Changing minds: computers, learning, and literacy*. MIT Press.

Faidutti, B., & Gontier, J. (2008). *Red November*. Fantasy Flight Games.

Harel, I., & Papert, S. (1990). Software design as a learning environment. *Interactive Learning Environments*, 1(1), 1–32.

Leacock, M. (2008). *Pandemic*. Z-Man Games.

Mateas, M. (2008). Procedural literacy: educating the new media practitioner. In *Beyond Fun* (pp. 67–83).

Mercer, N. (1996). The quality of talk in children's collaborative activity in the classroom. *Learning and Instruction*, 6(4), 359-377. doi:doi: DOI: 10.1016/S0959-4752(96)00021-7

Papert, S. (1980). *Mindstorms : children, computers, and powerful ideas*. New York: Basic Books.

Steinkuehler, C., & Duncan, S. (2008). Scientific Habits of Mind in Virtual Worlds. *Journal of Science Education and Technology*, 17(6), 530-543. doi:10.1007/s10956-008-9120-8

Teuber, K. (1995). *Settlers of Catan*. Mayfair Games.

Zagal, J. P., Rick, J., & Hsi, I. (2006). Collaborative games: Lessons learned from boardgames. *Simulation & Gaming*, 37(1), 24 -40. doi:10.1177/1046878105282279

---

[89] In this work, we use computational and procedural literacy interchangeably.

[90] The rules of *Settlers of Catan* are addressed in more detail in "Settlers of Catan," p.93.

BOARDGAME AESTHETICS
Greg Costikyan

Wittgenstein famously believes that no definition of "game" is possible, because so many human activities are called games. This is nonsense, of course – but there is an underlying truth. Because games are so diverse, players of one kind of game often have trouble understanding why players of other game styles enjoy them. As a trivial example, the players of first-person shooters rarely enjoy board wargames, and wargamers rarely like shooters. The aesthetics of the two styles are very different.

The problem of aesthetic diversity is true even in so restricted a form as the boardgame. Even if we focus down from the vast universe of all games to the apparently small subset consisting of games played on a printed surface by people seated around a table, we run into a diversity of tastes. There are multiple boardgame aesthetics. My intention here is to explore them.

The Abstract Strategy Game

Let us consider the serious player of *Chess* or *Go*. He (less commonly she) will have spent long hours pondering the strategy of the game, quite possibly reading books on the subject and studying games played by masters. He will have a conception of the game as a clean, utterly non-random contest in a purely mental sphere. He is likely to believe that this is how games should be – that games of this type are pure, cerebral, by nature the noblest of games, and that the sort of froth that appears on the shelves of toy and department stores is degraded piffle, perhaps suitable for children, but unworthy of study by any sophisticated person.

The very abstractedness of abstract strategy games is itself a virtue; *Go* is nothing but stones and a grid, and while the shapes of *Chess* pieces have historical value, the game is in the forces they project, with their variable movement capabilities, and it matters not a whit that one is shaped like a horse and another like a castle. The abstract strategy gamer is likely to believe, with Parlett, that modern commercial games:

> *"...rely for their underlying mechanics on well-established formulae, the least imaginative being variations on a theme of Goose -- roll dice, move there, miss turn, get home first. Being designed for family fun rather than for genuine game enthusiasts, procedural originality is irrelevant. They rely entirely on their theme for whatever sales potential may be squeezed out of them, and their own makers do not expect a shelf-life longer than the topicality of the theme in question."*[91]

In short, to an abstract strategy gamer, the very theme-ness of "theme games," with their reliance on thematic color, is a suspicious attempt to distract attention from the mechanics and strategy of the game itself, which from the aesthetic of an abstract strategy gamer are really all that matters – and a game that does not focus relentlessly on these elements must do so because it is not really very good as a game *qua* game.

An abstract strategy gamer may find the occasional modern title that holds some passing interest – a game such as Randolph's *Twixt* or Tavitian's *Blokus* that eschews theme for strategic clarity, and that avoids randomness in all its forms – but will view virtually everything else as commercial dross.

The Board Wargame

The board wargamer is at heart a simulationist. To the wargamer, wargames are interesting because they portray the color and pageantry of the past; men pitted in terrifying and bitter struggle – "Compared to war, all other forms of human endeavor shrink to insignificance," as Patton said.

To a wargamer, wargames are not abstract, time-wasting pastimes, like other games, but representative of the real. They show history, or hypothetical conflicts that are nonetheless grounded in a real understanding of military affairs and the complexity of combat. You can learn something from wargames; indeed, in some ways, you can learn more from wargames than from reading history. A work of history can only tell about the events it depicts; a wargame can *show* the events, and give insight into why the commanders did as they did, and provide the player a gut understanding of the forces at play and the factors that influenced the outcome.

To an abstract strategy gamer (or for that matter to a Eurogamer), the idea that the outcome of a game might be determined by factors that the players cannot control is anathema; to a wargamer, it is a virtue. "No battle plan survives contact with the enemy," as von Moltke said. No commander can be certain of the outcome of any battle, or there would be far fewer battles, just as there would be far fewer horse races if horse racing were entirely deterministic. To a wargamer, randomness is not something to be viewed askance; indeed, a degree of randomness is almost essential in any game that purports to be a simulation. The easiest way to represent factors over which opposing sides have no control is with the roll of dice. Sometimes, indeed, this means that one player or another wins "by luck," something that an abstract strategy gamer would find intolerable – but a wargamer shrugs it off. *C'est la guerre.*

In other words, one of the chief aesthetic values of the wargame is its value as a simulation; a wargamer understands that there is sometimes a tradeoff between the "playability" of the game (its value as a game *qua* game) and its "accuracy" (its value as a simulation), and accepts this tradeoff as a necessary part of the genre – but a wargamer will tolerate, and even appreciate, a game that fans of other game styles might view as mechanically or strategically uninteresting, so long as it imparts an accurate and insightful understanding of the conflict it simulates.

To a wargamer, complexity is understood as a requirement of simulation. Complexity is not a virtue in itself; if two systems, one simple and one complicated, simulate the same things equally well, the simple is preferable. But complexity does not daunt the wargamer; wargames are the most complex tabletop games of all, and a wargamer may take a macho pride in his ability to master even the most complicated of systems. A Eurogamer may blanch at rules of more than a dozen pages, but the wargamer assumes that any game with fewer is simplistic, in all likelihood a poor simulation, even if perhaps an enjoyable game. The wargamer may play it, just as he may play Lamorisse's *Risk*, but knows full well that this is not, by his standards, a *real* game.

Games such as *Chess* and *Go* are, to a wargamer, musty relics from an almost prehistoric past – suitable enough mental challenges, no doubt, but devoid of color or any intrinsic interest. Supposedly *Chess* began as a sort of simulation, and supposedly *Go* teaches something about the strategy of maneuver, but they are so far divorced from anything real as to lose all meaning. The players of abstract strategy games learn nothing from them, other than how better to play a game – and what, ultimately, is the virtue in that?

And the Eurogame is hardly any better. Eurogames are completely divorced from their themes, the mechanics shaped for the demands of their market rather than by the demands of simulation. You can take a Eurogame and reskin the theme entirely, and it would be no different; by contrast, if you take say, a World War II game and reskin it as Napoleonic, the players will at once realize that something is amiss. Armor does not play the same role as cavalry. The concerns of commanders in the two eras are quite different. It will be quite a strange Napoleonic game indeed.

Despite the complexity of the games he plays, and despite their inherently strategic nature, the wargamer is paradoxically less concerned with the kind of strategy that abstract strategy gamers and Eurogamers find essential. In a European Theater of Operations game, there are really only two strategies for the German player – Russia first, or Britain first. The wargamer doesn't care, so long as that is realistic. The game is in the execution, and in the simulation's portrayal of the real, not in the ponderous pondering of strategy and goals that are typical of more deeply strategic games.

The Eurogame

The Eurogame is so called because the instances to which most gamers are exposed were first published in Germany. Paradoxically, however, the game style owes its origins to games published by the American conglomerate, 3M, in the 1960s – the fabled 3M games, in which Sid Sackson and Alex Randolph, acknowledged by Eurogame designers as the inspiration of their form, came to prominence.

Like abstract strategy gamers, Eurogamers prize strategic depth; if you listen to Eurogamers talk, again and again you will hear the phrase "interesting choices." They expect games that provide a limited number of options each time the player has an opportunity to act, but which make deciding among those options interesting, and non-trivial. If the best option is obvious, there's really no choice at all; but for the choice to be meaningful, there must be ramifications expanding from it. Choosing one option closes off some avenues and opens others. This requires a system of sufficient complexity, with a degree of uncertainty in terms of outcome – and yet, perhaps paradoxically, Eurogamers dislike games where "uncertainty of outcome" depends on random factors.

This dislike of randomness applies only to randomness that can dictate outcomes; that is, a Eurogame would never contain something like a wargame's Combat Results Table. But randomness is commonly used in Eurogames as a way of providing variability in outcome, or to break symmetry to ensure that players have different objectives or strategies; Eurogamers accept this, so long as random elements either expose all players to the same opportunities and disadvantages, or else confer no strong advantage on any single player. As an example, distribution of cards at the beginning of play does not confer a strong advantage on any player, so long as all cards are of equivalent power, but do 'break symmetry' by giving players' different starting vantages.

In general, however, to a Eurogamer, as to an abstract strategy gamer, a game that can be won "by luck" is by nature an inferior game – and if luck is a strong element, hardly worth playing, and suitable only for children.

Eurogames are strongly shaped by their market; they are mass-market products in Germany, after all, if relegated to hobbyists in North America. An ideal Eurogame is played in an hour or less and supports between three and six players. It has a low level of complexity by the standards of the wargame (or by the standards of Ameritrash), but somewhat more than is typical of the American mass market game (most of which are marketed primarily to children). Ideally, it is accessible to fairly young players – many Eurogames are played by families together – but rewards the intellectual maturity that older players bring to bear, and the evolution of deeper strategic thinking by younger players.

The Eurogamer prizes clever simplicity; while he will not flinch at a degree of complexity, he admires a game that creates strategic depth with a minimal investment in learning the rules.

By and large, Eurogamers find games that pit players too directly against one another disturbing; such games are "nasty," hurtful, games that cause harsh feelings. Instead, the ideal game is one in which people injure or aid each other only at the margins, where each is building toward a win, perhaps competing for resources but not stabbing each other in the back. They prefer positive sum games, not zero sum games. Only one player can win, of course, and win conditions are necessary to motivate play, but winning should come from strategizing more efficiently, not crushing your opponents.

Like wargamers, Eurogamers enjoy novelty. They consider themselves followers of an artistic form, and often know the names of the game designers whose work they enjoy, looking forward to new works from these *spieleautoren*. They too typically have large game collections.

Eurogamers enjoy the themes of the games they play, though they know the actual gameplay is divorced from the theme, that the theme is a mere marketing appendage on what is at heart an abstract strategy game. They view games as more than their mechanics, but as *objets d'art*, products whose art style, component value, and graphic design affect and inform the experience of play. Just as digital game players have problems divorcing an understanding of mechanics from the visuals to which they are exposed, a Eurogamer's judgment of a title may be as much informed by its production values as its actual gameplay.

For this reason, Eurogamers view traditional abstract strategy games as – well, historically important, no doubt, and undeniably excellent games in their own way; but curiously colorless, without texture, and because they're not involved in an ongoing tradition of artistic evolution, less interesting than modern games. As for wargames – they are simply not worth playing: far too complex, far too lengthy, nastily competitive, too random, and without that tasty sense of strategic depth that Eurogamers prize.

Ameritrash

"Ameritrash" is a back-formation from "Eurogame," and is used to describe games, not all of them created by Americans, that hearken to titles published by Avalon Hill, Hartland Trefoil, and some others in the 1970s through 1990s. Perhaps originally intended as insulting, the term has been adopted with perverse pride by fans of the form.

Just as Sid Sackson's *Acquire* – first published in the US by a US publisher – is among the most "Euro" of "Eurogames," so many "Ameritrash" games are by no means American in origin: Hostettler's *Kremlin* is Swiss, Lamonisse's *Risk* is French (originally *La Conquête du Monde*), McNeil's *Kingmaker* is British, and so on. Ameritrash games are not limited to these older examples, however; publishers like Fantasy Flight continue to produce excellent Ameritrash games today, with titles like *Arkham Horror* and *A Game of Thrones*.

What, then, makes a game "Ameritrash?" First and foremost is a tight connection between theme and mechanics. To Ameritrash gamers, Eurogames are oddly colorless precisely because their themes are irrelevant, mere marketing drapery for games of abstract strategy. Ameritrash gamers like games where the mechanics emerge from the themes, where railroad games have a historical connection to the 19th century, where zombies eat the brains of their victims and gain some game benefit therefrom, where goals are related to what people in the situation of the game would actually try to do. Ameritrash gamers are not as fanatic about simulation as wargamers, but think that if a game is set in the Stone Age, it should have clubs in it. Obviously. Dinosaurs optional.

Ameritrash gamers like to plan and plot as much as Eurogamers, but they also like to bounce dice. In real life, shit happens, and sometimes you roll snake eyes. Sucks, but there it is, and you're playing the game to have fun, not to demonstrate that you are the True Mastermind whose clever stratagems render all opposition futile. Ameritrash gamers don't like games with random, arbitrary outcomes, but they tolerate a far greater degree of randomness than Eurogamers, particularly when the randomness is for the sake of color – random events cards, for example.

Ameritrash gamers also like games with conflict – games where you go head-to-head with others, where you can elegantly screw your opponents – where you can crush your enemies, seize their cattle, and hear the lamentations of their women. They view negotiation, trading, backstabbing, betrayal, alliances, and just general tabletalk as strong positives, and find the "niceness" of Eurogames somewhat irritating. If only one can win, why shouldn't the game let you screw up your opponents? "Nice guys never win" – surely an American sentiment.

Ameritrash gamers, like Eurogamers, are a kind of hard core; but because Eurogames are designed to appeal to one kind of mass market, and Ameritrash games are designed for a hobbyist market, Ameritrash games tend to be geekier. They often take multiple hours to play, rules complexity is tolerated, and classic geek themes (sword and sorcery, space war, monsters) are more common.

An Ameritrash game, like a Eurogame, is typically designed for 3 to 6 players, but has a far tighter connection to theme, a higher degree of reliance on randomness, and pits players more directly against one another.

The Beer-and-Pretzels Game

The phrase "beer-and-pretzels game" was originally coined by wargamers to describe relatively simple, quick-playing wargames, the implication being that they were less intense games with fairly simple rules that did not require extraordinary focus to play. Or sobriety, for that matter.

It's since been adopted by gamers in general to mean casual, short, fun, simple, easy-to-play games, often with light-hearted themes. You might play beer-and-pretzels games at a party, or after a long and more intense gaming session, to relax. They do not require deep thought, but may not be entirely devoid of strategy; and a high degree of randomness may prevail. Classic examples include Rosenberg's *Bohnanza*, Jolly's *Wiz-War*, and Cayce's *Pit*. Virtually all US mass-market boardgames geared toward adults fall into this style: Osterhaus & Kirby's *Apples to Apples* and Alexander & Tait's *Cranium*, for example – no great surprise, given the reflexive anti-intellectualism of most American adults.

There's no real stereotype of the beer-and-pretzels gamer; typically, people who play games like this are either hardcore gamers of one type or another, or people who do not self-identify as gamers but are happy to play a simple, fun game for social purposes.

Beer-and-pretzels games tend to have a set of common characteristics, however. The rules need to be explainable in just a few minutes, possibly to inebriated people. Turns must pass quickly so no one gets bored. Humor – something virtually non-existent in Eurogames – is common. There cannot be elaborate board layouts, because no one can be bothered, and in the quick, frenetic action typical of such games, pieces would probably get knocked over anyway.

In beer-and-pretzels games, fortunes often reverse quickly, with one move or the turn of a card launching a trailing player to the lead. They often end suddenly and unexpectedly – a stark contrast to Eurogames, which tend to build slowly and inexorably to the end-game. Randomness, either in the form of cards or dice, or sometimes both, is almost essential. Hidden information is common. Scoring never requires anything more than the simplest calculation.

From a design stand-point, beer-and-pretzels games are actually non-trivial to create; despite the "anything goes" feeling of the form, the games have to have enough depth to encourage repeat play without a stiff learning curve, and need to be enjoyable in quick sessions.

Conclusion

From Metacritic to Boardgamegeek user rankings, people tend to try to cram all works into a single scale of merit. While it is unquestionably true that some games are bad and some games are good, it is equally undeniable that tastes vary -- and that a games-literate and nuanced view of games makes such unitary scales questionable. For reasons both of culture and personal preference, people bring different aesthetics to games, and the virtues they find in the games they play are often quite different.

From a design perspective, it's useful to understand what audiences exist for games; and how diverse the form actually is. And while success can be achieved by catering to the aesthetic of a particular audience, games that break the mold are often the most interesting. Still, it is worth contemplating what pleasures gamers draw from the games they play, and why they enjoy them.

---

[91] David Parlett, *The Oxford History of Board Games*, Oxford University Press, 1999; p. 349. Note that Parlett is not describing all modern games this way, but "games at the lower end of this market." He is himself an eminent board game designer.

IMPROV
Brenda Bakker Harger

While improvisational acting cannot be strictly classified as a tabletop game, there are enough similarities to make it worth examining. Like a tabletop game, improvisational acting takes place in real time, requires more than one participant to be present in the same room, and asks those participants to be willing to play adhering to an agreed upon set of rules. Improv differs in that there is rarely a "win" state, there is usually no score, and even when presented as "competitive" (i.e. Theatresports), it is always cooperative. In both cases, the experience is ephemeral – it is something that exists for a period of time, then is gone, perhaps to be repeated, but never in exactly the same way. What follows is an introduction to improvisational acting – the basic paradigm along with several exercises that illuminate that paradigm through immersion. Improvisational acting is part of the core curriculum at the Entertainment Technology Center (ETC) at Carnegie Mellon University. The students in this program are not only interdisciplinary – 40% fall under the "Art" moniker – which includes everything from visual arts – 2D 3D, design, drama, music, etc., 40% are technical – primarily computer science, but also engineering, and 20% are other – business, philosophy, English, etc...., they are also international. Improvisational acting forces them to reexamine their starting points, creating a level playing field where they begin with an agreed upon set of rules to create in a new way.

What is Improv?

There is a clear relationship between improvisation and games. A relationship that includes storytelling, story structure, character development, movement, team building, listening, focus, basic acting, and most of all a paradigm and heuristic that serve both the process of game development as well the games themselves. Improvisational acting is a method of expression through performance which brings participants to a common starting place enabling them to put aside egos and create together. Most famously known as a comedy performance vehicle (*Second City, Upright Citizen's Brigade, Who's Line is it Anyway?*), improvisational acting techniques are also useful in other applications. Improvisers learn through playing games and exercises to develop a set of hard skills and soft skills that help them to create. Animators can benefit from character movement and behavior exercises, producers from effective team communication and idea generation, programmers from exercises and patterns that can be replicated in code to inform A.I., game designers in the heuristic and emphasis on real-time problem solving. The hard skills improvisers practice include exercises in the basics of storytelling – what makes a story, how to create a story arc, how do you build suspense; in character development – what is a character, how to build a character from an external perspective through body language, how that translates into personality, psychology, and archetypes; in the character's objective – how what they want informs behavior, choices and actions that further develop that psychology. Improvisers practice creating sections of story called scenes which are the building blocks and parts that form a greater story. These blocks may be defined as CROW; Character, Relationship, Objective, and Where. We need to know who we are, who we are with, what we want, and where it all takes place.

The soft skills (those more related to personal interaction and emotional intelligence) practiced are in the form of listening to each other, of working in teams, of exercising spontaneity, of adding to each other's ideas, and becoming great observers – all essential skills for an actor. Improvisers use games and exercises to practice these skills. Because the focus is on taking risks and exploring the moment to moment, improvisation allows participants to once again access the aspect of self that creates in the form of play. In the ETC, all of the first year students are required to take improv. The aim is not to teach them how to perform (although many of them are perfectly capable by the end of the semester), but to teach them how to use the skills they develop in improv in their future work. By placing the emphasis on creation rather than performance, we are able to focus on the application of skills rather than on achievement.

The Paradigm and the Rules: Why They are Important.

Improvisational acting and games both function by agreeing to follow a set of rules. In tabletop games, the rules vary from game to game, but the need for all to agree to play by the rules is constant. In improv, the rules will vary according to the focus or goal of the game or exercise, however, there are three universal rules that all improvisers need to follow if they are to move forward in their work together. These rules define the paradigm. The first rule is: Be fun to play with. This means having a spirit of generosity, a willingness to share with others and to not take yourself and your own ideas too seriously. It's being able to incorporate other's ideas. This is different than, "Have fun playing," there are plenty of people who have no problem having fun but are not fun to play with. The second rule is: Serve the narrative. In improv, the narrative is often the story or scene that is unfolding in real time. It also however refers to anything at all that you are working on that is group-generated and outside of yourself. Your focus should always be on that – the narrative – rather than your own ideas or agenda. The final rule is: Make your partner look good. Simply, if you are concentrating on the people you are with and on helping them perform the best they can by setting them up and supporting them, you will be keeping the other rules. If you agree to this rule, you can be assured they will also be doing the same.

Making Offers and Assumptions.

Improvisers move the story or the game forward by making offers and making assumptions. An offer is anything an actor does. Period. An offer can be something an actor does, says or emotes. An offer is a gift – early in our ETC Improv class, we play a game called Presents. One improviser starts by making an offer of something that has size and weight – they give this to a partner who treats it like a present and opens it, naming what's inside. An offer can be an actor walking on to a stage with a suitcase, setting it down, and looking around. Suddenly the audience has questions. Who is that? Where are they? Why are they here? Why now? Where did they come from? The actor answers these questions, a moment at a time, but making small advances in her actions. She might sigh, or look at her watch, or straighten her skirt, or her hair. She might be sad, or excited, or resigned. Everything she does is an offer to make more sense of the narrative – to move it forward. The important thing to remember is that the actor has no more idea of where the narrative is going than the audience. They are discovering it together a moment, an action, an emotion at a time. Like games, the player only has what is in front of him, and has to make offers in return to move forward. In order to serve the narrative, we listen for three basic elements: Facts, Feelings, and Intentions: facts – what?; Feelings – emotions; and Intentions – motivations and justifications.

An assumption is also an offer – usually verbal. The most important thing to remember about an assumption is that whatever is assumed in improv is true. If I say you are my mother, you are. If you say we're on the moon, we are. Once an assumption is made, the other actors have to accept the assumption and work with it.

Presents

There are many variations on this game, but the basic principle is the same: Two people take turns giving each other imaginary presents. The first person decides the general characteristics of the present – how big it is, how much it weighs, what kind of package it comes in, etc., but makes no attempt to assume what it is. The second person "unwraps" the present and names it according to the information he/she has received. Then they switch. The game continues as long as anyone wants it to. The only way this game will work is if the participants are both saying "yes" to the other's offers.

Saying Yes...

Saying Yes is the key to serving the narrative. In the Presents game, one offers a size and weight without knowing what the present actually is, the other

IMPROV AND ROLEPLAYING GAMES
Greg Costikyan

Tabletop roleplaying games began as an outgrowth of military miniature wargaming, and the earliest RPGs, like *Dungeons & Dragons* were typically played as a sort of boardgame without the board, with careful calculations and dierolls determining outcomes and players working primarily to maximize their experience point gain. As they moved to digital media, RPGs continued more or less along the same path, since computers are good at performing careful calculations and generating random numbers.

In the world of tabletop and live action roleplaying, however, the trend has been in a different direction. In a roleplaying game, by nature, each player controls a single character, and even though the rules of early RPGs did not reward or provide systems to support actual roleplay, that is, improvisational acting in character, the mere fact of having individual characters, and their existence within an imaginary world, encouraged players to explore the improvisational aspects of the milieu.

Over time, a number of independent movements have arisen among roleplaying gamers and designers to push roleplaying games more in the direction of theater; and indeed, in some cases the sorts of games these movements create are hard to distinguish from "acting games," the improvisational exercises some acting schools use to develop actors' skills.

One such movement is the indie RPG movement, whose enthusiasts often participate in the forums at The Forge (http://www.indie-rpgs.com/). In principle, any tabletop roleplaying game that is self-published or distributed in ways other than the conventional hobby market is considered "indie," but the practitioners of these games generally move in a "narrativist" directon. The term "narrativist" derives from Ron Edwards's "gamist-narrativist-simulationist theory" (GNS theory), which characterizes roleplaying games by their tendencies along each of these three dimensions. Edwards is himself the designer of one of the best known indie RPGs, *Sorceror*, a game in which each player is literally demon-haunted and may perform powerful magic – but only at the expense of losing an element of his or her humanity.

The focus of narrativist RPGs is on story-telling rather than improvisation per se; but their systems are often quite different from those of conventional tabletop RPGs. In a conventional RPG, accepts those parameters and completes the transaction by naming what it is. In doing so, the participants are not only saying yes, but they are fulfilling expectations which were created in the initial offer. When the expectations are not fulfilled, the audience (and the participants) become confused. This non-fulfillment can take several forms. Blocking (saying no), breaks all of the rules. If the receiving partner names something that does not coincide with the initial offer – a large heavy present is a named a feather for example – the offer is blocked. If I say you are my mother and you reply with "I'm not your mother", we have to stop and figure out, well, then who are you? We are not serving the narrative. The actor who is blocking also is not (in this moment) fun to play with. Blocking in improv is almost always done out of fear. An occasional block will be forgiven by the audience, but too many will result in confusion and negativity. Another exercise in saying yes is in a game where we describe a painting. Three participants make statements about a painting they see (of course, imagine) on the opposite wall. The first person makes a statement: "I see a meadow....." The second person agrees to that statement and adds on by saying "Yes, and...there is a blue sky above." The third person agrees and adds "Yes, and....there are puffy clouds in the sky." The first person picks up from there "Yes, and....there is a large oak tree on the left hand side," and so on. Until the participants run out ideas (never!), or fumble in some way - by hesitating, by adding "I think..." or turning the statement into a question...or by saying Yes, but... instead of Yes, and... Yes, but is the same as blocking. You "pretend' to agree by saying yes, but you don't really accept the offer. Think about it this way; have you ever received a Yes, but apology? I'm sorry, but … (endless qualifiers) It's difficult to discern what is true. Waffling is a milder form of blocking. A participant waffles when they refuse to define something that needs definition. If you receive a present and respond with "Wow! I love this!" or "It's just what I wanted!" without naming what it is, we stall the narrative instead of moving it forward. Students learn to add to ideas rather than judge them, an all too common problem in any kind of group work – especially regarding brainstorming. This does not mean that ideas eventually should not be judged...just not before they have been pushed to their maximum potential.

Problem Solving in Real Time.

One obvious aspect where games and improv are most alike is in the need for real time problem solving. Problem solving could be seen as the basis of all creative processes, the difference with improv is that it is performed live in real time in a designated space without writing anything down. Like taking turns in a game, improvisers move the narrative forward by focusing on these three principles:

1. Use small amounts of information

2. Use what's in front of you – you only have what has been introduced in the scene or what has been named explicitly.

3. You need to be present – Observe, Listen....and go slow.

By taking turns, the improvisers ensure that no player is forcing their ideas on the narrative. By going slow, the improvisers ensure that they are incorporating everything that has been introduced. The audience sees everything that is offered and is disappointed when an improviser misses something that they – the audience have seen. At the very least, students learn to appreciate the power of details – in their stories, their worlds, their pictures, their work, and their lives. They also learn to recognize the power of the moment – how an ordinary activity can become extraordinary by paying attention and committing to the action.

Team Work / Group Mind

At the ETC, the Improvisational Acting class meets for two to three hours a week. For most of our students, this course is unlike anything they have ever done before and for many it is one of the most difficult classes they have ever taken. There are different reasons for this, but the primary reason is that although they are usually extremely intelligent, they find that they cannot rely on the skill sets they have developed, or any book knowledge they may have acquired. The best way to learn and understand these processes is by engaging in them – in doing; so in improv, the students learn by participation. The class takes place in an empty room – there is no power point or note taking. The students are asked to dress comfortably and leave their belongings (and egos) at the door. For any theatrical experience to succeed, the ensemble must understand and be able to communicate the common

game systems are primarily concerned with determining the success or failure of specific actions taken by the player characters. In a narrativist RPG, quite often the game system is used to determine whether a scene or confrontation is "successful" or not from a player's perspective, but with players having great freedom to narrate the events of the scene, without additional die rolls or the like to determine whether or not specific actions succeed. E.g., in a conventional game, the outcome of a fight would involve many dierolls to determine whether a character hits and then how much damage he does; in a narrativist game, a dieroll might be used to determine whether a characters wins or loses the fight, with the players then describing how this happens freely.

Narrativist RPG designers are primarily interested in shaping the arc of a story, rather than in improvisation and roleplaying; but this inherently produces improvisation and roleplaying by the players.

Story games (see http://www.story-games.com/forums/) are subtly different from indie RPGs. A story game is a framework for shared story creation; quite often story games entirely dispense with the idea of a "gamemaster" entirely, instead providing a set of rules for determining who "controls" the narrative at any given time. The rules tend to tend to be more robust than those of "acting games;" indeed, the rules of acting games are rarely described as "rules," but instead in terms of instructions from a director or teacher. Because story game creators emerged from the tabletop tradition, they think in terms of using rules to shape an experience, and of modifying those rules over time to improve the outcome. Perhaps the main difference from "acting games," however, is that players role-play and improvise while sitting around a table rather than while standing and moving as their characters would; story games still transpire in the imagination, not on a stage, and the characters played may look nothing like the players who take their roles. The improvisation, in other words, is primarily verbal, not in terms of action and stance.

Live action roleplaying games (LARPs), by contrast, make a virtue of physical performance as well as character improvisation. There are, however, many different kinds of LARP. One common form is the "bopper LARP," a game, generally in a fantasy setting, in which physical combat, often with padded weapons, is the main focus of the game. Even in such games, however, costuming and adopting a persona, remaining in character, are considered important.

At the opposite end of the spectrum is the Dogma 99 larp (http://fate.laiv.org/dogme99/en/index.htm) , a larp designed in accordance with a manifesto promulgated in 1999 by a group of Scandinavian larpers. (In the Scandinavian larp community, "larp" is considered a word in itself rather than an acronym, and is rendered in all lower case letters). One of the rules of the manifesto is that

goal. In improv this is referred to as "group mind". Group mind is not all thinking alike, but rather focusing on the same goal – serving the narrative. Exercises in group mind focus on getting the partipant to let go of an individual idea and give themselves over to the collective narrative.

Here are a few simple group mind exercises and games:

Pass the applause: Participants get in a circle. Each person claps simultaneously with the person to the left, passing the clap around the circle. It should eventually sound like one person clapping. This exercise helps to teach and practice focus, clear communication, speed and precision. Eye contact is key to receiving as well as sending. Speed and precision help the participant to 'give up" control and be ready for anything - just respond. The game teaches participants the importance of being alert, being present, and communicating clearly.

Organic Circle: The group stands in a circle. One person offers a sound and a gesture to the person on his/her left. The next participant repeats the sound and gesture and passes it to the left. The sound and gesture are accepted and sent on in one motion, so each participant only repeats it once (unlike pass the applause). I usually side coach (giving instructions while they continue to play) to have the group speed up or slow down or reverse the action. The sound and gesture usually change - naturally - no one should change it deliberately. This game teaches attention and being accepting and open to offers made.

Who are we? What do we make? What's our Slogan? The group stands in "blob" formation - and answers these three questions in order: Leader points to one person at a time who answers with whatever comes to mind in the moment. The questions are : Who are we? (one person answers) What do we make? (another person answers) and What's our Slogan? (third person answers). The rest of the group repeats the answer enthusiastically all together as though they are at a rally. Repeat several times through. This helps teach a group to work around each other's ideas and the narrative they're creating together. A more sophisticated group mind exercise is:

Counting to twenty as a group: The group can sit or stand in whatever formation they like - a circle works well. The group simply counts to twenty as a group, one person at a time. If any number is said by more than one person, the group needs to go back to the beginning. The group should count randomly, without any assistance like forming patterns, pointing the next person to speak, going around the circle, etc. The more control any individual tries to exert over the exercise, the harder it is to accomplish. This teaches a group to be alert to each other and give themselves over to the task together.

Storytelling Foundations: How Improvisers Tell Stories.

Storytelling is key to almost all improvisation. Whether a story is told from start to finish, or we see just a glimpse of the overall in the form of a scene, creating a narrative is one of the main goals. In order to tell a story, improvisers know that you need to be very clear on the definition of a story. No matter how you describe the structure, the principles are the same. There needs to be a world that has its own laws and properties. A character or characters inhabit that world. Something happens that interrupts the character's world; tension needs to build and continue to build until something changes. After the change happens, the character continues in the world, but something has been transformed. Whether the character's transformation is internal (the character has an attitude adjustment, a new view of his circumstances, knowledge he did not hold before), or external – the circumstances around the character have changed and forces a reaction by the character that is transformed from before. These aspects need to be in place to make it a story. Keith Johnstone's circle of expectation specifies additional requirements - whatever you introduce into your story needs to be within what the audience might expect in that world. Too many "unusual things" make it too difficult to justify and pull together. Keep the main thing the main thing – stay with the story!

The best template for checking to see that all of the elements of story are present was developed by Kenn Adamss of Bay Area Theatresports:

> Once upon a time…..
>
> Everyday…
>
> But one day…
>
> Because of this…

"there are no rules," which seems paradoxical, but by which they mean that such larps are not to have any game-y systems to handle things such as combat; all action must be live and real, and the larp should be structured to avoid situations, such as combat, that cannot be readily handled in a pure roleplaying context. Another rule is that all players must remain in character for the duration of the larp, except in specifically designated "cool down" areas, and that suspension of disbelief must be sustained to the highest degree possible.

An equally interesting larp type is the "jeepform," a style pioneered by the Swedish group Vi åker jeep (http://jeepen.org/). A jeepform is intended for play by a handful of players in a short period of time, along with one or more gamemasters, who often have roles to play within the jeepform itself. Jeepforms are shaped toward the creation of story rather than 'roleplaying for show,' and are often designed so that characters emerge over time through play – and often so that the player of a character has only partial input into the nature of his or her character, with both the gamemasters and the other players able to establish things about the character. As a result, they tend to foster wild and rapid improvisational roleplay.

LARPs are sometimes highly structured, with characters designed in advance and with the game operators shaping a pre-determined story arc; others are far more freeform (and indeed, the "freeform" is a kind of LARP, characterized by a minimal rules set and no predetermined outcome). Even in the most structured LARP, however, all conversations are improvised by the players; and in less constrained LARPs, the experiences of the players are highly improvised as well, within the context of a preestablished setting and tone.

The nature of digital games, with their predesigned art assets and precoded capabilities, make anything beyond the merest conversational improvisation impossible (and that only in online games). The nature of boardgames, with their tradition of formal and complete rules, also mitigate against improvisational play. But in roleplaying games, particularly in their more experimental forms, the techniques of improv have been enthusiastically adopted and extended to create games that are artistically exciting mergers between theater and "the game."

Until finally…

And ever since then…

The moral of the story is…

The first section; "Once upon a time…" and "Everyday…," is the exposition. "Once upon a time…": we are introduced to the world and characters in that world. "Everyday…": we are introduced to the routines in that world - what they do and what happens to them normally. "But one day…": is the inciting incident – what happens that interrupts that world and routine. "Because of this…": are the consequences of that incident, and the beginning of the rising action. The "Because of this…" section can be repeated – consequences beget consequences. "Until finally…": the climax, the consequences reach a point that there is no turning back. "And ever since then…": is the resolution - the climax has rendered a change in the character or the world that will remain forever. At this point, there is no going back to the world that existed in the exposition. The moral of the story gives one last opportunity to tie everything together – to reiterate what was potentially learned (or not) and to justify the reason we told the story in the first place.

Improvisers tell stories in many different ways. One is from start to finish – from "Once upon a time…" to "And ever since then…". A scene is the story delivered in part. Scenes can be presented as part of a greater narrative (in long form, there are many scenes played which eventually all relate to each other) or they can exist as a very small glimpse into a world at any given time and place. As stated earlier, improvisers need to communicate to each other the basic parameters of the circumstances, CROW (Character, Relationship, Objective, and Where), in order to have a scene. In addition to CROW, all scenes have these characteristics in common.

- They usually start in the middle (In media res). Scenes usually don't start with "Once upon a time…," we are usually thrust into the middle of a relationship, an event, a problem, a place, etc, but we don't know initially how we got there. Furthermore, we don't always see the resolution in the scene. Improvised scenes don't take the time to go through the entire exposition. Improvisers become adept at giving us just enough information to let us know what is about to change in the scene.

- The story can only be shared a moment at a time.   Actors work very hard to take the actions and dialogue of a character within a given story and make them real – as though they are truly happening in that moment, not replicated. Because improvisers do not use a text, they have to pay closer attention to the moment they are in and react to each other and what is offered – everything is unfolding at the same time –

character, story, needs, wants – so much information to incorporate. The only way to manage this is by paying attention to what is happening in that moment, not worry about the moment after. The result is a truth in response that is perceived as genuine. These exercises help/force actors to stay in the moment.

Two exercises that help to achieve this are "Without a Letter", and "Leave for the Same Reason." The first, "Without a Letter," incorporates dialogue, the second, "Leave for the Same Reason," uses no dialogue, but asks the participants to be fully present in the moment and by doing so, be fully aware.

Without a Letter. (from Keith Johnstone) 2 actors start at scene with CROW. They can either initiate it themselves, or get a suggestion from the audience or the instructor. It is important that the characters each have a strong objective. If I give the actors a suggestion, it is something like this:

> Aa son comes home from his first semester away at university. His father or mother is anxious for his return – proud tht he is following in the family's academic footsteps. The son however has made a decision he needs to share with his father/mother. He has decided to become a hairdresser.

The actors then get an additional challenge to the scene – they must perform the scene without using a letter of the alphabet – say "s" (the letter should be a consonant – vowels are too difficult). The result is that the actors are forced to take their time, and the challenge of avoiding the utterance of a particular letter is seen by the audience as thoughtful, sometimes emotion-filled responses to difficult news.

Leave for the Same Reason: (Johnstone) 3 players sit side by side onstage. Without speaking to each other, they must make offers that escalate a situation to point that all three must leave the stage at exactly the same time for exactly the same reason - without any of the players leading the others. Anyone can start – i.e. someone might make an offer of a slight cough. The others would accept that offer by mimicking that cough and exaggerating it slightly. This game teaches the importance of careful nonverbal listening which relies heavily on the player's periphery. It also emphasizes the importance of accepting offers and taking your time in figuring out what's going on. And it emphasizes very clear moment to moment acting (seeing what happens next) with rising stakes, careful listening and observing, and finally, accepting offers and building on them.

Both of these games force the improvisers to move forward slowly and more carefully than they might otherwise. When improvisers slow down and pay attention to moment to moment actions and reactions, the result is very real and satisfying – what improvisers often refer to as a moment of truth. A moment of truth is an empathic connection through a specific incident in a story. These moments of truth are the moments that elicit a reaction from the audience – whether it's laughter, a gasp, or a sigh doesn't matter, it's a recognition that something has happened. Satisfying stories are created by evoking moments of truth within the audience. A moment of truth does not have to be profound. Moments of truth can occur at any time during a story. Sometimes the greatest realizations occur in the details of everyday life.

In improvisational theater, moments of truth, from the most profound to the most simplistically humorous, are the goal of each story, and CROW (Character, Relationship, Objective, and Where) is the foundation - the rules - towards achieving these moments. So the above all leads us back to CROW, the building blocks of a scene, or what do we need to know to move forward.

While the rules, assumptions, offers and saying yes define the process of how we are to tell stories as a group, we also need to name what we need to know with CROW. Characters are the people in the scene – they are defined by external characteristics as well as internal characteristics - how they more through space, what they say and do, and how those things define their personalities and psychological makeup. The characters have relationships to each other. Relationships can take many forms – familial, professional, etc. Relationship is the most important component to name as quickly as possible – it is always more interesting for characters to know each other. And all characters have objectives. An objective is what the character wants. An objective is either a physical or a psychological goal, and is crucial to the creation of satisfying stories. Objectives should be thought of as verbs, and must lead to action.

A simple physical objective may be something as basic as, "to take a single step." A complex, physical objective consists of several simple objectives and may be something such as, "to follow the yellow brick path to its end." A psychological objective will add a layer of inner significance, such as "to follow the yellow brick road in order to find a way back home."

Through layering and mixing complexities, these kinds of objectives become critical to creating satisfying stories. The physical objectives can be made more dynamic with the addition of psychological components. The psychological objectives can be made more concrete by adding physical goals. An objective that is moving and motivated, active and attractive, and grounded in story will resonate.

All objectives in a story should lead toward the achievement of the overarching character objective. This is the single most important objective that carries a character through the story. The overarching objective helps to structure most smaller physical and emotional objectives. It is not always apparent and does not always take precedence over the immediate objectives. However, it will constantly come back into play and often times acts as a framework for the lower level objectives.

To help us wrap up, here are two games that help to define and understand objective:

Outta that chair. A game to teach objective. One person sits in a chair. One by one improvisers enter with one objective - to get the person out of the chair and take their place. The person in the chair also has an objective - to stay in the chair. Any offer is legitimate, so long as the improviser doesn't threaten or use force. To stay in the chair, the person needs to reply with a compelling response to the offer on why he/she must remain. If they cannot come up with a compelling reason to stay, they must leave.

Red Light Green Light A classic children's game. Divide a group in half - one half watches while the other plays. One player (the light) stands at the opposite side of the room - the rest of the group starts behind a line. When the player turns his or her back to the group and says, "Green light," the group can move forward. When the player turns back and looks directly at the group and says, "Red light," the group must freeze in place. The player as the light determines what constitutes "freezing." If the person catches anyone moving, they will be sent back to the original spot behind the line. The objective of the game is to be the first to reach the player (light) without getting caught, tag them, and take their place. Variations: Players proceed as partners - linked up with one or two others – and they must be connected (touching) at all times. Players can also proceed as one group (all touching). Metaphorically, the game follows classic story structure. If the playing area is divided into three sections, each section represents how the emotional stakes change while working to achieve the objective. Using story structure terms and Kenn Adams's story spine, the first segment is the

Exposition ("Once upon a time..." and "Everyday...") The players are testing their space, the objective is far off, the player as the light is comfortable, and far from getting caught, and the audience (the group watching) is getting to know the players. The attitude is carefree and fun - loose body movements and low commitment. The emotional stakes are low. The middle section is the Inciting incident and the beginning of the rising action ("But one day..." and "Because of this..."). The consequences for getting caught are greater, so the emotional stakes become higher. The players become more serious, more committed - body movements become more balanced and rigid, and the audience begins to look for the potential "winners." The player as the light starts to become more "paranoid," watching more closely and even stepping back some. The third segment picks up at the end of the rising action and up to the climax ("Because of this..." and "Until finally..."). The climax is the actual tagging of the player as the light. Substitute "characters" and story situations (teacher/students, guard/prisoners) to explicate further. The theme of justice also emerges.

The last element of CROW is Where. Where is defining the space. There are several ways to communicate the where. The simplest is to ask the audience where you are. Or you can name it in the dialogue, or you can show it by creating and using a object that would exist in the location, or you can create sound effects that give clues and give actors an opportunity to react, or add music as a soundscape (live musicians are best), and so on. Defining where you are is the easiest way to begin a scene – you suddenly have a wealth of possible expectations and activities that could be useful.

These are the basic principles that create the paradigm of improvisational acting. Building on these principles, improv goes in many different directions.; from comedy-based, to serious, to short games and short form (scenes), to long form and full narratives. The interactions change constantly according to the groups of improvisers, but the principles and rules remain the same. Like a hundred variations on *Scrabble* or any role playing game, improv is at its core a fluid experience focused on the present time, in other words, play. Which brings us back to the relationship of improvisational acting to tabletop games. Play is what we do in both. We play in groups with clear goals and parameters, and while the results of our play are not exactly quantifiable, they work parts of our brains that call us to reason in creative ways. In the ETC, we think this is important, and so play is a part of our curriculum. Not only do we create better teams, we create leaders who know how to problem solve in real time and to be comfortable with what they don't know, rather than clinging desperately to what they do. Improv naturally produces risk takers and innovative thinkers who work well with others, and it provides a performative perspective on how we can best play well with others, whether it's on the stage or around the table.

AUTHORS

Brenda Bakker Harger

Brenda Bakker Harger is a theater director (MFA Carnegie Mellon University), improviser, and professor of Entertainment technology at Carnegie Mellon University's Entertainment Technology Center where she teaches improvisational acting and leads diverse interdisciplinary projects. As an improviser, Brenda has performed with Pittsburgh Theatresports and SAK Theatre, and has led improv workshops nationally and internationally from theater improvisers to executive leadership training (Carnegie Bosch Insititute) to video game companies. Bakker Harger is also director of a unique award winning theater company at Carnegie Mellon, which uses live interactive theater to address controversial issues in the workplace and classroom. She has produced an exploratory DVD-ROM for interactive theater, and is currently pursuing her interest in further exploring her theory and skills in directing and improvisation with technology, both in gaming and theater.

Recent projects include: making a demo/prototype of a game based on the film *Night of the Living Dead* (with George Romero); creating a toy/exhibit featuring virtual representations of The Pittsburgh Children's Museum's Puppet collection; and interactive robots - creating a robot which had distinct character and was able to convey emotion and intention. In theater, Harger has directed and developed plays as technologically based interactive experiences, one which premiered at the Humana New Play Festival at the Actor's Theatre in Louisville, *Virtual Meditation #1*, and another, *Full Spectrum*, which premiered at the Ensemble Studio Theatre in New York City. In addition, Harger engages in ongoing research on using improvisational methods to create more believable virtual characters.

Matthew Berland

Matthew Berland is an assistant professor in the Department of Interdisciplinary Learning & Teaching at the University of Texas at San Antonio. He received his Ph.D. in Learning Sciences from Northwestern University in 2008, studying computational literacy, systems literacy, and the design of constructionist learning environments. In 2009, he completed a postdoctoral fellowship in the Institute for Computational Engineering and Sciences at the University of Texas at Austin working on AI systems and human-robot interface design. His current projects include an NSF-funded handheld robotics project; a computational thinking project using tabletop boardgames; a project to investigate the learning processes of novice programmers; and novel assessments for constructionist classrooms.

Greg Costikyan

Greg Costikyan has designed more than 30 commercially published board, roleplaying, computer, online, social, and mobile games, including five Origins Awards winners (ludography at www.costik.com/ludograf.html); is an inductee into the Adventure Gaming Hall of Fame; and the recipient of the Maverick Award for his tireless promotion of independent games. At present he is a Senior Designer at Playdom, a social game developer, and also runs Play This Thing!, a review site for indie games. He is also the author of four published science fiction novels.

URLS:

www.costik.com - personal website

playthisthing.com - a review each day of an indie game

James F Dunnigan

Jim Dunnigan writes books on military affairs, technology and history, builds his own computers, considers risk management a splendid leisure time activity, manages software development, can conjure up simulations on anything and considers problem solving a favorite indoor sport. He studied to be an accountant and during his time in college he got involved in designing wargames for Avalon Hill. He also got involved in developing online games, and continues this, along with writing a book or two a year. To find out more about playing wargames and have some fun, visit: http://jimdunnigan.com/.

Ira Fay

Ira Fay is a Senior Game Designer at Pogo.com, where he has lead Pogo iPhone game development, released several top web games, and championed playtesting and telemetry. Prior to Pogo, Ira worked at Z-Axis on *X-Men 3*, at Maxis on *The Sims 2*, and at Walt Disney Imagineering on *ToonTown Online*. Ira graduated from Carnegie Mellon University with a bachelor's degree in computer science ('00) and master's degree in entertainment technology ('04). Ira has given guest lectures at various universities worldwide, including USC Interactive Media, ETC Osaka/Silicon Valley/Pittsburgh, and GNW Digital Media Vancouver. In his spare time, two of his favorite activities are playing and designing boardgames with friends.

Simon Ferrari

Simon Ferrari is a doctoral researcher in digital media at the Georgia Institute of Technology, where he studies expressive game design, criticism, and competitive play. His first book, co-authored by Ian Bogost and Bobby Schweizer, is *Newsgames: Journalism at Play* (MIT Press, 2010).

Richard Garfield

Richard Garfield designed the first trading card game, *Magic*, in 1993. At the time he was a math professor, but the success of *Magic* led to him leaving academics and going into game design full time. Since then he has published half a dozen other trading card game designs, as well as a number of board and card games. Since 2001 he has been consulting on game design with companies including Microsoft, Electronic Arts, and the Pokemon Company. His recent games include *King of Tokyo* (boardgame), *Let's Jet* (boardgame) and *Spectromancer* (PC). In the last 5 years he has been teaching a class "Characteristics of Games", the material for which has been made into a textbook published by MIT Press. He continues to play, study, and design games out of an academic interest for what makes great games.

Pat Harrigan

Patrick Harrigan is the co-editor of the MIT Press volumes *Third Person: Authoring and Exploring Vast Narratives* (2009), *Second Person: Role-Playing and Story in Games and Playable Media* (2007) and *First Person: New Media as Story, Performance, and Game* (2004), all with Noah Wardrip-Fruin. He is a former marketing director and creative developer for Fantasy Flight Games, and co-edited FFG's *The Art of H.P. Lovecraft's Cthulhu Mythos* (2006), with Brian Wood. His work has appeared in Pagan Publishing's *The Unspeakable Oath*, Chaosium's *Arkham Tales*, and in the Gameplaywright volumes *The Bones* and *Things We Think About Games*. He has also written a novel, *Lost Clusters* (2005).

Kevin Jacklin

Kevin Jacklin is a long-standing member of Reiner Knizia's playtest/design circle, receiving credit on several dozen Knizia game titles. He is the co-designer with *Knizia of Hollywood Lives – the Movie-Making Party Game*.

John Kaufeld

John Kaufeld believes that great boardgames can change the world, one family at a time. He loves helping parents -- especially dads -- build connections with their kids through family time around the game table. He's a best-selling author, long-time boardgame evangelist, and self-proclaimed Chief Elf (whatever that means). You can reach him at jkaufeld@aol.com.

Chris Klug

Trained as a theatrical lighting designer, Chris Klug worked on Broadway, in regional theater and opera, and toured with various 70's rock n' roll bands. Through the intercession of a photographer friend, Chris took a part-time job designing RPG adventures for a NYC game company, Simulations Publications, Inc. After delivering a handful of freelance assignments, he was asked to join the design staff in 1981, and assisted with the design of *Universe*, then designed the 2nd edition of *DragonQuest*, *Horror Hotel* and *Damocles Mission*. While at SPI he edited the role playing section of Ares magazine. When TSR bought SPI in 1982, Chris and the rest of the SPI staff moved on to form Victory Games. There Chris headed up the role playing games group, designed the *James Bond 007* role playing game and oversaw the entire Bond product line. At Victory Games, Chris designed a half-dozen more titles and was, for a time, Design Director.

After leaving Victory Games, Chris became a freelance computer game designer and worked for SegaSoft, TSR, Hasbro Interactive, 3W, THQ, Simon and Schuster Interactive, Target Games, h2o Interactive, Gizmo Games, Westwood Studios, EA, GT Interactive and

Cheyenne Mountain Entertainment. Some of his computer game design credits include *Star Trek DS9: Dominion Wars, Europa Universalis, Duke Nukem: Time to Kill, Diamond Dreams Baseball, Aidyn Chronicles: First Mage, Earth & Beyond,* and *Stargate Worlds.*

In academia, Chris is currently a faculty member at Carnegie Mellon University's Entertainment Technology Center. In addition to teaching at the ETC, Chris has taught Interactive Storytelling at the Art Institute of Pittsburgh as well as the Art Institute in Phoenix. Chris is a playwright and member of the Writer's Guild of America West.

Stone Librande

Currently working as Creative Director at EA/Maxis, Stone Librande, (M.S. MIT Media Laboratory, B.F.A. California Institute of Arts Film/Video School), has worked in a wide variety of technical and creative fields. He has been employed as an art director, video producer, software engineer and freelance illustrator. On weekends he is either teaching a game design course at Cogswell College in Sunnyvale, CA. or creating his own custom card and board games.

Brian Magerko

Brian Magerko, Ph.D. is an Assistant Professor of Digital Media in the School of Literature, Communication, and Culture at the Georgia Institute of Technology. He received his B.S. in Cognitive Science from Carnegie Mellon in 1999 and his Ph.D. in Computer Science and Engineering from the University of Michigan in 2006. His research, funded by the National Science Foundation, NASA, and other federal institutions, focuses on the use of AI to personalize digital game-based experiences and the design of educational games. His blog project, *The Digital Tabletop,* is a multi-year transmedia comparison of the game mechanics employed in modern boardgames and digital games. His interest in boardgames has influenced both his design research as well as his approach to teaching. He has recently incorporated boardgames as a core component of his Game AI course, which prompts students to develop AI approaches for opponents for boardgames as a means of focusing on deep Game AI problems. Dr. Magerko has recently been spending his spare time playing copious games of *Dominion* online and testing the capabilities of the AI in the new release of *Ra* on the iPad.

Ray Mazza

Ray has degrees in physics, computer science, and entertainment technology. He enjoys writing, random skills (like shuffling a deck of cards with one hand), and long walks in game stores. If he can entertain and enlighten, he is a happy guy. Ray was last seen working as a lead designer on the hit videogame franchise *The Sims.*

Peter Olotka

futurepastimes.com/peterolotka

Experienced in the development and design of games, activity kits, museum exhibits, public programs and products.

Worked in multiple media and platforms including: board, card, computer, web, CDROM, radio, TV, print. Served as creative consultant for multiple science museums for staff and program development. Responsibilities range from providing conceptual design, researching and writing content to managing entire projects - budgeting, hiring subcontractors, etc. Projects involve meeting with the client's designers, marketers, technical staff and outside contractors in order to synthesize and unify competing interests.

Highlights
Founded Eon Products, Inc
Founded Future Pastimes, LLC
Founded Creative Consultants
Designed over 70 published games, products, exhibits and public programs
Clients include Fortune 500 companies as well as leading non profits
50 Game Design Awards

Education
MA Mass Communication,
Thesis: Telecommunications Event Design, Emerson College, Boston, Ma.
BA History, University of Colorado, Boulder, Co.

David Parlett

A Londoner by birth and residence, David Parlett has a degree in modern languages and was a high school teacher and then a technical writer before joining *Games & Puzzles* magazine in 1972 as a contributor and subsquent editor. He has been inventing games since childhood and has always delighted in recreational mathematics. Involvement with *Games & Puzzles* led to the first of many books on games, especially card games, that he has written down the years, and to the invention of his first and most successful game, *Hare & Tortoise*, which was first published in 1974, won the first ever German Game of the Year award in 1979, and has been in constant production ever since. His best-known books are *The Penguin Book of Card Games* (1979, latest edition 2008), *The Oxford Guide to Card Games* (aka *A History of Card Games*, 1991) and *The Oxford History of Board Games* (1999). His advice is often sought on the staging of historic games in period films and dramas. An active member of the International Board Games Studies Association, he has written many papers on the historical and philosophical aspects of games and play in general. Full details of his productions, together with the rules of many of his original card games, can be found on his website at http://www.davpar.com.

Lewis Pulsipher

Dr. Lew Pulsipher started playing boardgames more than 50 years ago. He designed his own games, then discovered strategic "realistic" gaming with early Avalon Hill wargames, and ultimately earned a Ph.D. in military and diplomatic history at Duke University. His first commercial title was published in 1978. He is designer of *Britannia, Dragon Rage, Valley of the Four Winds, Swords and Wizardry*, and *Diplomacy Games & Variants*.

After a 20 year hiatus from game design to teach himself computing and work as a programmer and chief of PC support at a major Army medical center, Lew has come back to designing games. *Britannia* (2nd edition) appeared in 2006, with foreign editions (German, French, Spanish, Hungarian) in 2008. *Britannia* is among the games covered in the book *Hobby Games: The 100 Best*, edited by James Lowder. It was described in an Armchair General online review of a 2006 edition as "ready to continue on as one of the great titles in the world of games". Players of *Britannia*, a strategically deep, four-player game depicting the history of Great Britain from the Roman invasion to the Norman *Conquest*, play primarily for entertainment, but some schools use it to teach Dark Ages history. Other games are forthcoming, among them an abstract boardgame from Mayfair Games.

A former contributing editor to several role-playing game magazines, and author of over a hundred game magazine articles, he is now a monthly contributor to *GameCareerGuide* and Gamasutra. These sites, owned by *Game Developer Magazine*, are the premier Web sites for those interested in videogame creation.

He is a contributor to the books *Hobby Games: the 100 Best* and *Family Games: the 100 Best* (Green Ronin), and to the forthcoming *Tabletop Game Design* (ETC Press). He is finishing his "howto" book, *Get it Done: Designing Games from Start to Finish*.

"Dr. P's" day job is teaching game design and other videogame creation topics in the southeastern US, where he has 17,000 classroom hours of experience, mostly teaching computing and especially computer networking, in college and graduate school. Current projects are at PulsipherGames.Com. Blogs: http://pulsiphergamedesign.blogspot.com/, http:// teachgamedesign.blogspot.com.

Some of his recent Web articles that have received widespread comment include "All I needed to know about games I learned from *Dungeons and Dragons*", (http://gamecareerguide. com/features/775/all_i_really_needed_to_know_about_.php) and the controversial "Too Much Like Work" (http://gamasutra.com/php-bin/news_index.php?story=25122 and also (extended) http://www.spitefulcritic.com/2009/09/too-much-like-work/).

Ian Schreiber

Ian Schreiber has been in the game industry since the year 2000, first as a programmer and then as a game designer. He has worked on five published titles, two serious game simulations, and several other things he can't talk about without breaking NDA. Ian has taught game design and development courses at Ohio University, Columbus State Community College, and Savannah College of Art and Design.

John Sharp

John Sharp is an interaction designer, game designer, art historian and educator. He has been involved in the creation and study of art and design for twenty years. John's design work is focused on social network games, artgames and non-digital games. His current research is focused on game design curriculum for after-school programs, the artgames movement, the history of play, and the early history of computer and video games.

John is a professor in the Interactive Design & Game Development department and the Art History department at the Savannah College of Art and Design-Atlanta. He is also a member of the game design collective Local No. 12, a group of academics including Mike Edwards (Research Faculty, Design & Technology, Parsons the New School for Design), Colleen Macklin (Associate Professor, Design & Technology, Parsons the New School for Design) and Eric Zimmerman (Professor, New York University Game Center) which focus on Twitter as a game and research platform. John is also a member of the Leisure Society, a group dedicated to the intersection of games, narrative and art. The Leisure Society is composed of Jesper Juul (Professor, New York University Game Center), Colleen Macklin, John Sharp, Michael Sweet (Associate Professor, Berklee College of Music) and Eric Zimmerman. John is also a partner in Supercosm, where he focuses on interaction and game design for arts and education clients.

JT Smith

JT Smith has founded a dozen businesses, three in the gaming industry. In his spare time he speaks internationally on technology and business, and has also authored several books, and dozens of articles on those subjects. He lives with his wife Sarah in Madison, Wisconsin where they both enjoy the food and fun that the city has to offer.

Noah Wardrip-Fruin

Noah Wardrip-Fruin is an Associate Professor of Computer Science at the University of California, Santa Cruz, where he co-directs the Expressive Intelligence Studio, one of the world's largest technical research groups focused on games. He also directs the Playable Media group in UCSC's Digital Arts and New Media program. Noah's research areas include new models of storytelling in games, how games express ideas through play, and how games can help broaden understanding of the power of computation. Noah has authored or co-edited five books on games and digital media for the MIT Press, including *The New Media Reader* (2003), a book influential in the development of interdisciplinary digital media curricula. His most recent book, *Expressive Processing: Digital Fictions, Computer Games, and Software Studies* was published by MIT in 2009. Noah's collaborative playable media projects, including *Screen* and *Talking Cure,* have been presented by the Guggenheim Museum, Whitney Museum of American Art, New Museum of Contemporary Art, Krannert Art Museum, Hammer Museum, and a wide variety of festivals and conferences. He is a member of the Board of Directors of the Electronic Literature Organization. Noah holds both a PhD (2006) and an MFA (2003) from Brown University.

Made in the USA
Middletown, DE
26 December 2023

46807769R00117